Measuring the Value of Partnering

How to Use Metrics
to Plan, Develop,
and Implement
Successful Alliances

Larraine Segil

Partner, Vantage Partners

AUTHORS CHOICE PRESS

iUniverse LLC
Bloomington

MEASURING THE VALUE OF PARTNERING
How to Use Metrics to Plan, Develop, and Implement Successful Alliances

AUTHORS CHOICE PRESS

iUniverse books may be ordered through booksellers or by contacting:

iUniverse LLC
1663 Liberty Drive
Bloomington, IN 47403
www.iuniverse.com
1-800-Authors (1-800-288-4677)

Originally published by American Management Association

ISBN: 978-1-4917-3011-9 (sc)

Printed in the United States of America.

iUniverse rev. date: 04/03/2014

Acknowledgments

Although the interviewees of the companies featured in this book are their senior executives, the real key in ensuring that I feature the company with balance and knowledge lies in the hands of those who arrange access and meeting opportunities. Few can compare with Jan Jurcy of Avnet and her colleague, Al Maag in the public relations and communications group. Jan not only arranged for individual meeting times with the entire top management team of Avnet but ferried me back and forth, to and from the airport to meetings on numerous occasions. Thank you, Jan! Terri Johnson, Hank Suerth's assistant at Starbucks was always there to make sure every meeting and interview was perfect—thank you! Also thanks to Phyllis Bazner, executive assistant to Ron Sargent, Chief Executive Officer of Staples, who made the way clear for interviews which enabled me to present Staples appropriately.

The executives whom I interviewed in the book were all extremely generous with their precious time, and they were open, forthcoming, and enormously welcoming to me. This made my job so much easier. My thanks go to each and every one of them, along with my admiration for their excellence in this field.

Raquel Green, our executive assistant at Vantage Partners, is the key to all my writing because she enables me to hide when I absolutely have to write and arranges every single trip, interview, meeting, and much more with great accuracy and tact. Thank you, Raquel.

Marianne Kruse, graphics expert extraordinaire, enabled this book to reach the visual quality of excellence. My grateful thanks for her commitment and to my partners at Vantage Partners for this resource. Thanks to Nancy Ellis, partner, agent, and most of all, my friend—you are the reason everything gets published! Also to Emilio Fontana, my former partner at Lared, thanks for all the experiences that we have had in our alliance journey together for the past 20 years at Lared and for the client examples that I have used in this book.

My editors Adrienne Hickey and Christina McLaughlin from AMACOM, a division of American Management Association, have been of huge value—thanks to you both.

Finally, my beloved husband Clive, still my biggest supporter after thirty-four years of marriage, and our son James Segil, president of Knowledge-base.net, who is my best critic. There is no way to thank either of you enough—you are the loves of my life.

Larraine Segil

Contents

Acknowledgments vii

Introduction xi

PART I   THE BASICS OF ALLIANCE METRICS 1

Chapter One   The Alliance Life-Cycle Stages 3

Chapter Two   The Five Stakeholders 29

Chapter Three   Alliance Development Metrics:
The Partners 39

Chapter Four   Implementation Metrics:
The Partners 63

PART II   EXCEPTIONAL EXAMPLES
OF PARTNERING 85

Chapter Five   Avnet: The Master Distributor 87

Chapter Six   Women and Big Brother:
Strange Companions 117

Chapter Seven   IBM and Alliances 135

Chapter Eight   The Hewlett-Packard/Compaq Merger:
An Integration Process Managed as
an Alliance 159

Chapter Nine   The Large Companies That Act Small 193

Chapter Ten   Hotels and Hyundai 215

Chapter Eleven   Starbucks 237

Chapter Twelve   Computer Games and Alliance Metrics:
The Un-Metrics 255

Chapter Thirteen Wrapping It All Up:
Summary and Action Items 261

Postscript 267

Index 269

Introduction

Why Metrics?

Measurement is intrinsic in everything we do. Simple comparison and contrast is an everyday event from the time we were children. The concept of measurement for managers is a natural—if not underutilized and misperceived—aspect of managing their businesses, large or small. Measuring alliances is therefore the everyday arithmetic of business—not physics, just basic math using both concepts and numbers. Many managers believe if you can't measure it, it doesn't exist. I don't agree.

You can measure many aspects of alliances. However, there is also an element of art in an alliance, the magic and the flow of what happens when partners come together. So, first I will talk about what can be measured. Then, we'll look at some of the more unique elements of alliances that fall into the realm of the *art* of alliance management.[1]

Here is the way we will think about alliances and alliance metrics in this book: First, we will look at the life cycles of an alliance and introduce you to an approach called the Mindshift[sm] approach that you will find very useful. Then, we will examine the two main groups of alliance metrics. The methodology ensures that you don't leave out a critical metric tool that could be helpful in making your alliances more successful. The term "metric" refers to that which should be measured.

1. Alliance Life Cycles—the *activities* in each life cycle, the *culture* of each life cycle, the *managerial personality* most suited to each cycle, and the *priority* of the alliance and how it changes through each cycle.

2. Alliance Metrics Groups—Alliance *development* group of metrics and alliance *implementation* group of metrics.

---

[1]The Association of Strategic Alliance Professionals (ASAP) is the first professional association for this area of management science. I am proud to be a board member. For information, visit the ASAP Web site at www.strategic-alliances.org.

These two themes will run through the whole book, which means that you can make sense of alliances and their metrics by always asking and answering the following questions:

What is the stage of the Alliance Life Cycle and what does the Mind-shift analysis tell me?
This will tell you the main tasks which are appropriate for that stage, the culture of the alliance or the way that the alliance and those related to it will behave, and the priority of the project to you and your partner.

What is the metrics group that this alliance falls into?
This will tell you if you should be checking the list for alliance development metrics (Chapter Three) or alliance implementation metrics (Chapter Four) or a combination of both.

The Alliance Life Cycle

Here are the major life-cycle stages into which metrics will be organized. These form the baseline that establishes the best practices which will be further supported and illustrated by the chapters that follow. A generic example of the alliance life cycle approach is in Figure I.1.

The first two stages of the alliance life cycle include development metrics, such as conceptualization, strategic development, planning, buy-in, the operating plan, and implementation metrics, such as launch and startup into the growth cycle called hockey stick (because it looks like a hockey stick on the graph). These are covered both in Chapter One and in Alliance Development Metrics (Chapter Three). The following stages seen in Figure I.1, from hockey stick (high growth) to decline, termination, or value-add or re-launch, are also covered in Chapter One but are referenced again in the Alliance Implementation Metrics section of the book (Chapter Four).

Measuring alliance metrics requires a balance between the external needs of shareholders, customers, and suppliers and the internal business procedures that management must take to perform the tasks identified, learn from the tasks, and innovate over time. Once balance is established, the other aspect of this approach is to evaluate the results of alliances (whether quantitative or qualitative) that evolve from past activities and then to decide how to drive those activities needed to achieve future (and possibly different) results. This may also mean balancing the quantitative outcomes from the alliances with their desired outcomes.

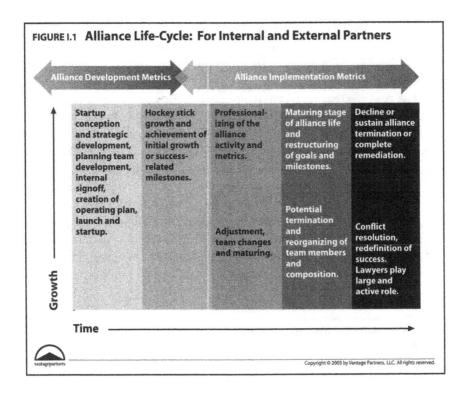

FIGURE I.1 **Alliance Life-Cycle: For Internal and External Partners**

The Alliance Players

Five groups have differing, and often, conflicting interests in alliance metrics. Each group wants their own interpretation of the metrics, and must be satisfied or the alliance will be affected. They are:

1. Partners.

2. Management.

3. External analysts, competitors, and the marketplace.

4. Other functions within each partner's company.

5. The alliances group and the individual alliance manager.

Throughout this book, I will take into account the quantitative and qualitative issues that affect the alliance from all directions and perspectives. When alliances succeed, there are many who will take credit for them. When alliances fail, blame is allocated to a few. My approach will show that the failure or success of an alliance is a multifaceted situation which can be dramatically affected by understanding who has *skin in the game* and, therefore, which constituencies must be served.

The result is that there are many metrics for many masters. Not every group or individual who wants to measure something in the alliance wants to measure the same things. For example, just look at the various metrics that have different priorities for some of the stakeholders in a simple sales or distribution alliance. Some want to measure growth in sales (the salespeople will because their bonuses are based on that number), others are more interested in market share (those in marketing), others are more focused on the transfer of knowledge and learning (the chief knowledge officer as well as the head of the alliance department and other alliance managers), and still others may be looking at the change in competitive advantage from the alliance and its external impact (the analysts and competitors).

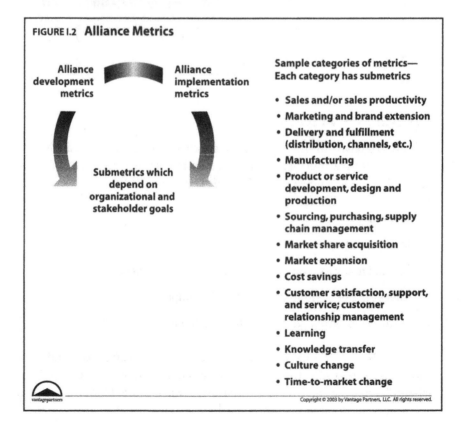

FIGURE I.2 **Alliance Metrics**

Alliance development metrics

Alliance implementation metrics

Submetrics which depend on organizational and stakeholder goals

Sample categories of metrics— Each category has submetrics

- Sales and/or sales productivity
- Marketing and brand extension
- Delivery and fulfillment (distribution, channels, etc.)
- Manufacturing
- Product or service development, design and production
- Sourcing, purchasing, supply chain management
- Market share acquisition
- Market expansion
- Cost savings
- Customer satisfaction, support, and service; customer relationship management
- Learning
- Knowledge transfer
- Culture change
- Time-to-market change

vantagepartners

I dedicate this book to my former partner
and co-founder of The Lared Group,
Emilio Fontana.

So the alliance may serve many interests and may also change in its importance to the various parties during the life of the alliance.

Figure I.2 describes the potential for metrics within the alliance framework and the categories of metrics. These categories also expand into subcategories for greater detail. This schematic will form one of the linchpins of my analysis in this book, along with the life cycle chart in Figure I.1. Each subcategory is a gold mine of all kinds of information, which will enable you to drill deeply into the various details that are important to you. For example, in sales there are numbers (increasing or decreasing) of sales calls in the sales cycle. These are compared to "growth in sales" which relates to the "cost of sales" and the potential for upselling in existing customers rather than costly acquisition of new customers. The comparison of all these numbers could be used to increase margin and so on.

I will summarize each of the categories in Figure I.2 and delve into them in detail again in the chapters that follow.

In addition to using the life cycle of the alliance as a guide to the differences that occur as an alliance starts, launches, professionalizes, matures, declines, re-launches or terminates, alliance metrics can be divided into two distinct groups.

The Alliance Development Group of Metrics

The alliance development group covers all aspects of alliance creation, strategic alignment, and more. Figure I.3 describes the development process in broad terms.

Each of these activities will generate its own set of metrics, and I will present them as a summary of best practices in Part II.

What is a best practice? It is a process or approach that has, over time, proven to be highly effective in achieving definable and stated goals. For the early life cycle stages of alliance development, the best practice is the most efficient, effective, and transparent way to conceptualize, strategize, create, plan, select, structure, and negotiate an alliance.

Defining a best practice is a necessary threshold step to any book about alliance metrics because so little is known about this field. There are so many self-appointed experts in it that it is difficult to know which assertions are based on considerable experience and which come from those who are still learning the field. No matter the level of reader expertise, the focus of this book and my goal in documenting these approaches is to give all those who have any interest in alliances, real tools and a basis from which to recommend best practices.

FIGURE I.3

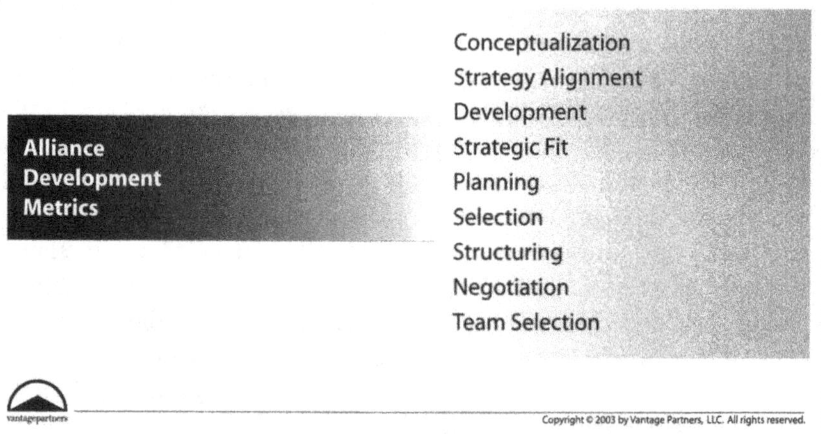

Alliance
Development
Metrics
Conceptualization
Strategy Alignment
Development
Strategic Fit
Planning
Selection
Structuring
Negotiation
Team Selection
Copyright © 2003 by Vantage Partners, LLC. All rights reserved.

The Alliance Implementation Group of Metrics

Figure I.4 lists the large categories into which implementation metrics are divided. These metrics address what happens when the alliance actually has to start delivering results. The nature of these metrics will also change over the course of the alliance life cycle.

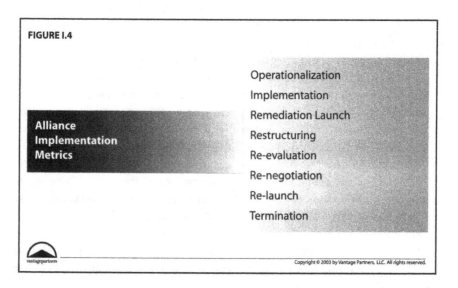

FIGURE I.4

Alliance
Implementation
Metrics
Operationalization
Implementation
Remediation Launch
Restructuring
Re-evaluation
Re-negotiation
Re-launch
Termination
Copyright © 2003 by Vantage Partners, LLC. All rights reserved.

Part I of the book will address the basics of alliance metrics, beginning with Chapter One and the effect and importance of the alliance life cycle. Part II will illustrate how some outstanding companies use alliance metrics.

The Basics of Alliance Metrics

The Alliance Life-Cycle Stages

Alliance metrics are really all about alliance management. In this chapter, I will examine how the life-cycle stages of every alliance change the way the alliance is managed. The tools I will use are the alliance life cycle stages and the Mindshift[sm] approach.[1] They will enable you to choose the right metrics for each stage of the life cycle. In Chapter Two, we will look at the five critical categories of people who have interest in your alliance's metrics and how to manage those sometimes conflicting interests.

Keep in mind that the process of creating and managing alliances is much like manipulating a large jigsaw puzzle, first pulling out all the pieces and then putting them back—that is the fun of creating and managing relationships.

The alliance life cycle stages and Mindshift approach are based on a concept I developed in my first book, *Intelligent Business Alliances* (New York: Times Books, Random House, 1996), which I strongly recommend if you are a novice to alliances. Whereas there I used Mindshift to look at whole organizations, divisions, or groups, here I will apply that methodology to the alliance itself, which can be considered from the point of view of its own life cycle and how its personality, culture, and priorities change during that journey.

Figures 1.1, 1.2, 1.3, and 1.4 lay out the Mindshift approach. As the alliance moves through different stages of its life cycle, the activities that

---

[1]The first publication of the Mindshift[sm] approach can be found in *Intelligent Business Alliances* by Larraine Segil (New York: Times Books, Random House, 1996) in Chapter Two. It was applied there to corporate or organization cultures.

are predominant in each stage change, the corporate personality or culture changes, and the kinds of individuals who will succeed change as does the project personality or priority.

My research into 500 companies at the California Institute of Technology (Caltech) over the past decade has shown how the life cycle stages of an *organization* affect the culture or personality of the organization. Now this same research has been applied and found valid regarding the life-cycle stage of the actual *alliance* itself. I have found that different life-cycle stages of the alliance will demand different kinds of activities. I have also seen that different life-cycle stages of the alliance demonstrate different cultural characteristics for that relationship (i.e., startup alliances behave differently from mature or declining ones). Additionally, I have discovered that different kinds of managerial personalities thrive (or fail) in various life-cycle stages of the alliance. (Some managers love the excitement of starting an alliance but get bored with the conflict resolution and repetitiveness of managing a mature one.) The final part of this approach is the all-important project personality, which examines the priority level of the alliance to all the stakeholders and how these priorities may change through the vari-

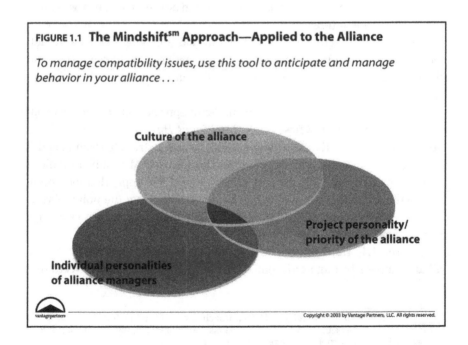

FIGURE 1.1 **The Mindshift^{sm} Approach—Applied to the Alliance**

To manage compatibility issues, use this tool to anticipate and manage behavior in your alliance . . .

Culture of the alliance

Project personality/ priority of the alliance

Individual personalities of alliance managers

ous life-cycle stages of the alliance (startup to decline). All of this analysis must take place in the context of looking at the actual organizations that are partnering and the changes they might be going through themselves.

Sound complicated? As we review the charts together, you will see how nicely the logic fits together so that it will become intuitive for you to see alliances in a different light, hence, the name Mindshift to shift your mind into a different gear about alliances.

Let me break down the various aspects of the Mindshift approach. The premise is based on the concept that alliances themselves have life cycles whether they are nonequity alliances or equity-based ones (joint ventures, equity investment, mergers) and that the culture of each alliance will change as its life cycle does. Figure 1.2 is a depiction of the activities that are most common for each life-cycle stage of the alliance, and it dovetails nicely into the description of the cultural characteristics of each stage of the life cycle which follows it in Figure 1.3.

Let me take you through the various stages, combining the information in Figures 1.2 and 1.3 for ease of explanation as we move through each life-cycle stage.

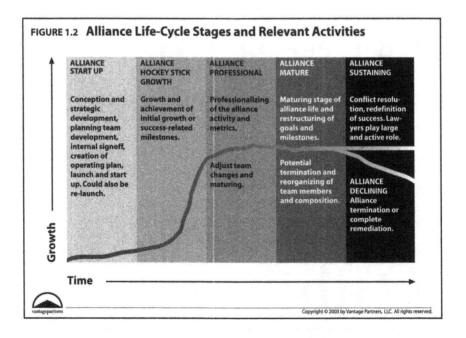

FIGURE 1.2 **Alliance Life-Cycle Stages and Relevant Activities**

ALLIANCE START UP	ALLIANCE HOCKEY STICK GROWTH	ALLIANCE PROFESSIONAL	ALLIANCE MATURE	ALLIANCE SUSTAINING
Conception and strategic development, planning team development, internal signoff, creation of operating plan, launch and start up. Could also be re-launch.	Growth and achievement of initial growth or success-related milestones.	Professionalizing of the alliance activity and metrics. Adjust team changes and maturing.	Maturing stage of alliance life and restructuring of goals and milestones. Potential termination and reorganizing of team members and composition.	Conflict resolution, redefinition of success. Lawyers play large and active role. ALLIANCE DECLINING Alliance termination or complete remediation.

Growth

Time

FIGURE 1.3 The Mindshift Approach—Alliance Culture or Personality

Startup	Hockey Stick	Professional	Mature	Declining	Sustaining
Insecure	Confident	Systematic	Complacent	Over-planning	Planning
Proactive	Quick to react	Planning/Predictive	Protective	Budget driven	Entrepreneurship
Emerging	Aggressive	Marketing, not just sales	Risk averse	Form over substance/ritualistic	Controlled
Single	Multi-focused	Cautious	Administrative	Hierarchical	Structurally systematic
Focused	Lack of management depth	Conflict resolving	Rigid	Non- active (less is more)	Aggressive
Risk intense	"Sales are first" philosophy	New hires/old fires	Profit driven (cost reduction)	Change makers seen as problem creators	Flexibility sufficient to be proactive
Founder (the champion)	Controlling	Consensus building	Middle management proliferates		
Driven		Team changes	Form over substance		
Non-continuous delegation		New metrics	Sclerosis begins		
Excitement					
New opportunities					
Trust					
Governance					
Hope					

vantagepartners

Startup Stage of the Alliance Life Cycle

The alliance startup phase includes conception and strategic alignment, development, strategic fit, planning, selection, structuring, negotiation, and team selection (all of which are also part of the Alliance Development Metrics seen in Chapter Three). However, certain Implementation metrics are also critical here such as Operationalization, which includes creation of the operating plan, continued team development, internal signoff, communication protocols, and launch and startup—many of the metrics that you will see in Chapter Four.

Startup alliances are emerging, proactive, single-focused, champion driven, and insecure, among other things, as seen on the left-hand side of the Mindshift chart (Figure 1.3). They also show:

➤ Excitement.

➤ Lots of new opportunities conceptualized—more opportunities than there are resources to cover.

➤ Trust (which in my interpretation of the word as it applies to alliances means that you said what you were going to do and you did it, namely, follow-through) is just beginning to form.

➤ Resources appear to be understood in terms of where they are coming from and who has the responsibility for providing them.

➤ Team selection is fluid but the champion is present and active.

➤ Reporting processes are fluid and not entirely clear—governance issues are evolving into decisions.

➤ Hope springs eternal!

The startup phase contains some contradictions. On the one hand, the partners are excited and anxious to make the relationship work and, most of all, to get it started. On the other hand, they don't really know each other as well as they will, trust is still evolving, or in some cases, it has already been affected by the aggressive negotiations that took place in which maybe some of the team members were not involved.

Because this is the first stage of the alliance, it is also the stage in which it is important to understand the executive sponsorship of the relationship so that support can be sustained and utilized throughout the relationship.

You may receive interest in the relationship from the senior executive level at this early stage, but keeping them involved and excited about it will be challenging unless the alliance becomes successful or they are requested to resolve conflict. This is a reactive way of managing the alliance life cycle. It is far healthier to manage it proactively, which means anticipating the various life-cycle stages that will evolve, and briefing, educating, and informing those who need to know when indications of change begin.

In Chapter Five on Avnet, you will see some of the interesting changes that happened suddenly in their relationship with one of their major suppliers, which dramatically changed one of the metrics on which they had depended for decades. They had to examine their entire business model as a derivation of that change and now have a more far-sighted picture and plan for this particular supplier relationship, rather than imagining that everything will ultimately stay the same. Because Avnet is a major distributor in the electronics field, their industry goes through major changes, it seems, every decade. Keeping in mind the life-cycle issues of all their alliances (whether with suppliers or with customers who are their two major stakeholder groups), has enabled Avnet to survive and evolve through one of the most difficult periods their industry has ever seen. The relationship that ensued could be seen also as a re-launch.

The re-launch aspect of the startup phase is an amalgam process. It has elements of startup combined with elements of the declining alliance. In that respect, it is an animal of a special breed. Remember that not all startups will include the re-launch phenomenon.

For that reason, I created a separate set of characteristics for the re-launch alliance as follows:

Re-Launch Characteristics

➤ Conflict resolution is still part of the discussion. Negotiation, mediation and resolution of areas of dispute are winding down into agreed upon compromises.

➤ New team selection is beginning—some of the old guard will be moved aside; those with commitment to success rather than revenge will remain. It is critical to have the right personalities on the team now—a slip of the tongue or poor body language that communicates a different message from the words that are said could flip the balance of this delicate re-launch process.

➤ New leadership of the team is important.

➤ Senior executive sponsorship will facilitate alliance re-launch.

➤ Re-alignment with the strategic goals of all partners, as well as strategic fit re-testing, will establish the priority of the alliance.

➤ Old mistakes should not be repeated though new ones are bound to occur.

➤ Alliance capability skills become a critical success factor. Some enhancement or training is probably necessary.

➤ Sensitivity is high. So all the development metrics that are in Chapter Three must have special attention (see subsets of conceptualization, strategic fit and alignment such as time to market, time to decision making, time to implementation) as well as those in Chapter Four (see Re-evaluation: Is this partnership still good for us to be in? If it is, then this information must be communicated to all parties and team members—and understood and accepted).

➤ Change management skills are important now. Team members must understand the need for flexibility and be willing to adapt to new circumstances, which could mean a change in the balance of dependency between the partners from the original agreement as formerly negotiated; adaptability will enhance the changes in markets, companies, and activities (e.g., the alliance may be less broad than originally conceptualized or more targeted).

The Hockey Stick Phase

The second stage of the alliance life cycle is the hockey stick phase, so named because the graph representing it looks like a hockey stick on the page. This aggressive, confident stage is where the alliance seems to be succeeding and action rather than process is king. It involves the beginnings of growth and the achievement of success-related milestones. Some alliances will never reach this stage. Others will skip this stage and go directly into another stage. However, if the alliance should go into the hockey stick phase, these are some of the things that will start to happen:

1. Others who may have initially been involved in the alliance idea development may come forward and take a deeper interest which could cause some turf issues.

2. Senior management may take a more intense look at the alliance and start to up the ante by increasing the metric expectations (e.g., "You are doing 20 percent growth. How about shooting for 30 percent?").

3. Credibility increases for the partner and their promises—and for you and your team's abilities and commitments. Leverage is your secret weapon at this point in the alliance life cycle.

The hockey stick phase is a great place to be and should be leveraged with:

a. Partner communications. Make sure that the good news is communicated both laterally across partner companies and vertically inside all partner companies. You have good news to tell and it's a lot better to set the minds of those who know little about the alliance with positive comments than to wait until the only news that they hear is of how things are going wrong.

b. Go for more resources. It's like going to the bank to borrow money when times are bad: It isn't going to happen without costing you a bundle. Go to the bank when your balance sheet is healthy and strong, and you will be likely to get the financing you need with the preferential treatment that a top quality borrower should have. Now is the time to go to those who control the resources for this alliance and propose your budgetary needs for the next cycle. The Mindshift approach will prepare you to look ahead to when the alliance is not growing as strongly and may well be entering the mature or even the declining stages. So think prospectively while things are good, plan for the fallow times, make sure resources are available.

c. Enhance team competency. When the alliance is in the hockey stick stage, this is a wonderful time to reward team members by enhancing their competency levels. Get them some process training and education on alliance management; don't wait for a crisis to understand the skills needed to add value to the alliance. The likelihood of support of such actions will be higher when things are going well, rather than having to plead or reallocate funds when the alliance is already under stress.

d. Integrate your alliance. The next opportunity that arises for you in the hockey stick phase is to start to integrate your alliance into the other activities of the company. This is the time to think about how to interact with other groups or divisions who may touch this partner. Why? Because you are growing and they will be more willing to talk to you now because you might have something to offer them through your success. If your alliance starts to lag, they will be less eager to share their information or success with you. Even the most collaborative companies tend to have areas of territoriality where either the compensation and reward systems don't support working together or people are afraid of losing the credit for their work. The integration process is multifaceted. It will include updating or gathering information on the various touch points of the partner organization (which should be information that you collected during the strategic fit and competitive analysis stage of alliance development metrics) and organizing a network of those who touch the partner, so as to share information and data. With one of our clients there were 30 people in the company who touched the partner in various ways; bringing them together added huge leverage. Power and knowledge were captured for the benefit of all present whether they were in supply chain management, sales, business development, the business units, or at corporate headquarters. This aspect of knowledge capture is important in every life-cycle stage of the alliance, but it is particularly possible in the hockey stick phase because success is evident and everyone in the organization who touches the partner will want a bit of that. Creating this network will enable you to share information with your colleagues and also, possibly even more important, to build internal goodwill that will put you in very good stead as your alliance transitions into other life-cycle stages that are perhaps a little less exciting than the hockey stick one.

The hockey stick phase has a series of metrics that tend to get skewed toward growth naturally because that is the most obvious characteristic here. However, it is critical to keep a level of discipline so that the value other than growth does not get lost in the excitement. For example, there might be:

➤ Technology learning.

➤ Process transfer (the way a manufacturing facility is laid out).

➤ Joint marketing development, which teaches a lot about how the partner perceives the market or understands the customer.

All of these items should still be valued, measured, expected, and encouraged, so that if growth should wane, the alliance will continue to be seen to have some value.

So keep in mind the following tips:

1. Growth is important. But remember to measure knowledge transfer, too.

2. Team enhancement. This means finding and adding some people who also have respect for and are good at process because growth will need to be disciplined, measured, and understood so that it can be sustained. So action-type managers will need to work well with those who are process oriented, too.

3. Prepare for more growth, prepare for less growth. This means thinking about and allocating resources that can be added in modules. You should partner internally to get added contributions of human resources. Don't increase your expenses any more than you absolutely have to; try to out-source parts of nonessential functions whether to a shared services group within the company or an external outsource provider. Keeping a lid on costs will make your growth more profitable within the alliance and prepare you for less exciting days should they evolve in a later life-cycle stage of the alliance.

4. Don't gloat. It's easy to become excited, but remember that alliances require the cooperation of many on all sides, both within the same company in different functions and in the partner's company. Being respectful and gracious will take you a long way in building the goodwill that will help in times of conflict.

A good example of a hockey stick stage alliance is that of Avnet and IBM. See Chapters Five and Seven for more information on how they worked through this phase.

The next stage is the professional stage, most suited to metrics and action combined.

The Professional Stage

This is, in my research, the most effective partnering stage. Why? Because in this stage, there is recognition that growth does not continue forever and requires continuing effort to be sustainable. In this stage, the alliance team and senior management also realize the value in metrics, process, and leadership.

The alliance will have proven itself to a large extent and will be moving along with the contributions of all sides fairly well understood.

Here are the characteristics of the professional stage of the alliance life cycle:

1. Team changes. At this stage the team starts to mature, possibly by natural attrition, by people moving on to other positions, or by design. Often as the alliance reaches this stage, it is no longer growing as aggressively as before, although there is still acceptable growth, and so those managers who were involved in the launch of the alliance and its initial success are getting a little jaded or even bored and that can be the death knell of a good alliance. From a leadership standpoint, it is important to move those people along. Some of the metrics good to introduce at this point are the following:

   a. *The alliance manager's enthusiasm level for the alliance.*

   b. *The resource allocation as it compares to the resources that were allocated at the beginning in startup.* This is a leading indicator of potential problems. If resources are beginning to become difficult to achieve from either the partner or your own company, this could be leading you into a resource crunch that could inhibit your activities in the alliance. Now is a good time to raise your awareness of this because the budget for the next year may require some innovative ideas in order to maintain interest and value in an alliance that is beginning to mature. Anticipate challenges rather than be in a crisis management mode with your alliances.

   c. *Trust issues.* Even though your alliance may be doing rather well, a new team that comes in may need some time to *buy in* and gain *ownership* of the alliance, as well as get to know their counterparts on the other side. It is important to have a good clean handoff process. Even the most secure alliance will be challenged when team members change too quickly because so much of alliance success depends on the people who are implementing them. When the team changes, you have to make a concerted effort to examine metrics once again.

   d. *Metrics that are the tried and true from earlier lifecycle stages are now worthy of another look, for example, the definition of success.* Has it changed? Is it Return on Investment (ROI), Return on Equity (ROE), and so on? Take another look at the alliance development and alliance implementation metrics and run through them again with a new view that comes from having worked together for a while, as well as having seen the market changes and company changes that are inevitable. One metric that we use a lot, and it always seems to give a clue as to what is to follow, is the executive sponsorship. If that has changed, look out! Especially if it has gone *down* (lower in the organization showing a lower level of commitment and interest) rather than *up*. If it has gone up, this is a great sign. For example when we were working with the former Compaq Computer Corporation (Compaq) on the creation of their alliance with the Walt Disney Company (Disney), the alliance discussions started in the western region with Leigh Morrison who was a vice president of $4-billion in sales for the Western United States. However, the executive sponsorship for the relationship soon migrated up to the very top of Compaq the Chief Executive Officer (CEO), Michael Capellas. He took a particular interest in this relationship, saw it as strategically important for Compaq (as indeed it was, since at that time Hewlett-Packard Company (HP) and IBM both wanted the relationship for the United States—HP clearly now has it). Once Capellas was involved, this ratcheted up the interest on the Disney side. Soon he started interacting with Michael Eisner, and we were off and running!

The Mature Stage

The mature stage is a time when senior management may well start evaluating the viability or legitimacy of the alliance. Its growth will have leveled off, and the initial excitement may well have faded. Sometimes we say that these alliances are moving into sclerosis in the mature stage because the alliance is not growing as expected. It is becoming of less value, and less attention is being paid to the growth aspects but lots more to the paper, process, and often bureaucratic waste of time.

Additionally, time has passed since inception. There is a high likelihood that those who launched the alliance are no longer involved, and the managers that are responsible for it are not as emotionally involved. Indeed, they may have little knowledge or corporate memory of the early, adrenalin-pumping stages.

On the other hand, there may be some very valuable outgrowths of the mature alliance that make it more valuable than its unimpressive lack of growth would indicate.

Your employees may have become so knowledgeable about their partner's business that should your company ever decide to compete, they would be a formidable competitor. Of course, this is an excellent reason to make sure that the alliance is well managed and well understood by both parties. Even though the alliance might enter the mature stage, or even if it was in the declining stage, there are so many other strategic and competitive considerations that both parties should strive hard to make the relationship work. This is a good example of why alliances do not lend themselves only to quantitative metrics. If you were looking mainly at growth as a factor for success, the strategic implications of terminating an alliance that could have educated a competitor would be downplayed and perhaps underestimated. Alliance implementation metrics that cross every life-cycle stage must include those in Chapter Four, with special attention to alignment with strategy, the competitive analysis, the future positioning of the partners, and the preemptive nature of the relationship.

Here are a number of the characteristics that are most often found in the mature stage of the alliance life cycle:

1. Slowed growth. This is the most obvious characteristic.

2. Changeover of teams on both sides. Those who feel more stimulated by growing opportunities and less by conflict resolution will naturally gravitate out of this stage of the alliance. Rather than trying to keep unwilling or (because they are unwilling) incompetent members on either team, anticipate this change and move some of them off into other positions, while planning the move well so that there is continuity of handoff and neither partner feels shoved aside.

3. Increased conflict. Often when growth slows, the pressure is on both sides to produce. Then the differences between management styles, cultures, and definitions of success become relevant. One company may be satisfied with even a reduced level of growth because the alliance with the partner is so strategic and prestigious for them, while the other may need more profitable results.

Do keep in mind that each life-cycle stage is distinct: Movement from the left-hand side of the chart (startup) to the right-hand side of the chart (decline and sustain) is *not* linear. Your alliance does not have to go from startup through each of the life-cycle stages. You could go from startup directly into decline! Or, you could go from startup into the mature stage without any of those great spurts of growth for which everyone is looking. When that happens, conflict is more likely to occur. Both parties may start to question the viability of the alliance, unless, as mentioned above, it is strategically important to one or all of them.

4. Restructuring of goals. The mature stage will invite restructuring of goals. Logically, few, if any, alliances have in their operating plan a protracted period of lagging growth. In most situations, there is an expectation somewhere that the project will *take off* and thrive, however that is defined. The significance of the mature stage of the life cycle is that the alliance, at that moment, is not *thriving*. The metrics for *thriving* should include many of those from the alliance implementation list:

➤ Detailed financial plans and ratios.

➤ Schedules for a variety of deliverables.

➤ Protocols for knowledge capture and transfer.

➤ Resource modifications.

➤ Customer relationship management and metrics associated with the customer such as upsells, acquisition cost, attrition rate, and lead conversion rates.

Because many of these measurements would have been launched along with the startup phase, it's their comparison and interpretation that will now be front and center stage for the partners' attention.

It is here that the disagreements could begin. There could be disagreements about: the definition of terms, one partner may want to change the terms if their position in the market has changed either with another competitor entering, a change in technology, even their own corporate restructuring or takeover, or general economic conditions.

The financial metrics that could be restructured at this stage may well be dependent on the outcome of other, less obvious, metrics such as the value of the brand enhancement by the association of one partner with another. If a partnership had reached the mature stage, the partner would have some hard decisions to make. First, would they be better off not partnering with this partner? Or, more critically, could they afford *not* to partner with such a powerful and omnipresent brand? Namely, would it be worth their while just to hold that preemptive brand association no matter what the growth outcome was for strategic reasons alone? The Eastman Kodak Company, decades ago, made the decision *not* to sponsor the Olympics for one single year. It was that year that Fujifilm slipped in and grabbed the opportunity. Strategically, Kodak made a wrong decision even though from a profit and loss standpoint, they avoided a large expense that year. Who could quantify the lost opportunity (ROMOC—return on market opportunity cost), the future competitive nature of Fujifilm's aggressive entry into the United States, and the commoditization struggles that both companies would face in the fight for the United States (and global) consumer as they moved into the digital world?

5. Intense mediation. The presumption in mediation is that the parties consider it worthwhile to actually continue with the alliance and to establish the ground rules for some sort of re-launch process. Just establishing these issues and getting them on the table are a challenge in itself. The parties may have stopped being honest with each other, they may be obfuscating or, worse still, moving into areas of total mistrust and recrimination. The job of the mediator is to start de-emotionalizing the discussion. He or she might list the following tasks as a mediation process: looking at the relationship as it was in the past, listing your expectations then, and determining how either the circumstances have changed or your companies or teams have changed, and then redefining the legitimacy and purpose of the relationship as it is now and will be in the future.

    The art of mediation is not very different from the art of negotiation; however, it includes a heavier emphasis on the historical behavior and experience of the parties in an already existing relationship, and it is a definite skill which should not be attempted by those who are not schooled in it. A delicate moment exists in the relationship when a mediator is called in, when it could go either way. Once the lawyers get involved, and the situation moves to arbitration, litigation, and downright war, resolution becomes much more expensive, difficult, and destructive to the future potential that could be salvaged from the alliance. So give mediation a chance. After all, you have invested so much in the alliance this far, and it may be worth a last effort to make it work.

6. Potential termination. One of the events that could happen in the mature stage of the life cycle is the termination of the alliance.

The Declining Stage

Unfortunately, the declining characteristics could pull the alliance into termination which could happen before it was planned, or some re-launch characteristics are applied. However, the alliance could recover some value and fall into the turnaround category, called the sustaining life-cycle stage on the right in Figure 1.3 which I will discuss next.

There are some similarities to the mature stage in the declining stage characteristics, namely, that mediation would be a preferable option if there is any slight desire to see the alliance re-launched. However, most of the characteristics deal with the recognition and management of this difficult stage of an alliance with regard to decisions about termination. Here are some of the metrics and considerations that you might want to think about:

1. Value proposition. What is it? Is there a value proposition that can be articulated at this stage of the relationship that will have meaning for all parties? (This is consultant language: What's the point of this alliance? Is there any value left in it that is substantial enough to warrant trying to turn it around?)

2. Can you afford to terminate? In other words, do you run the risk of releasing a competitor into the marketplace once you terminate with this partner who has now learned enough to become a competitor?

3. Has the market changed so that the alliance is no longer viable enabling you to terminate with good feelings and no damage to either partner (and even leave the door open to future collaborations)?

4. Is the declining of the alliance due to the personality clashes of certain alliance managers. Would changing managers help? We will cover some of the key individual characteristics in the next section regarding individual managerial personalities for alliance managers (Figure 1.4) to assist you in this evaluation.

These are just a few of the key considerations that will help you through the declining phase gracefully!

The Sustaining Phase

Many people interpret this as the stage that will perpetuate and sustain the ongoing existence of the alliance. I have a different interpretation. *Sustaining* in this context means a *transitional stage of life of the alliance as it moves back into one of the earlier stages.* Sustaining means turnaround. It is unhealthy to stay in turnaround for a long period of time. The characteristics of turnaround will prove that these are temporary measures coordinating closely with the characteristics discussed in re-launch. Here are a few metrics and considerations for the sustaining life cycle stage.

1. New team members who have visionary abilities. This means that leadership is critical. The leader of the alliance team now must be someone who has good credentials for the purpose of the alliance—either an engineer who is well respected by both sides if the project is research or a marketing whiz who is known to be innovative and aggressive. These leadership qualities should again be treated as measurements with assessment tools.

2. Tight milestones and defined budgets. This is not the time for long periods of pilots, flexible budgets, or financials. The visionary manager who is turning around a failing alliance doesn't have interminable freedom to make this alliance show some signs of success. Generally the milestones are shorter than normal, and a very tight grip must be kept on a couple of key metrics that are relevant to the substance of the alliance such as:

   a. In a sales and marketing alliance relevant metrics would be: the customer acquisition cost, the time to market, the cycle time of all relevant activities, and the sales increase from new customers as well as leverage of existing ones. A quarter will be the first measurement and probably no more than four quarters.

   b. In a research alliance, the milestones should not be unreasonable so as to expect definitive outcomes, but rather the achievement of a certain deliverable constitutes success (and that deliverable may not be the ultimate goal or outcome). There have to be some reality checks here as to what can be done in what period of time. And, in some instances, the entire project will need re-evaluation as to whether the risk, time, and resources required to get to the desired result are worth the effort and can be achieved in the short time-window available for most turnaround alliances.

   c. In a joint venture, the structure is probably already in place. One consideration could be to examine whether it's the right structure. Possibly having a separate legal entity is not necessary with all the accompanying legal responsibilities and liabilities such as cost of terminating such an entity. In some cases, a contract alone without the structuring of a new entity is sufficient.

3. Involvement of the lawyers. This is a part of every alliance at some point or other, generally in the beginning and at the end. The key point here to remember is that lawyers are your advisors, not the managers of the alliance, so it is good to keep them informed. In a regulated industry, you will have no option but to do that assiduously. However, the business decision should always remain yours and the relationship management issues with the partner are yours, even though legal counsel on both sides may be talking to each other. The turnaround scenario may well be a negotiated solution and compromise from the declining discussions that took place and the conflict resolution mechanisms that are being implemented. However, because this is tantamount to a re-launch, you are starting to build a relationship that may have some rifts in it but, nevertheless, requires the attention that a startup does and more. A turnaround alliance is on the cusp of decline all the time until it gets out of the turnaround stage and back into an earlier stage of growth. So the dance you do is between understanding the terms of the new agreement, being flexible enough to take into account the partner, your company, and market changes while you are implementing, keeping a very short fuse on all the metrics, while managing the expectations like an expert so that what is promised, gets done, and what is expected, happens most of the time. This rebuilding of trust will go a long way to remediation and the re-launching of a failing relationship, which is a large part of the job of the turnaround manager.

You can see that managing a startup alliance will require a very different mindset from managing one that is in the declining or mature stage. By knowing these characteristics before deciding on resources (both human and capital), your planning and execution of the alliance will become far more precise and comprehensive. This knowledge and Figure 1.3 can also act as a communication tool to underscore when differences in life cycle stage between you and your partners might be causing lack of clear communication.

When I performed the original research at Caltech examining two hundred thirty-five companies and establishing the Mindshift approach as applied to organizational life cycles, I also found specific individuals who are attracted to or detracted from various life cycle stages. They tend to thrive or fail depending on their fit or lack thereof. When applied to the alliance itself, the same findings hold true. Alliance managers tend to gravitate to the stage of the alliance that most interests them or fits with their personality. That is also where they are the most effective. This is important to know before placing them in this position and will also underscore the need for changing alliance managers as the alliance itself changes. Figure 1.4 describes the managerial characteristics as they change through the life cycle of the alliance.

I am sure you are now looking at these various personality types and recognizing your colleagues, bosses, subordinates, and even yourself! Let's walk through Figure 1.4 together.

The life cycle stage of startup begins on the left-hand side with the adventurer manager who is exciting to be around and has a real sense of urgency that is wonderful for championing an alliance. But he doesn't often have the staying power to continue with the details of growing or managing the relationship. The hockey stick phase is driven by the warrior manager—again, a good person for launching a new idea and growing it, but don't ask him or her to apply metrics because he or she can't be bothered with the details or paperwork. The professional stage alliance manager is an excellent resource—the hunter manager, who does a good job of action and process as well as resolving ambiguity and conflict. The farmer manager will have a tough time taking much risk and could *process* the alliance to death and accelerate it into declining on the right-hand side of the cultural chart in Figure 1.3. Sustaining would require a visionary-type manager who is both focused on the action items as well as the process ones of measuring what is critical to make the return from decline into growth again. Figure 1.3 is not meant to be all inclusive of every characteristic but gives you a good cross section of the actual personality characteristics of alliance managers. Understanding these characteristics will help you plan and re-juggle your team when necessary.

My research established in 1994 and more recently affirmed in 2002 that the professional stage of the alliance life cycle and the hunter personality (also in that stage) are the best for alliance value creation and management. Hunter managers are good leaders and team builders and can work well with those in the adventurer, warrior, farmer, visionary and even politician status. They are cognizant of metrics being important, but they also understand they should not include too much process or bureaucracy that might slow the pace of the alliance unnecessarily.

The point of the Mindshift approach as applied to the actual alliance is to assist you in the metrics environment with some of the *softer* cultural and people issues: It gives you an objective, measurable way to look at cultural and personality differences, a language of common terms and ideas that

FIGURE 1.4 The Mindshift Approach—Individual Managerial Personalities

Adventurer	Warrior	Hunter	Farmer	Politician	Visionary
Risk taker	Aggressive	Leader	Old boy network	Risk averse	Results oriented
Visionary	Self-confident	Good team and consensus builder	Formal	Isolationist	Assertive
Obsessive	Winning battles (may lose war)	More formalized	Risk averse	Bureaucratic	Confident
Driven	Abrasive	Systematic	Behavior is conforming	Polite but self-protective	Inspires hope
Sometimes unrealistic sense of urgency	Result focused			Form over substance in behavior	Team building
	Resistant to process			Paperwork is protection against reality	Risk taker
	Omnipresent				Flexible

vantagepartners

enables you to present and manage the differences between groups and individuals who may have difficulties in communication, measuring the same things, defining success, and working together in a multiplicity of ways. It is a way to anticipate behavior, manage the differences, and to dissolve cultural clashes and resolve impasses.

The final part of the Mindshift approach is the project personality or priority. Figure 1.5 can help you think about those differences. There can be significant differences among the priorities of different parties to an alliance. The priority will affect strategic impact, resource allocation, longevity of commitment, staying power, senior management level interest, sponsorship, and more. *Priority* is a critical piece of information for you to know and will assist you greatly in managing your relationship. It is a metric that should be viewed at the inception of the relationship, with a baseline set, similar to mutuality metrics, and then measured over time throughout the life of the relationship. When the priority is dropping for

---

FIGURE 1.5 The Mindshift Approach—Project Personalities or Priorities

Bet the Farm	Middle of the Road	Experimental
• Project is integral to future survival of corporation—fits into macro strategy and positioning	• Project is important but secondary to major market, e.g., USA is major thrust, international seen as secondary	• Project of limited importance to top management but vital to segments of organization, e.g., R&D
• Well financed	• Part of business strategy re: implementation—some macro elements	• Resources committed but limited vis-à-vis time and results
• Top management involvement	• Some top management involvement in inception—wanes—over time unless becomes hockey stick	• Conflict resolution mechanisms not well designed

one party of the alliance, you are looking at a leading indicator of alliance failure, which must be managed before conflict ensues. Figure 1.5 outlines the various levels of project priority—from "bet the farm" which is very important to the organization and indicates this alliance will probably be a strategic one, to the "middle-of-the-road" alliance which could be strategic to a business unit but not to the whole organization, to "experimental" which could still be important to a team or group or even a single individual but to the greater organization or even within the portfolio of alliances, it is of lesser value. The evaluation of different priority levels will be of great value as you measure change in your alliance. Although project priority is an element of alliances no matter their stage of the life cycle, in the declining stage it is particularly relevant because this metric will show you the way to turn your alliance around, especially if the priority level is higher for one party than for another. Remember to apply the priority analysis to every stage of the alliance life cycle.

Bet-the-Farm Priority Level of Alliances

The bet-the-farm level is where the project is of strategic importance, will be well-financed, the parties will not want it to fail, and it is integral to the future as well as the long-term positioning of the organizations involved. When a project is bet the farm there is a high likelihood that even if the growth factors are not there, and the project could be termed in the declining phase, the parties will fight long and hard *together* to make it succeed. This fight will mean re-evaluating every aspect of the alliance from cost savings, new team allocations, renewed market focus, different branding, changed resources, and so on. However, if only one party considers the alliance to be a bet-the-farm alliance, and the other party or parties don't, you will see a split of effort at this point. Earlier in the alliance, the party for whom the project priority was highest might have contributed more in effort, resources, and time to the alliances. After all, it's more important to them so that makes sense. However, when the project reaches a declining stage, it will be the time when the real differential in commitment will be obvious.

The golden rule is this: The party, for whom the project priority is highest, is the one that does all the work.

That partner will be looking for any way to continue the relationship. This may mean actually undertaking the cost and the effort of putting their employees, at their cost, into the location or operations of the partner so as to nurture and care for the alliance. It may mean accepting many slights, lack of attention, poor communication, inefficiencies, and possibly even being ignored by the partner, with equanimity. Because the main outcome is that the alliance continues and if that in itself is of value to the partner for whom the alliance is a bet-the-farm one, then everything else is irrelevant. The most important advice I can give you here follows:

➤ Don't have expectations that your partner will contribute what you think they should or even what they said they would.

➤ Keep the lawyers out of it.

➤ Keep positive communication going even if it is only one sided (i.e., from you to them).

➤ Keep your pride in your pocket.

➤ Be sure to measure the benefit that you believe make this a bet-the-farm project for you. If it isn't there, then there is no reason for you to continue being abused.

➤ But if it is, don't let personalities or misaligned expectations ruin a relationship you must have.

Middle-of-the-Road Priority Level of Alliances

The middle-of-the-road stage is not quite as obvious as the bet-the-farm stage. This means that the project will be of some importance to both parties, that is, if the alliance is seen as middle of the road in priority but if it is in decline, the decision will have to be made jointly regarding whether each party wants to contribute turnaround effort to re-launch the alliance. No one party may be willing to take the lead. Their interests in the alliance may be equally tepid. A mediator will be an alternative in that he might revive interest in the parties in the alliance which was at one time of some importance to all partners. There is another wrinkle here: The future analysis and prediction of the best case outcome for the alliance could change it into a more successful one for one or both of the parties—and that may involve bringing in another partner for whom the alliance could be bet the farm. That partner might arrive with renewed energy, resources, and strength to revive the lagging opportunity or project.

Experimental Priority Level of Alliances

Experimental is the third stage of project priority. Here the partners have gone into the project with fairly low expectations, and see the process as an experiment. Often, all partners don't always see the alliance in the same way. One may see it as experimental and another as bet the farm. In those cases, the golden rule will apply, that is, the partner with the highest priority for the project will be the one that does all the work. That goes for when one partner is experimental and the other is middle of the road, as well as if one is middle of the road and another is bet the farm, or any combination of all three levels. The issue here is this:

> *Are you using project priority as one of your metrics? If you are not, you will miss seeing this leading indicator of alliance failure. If you are, you will be able to anticipate issues before they arise and manage the differential in alliance priorities before they become problems.*

Experimental projects will rarely see the light of day if they are in decline because they will be cut. The only variable in that situation is if the partners see the alliance at different levels of project priority, in which case the golden rule applies.

The Mindshift[sm] approach is a helpful aid to anticipating the kinds of behaviors and cultural norms that companies and divisions and even groups use in dealing with each other, depending on their life-cycle stages. Once you understand the life-cycle stage and the anticipated behavior, you can take the amorphous concept of culture and individual personality, as well as the different priorities that the companies may have for the project and put these components into a methodology and context that enables you to select your partners with this added intelligence. In addition, potential areas of conflict could be anticipated and resources allocated to manage through them, rather than being in a crisis mode and reactive to your partnering situation.

We have covered the life-cycle stages of the alliance and how the Mindshift approach along with knowledge of the different activities to be done in each life-cycle stage can help you plan and manage your alliance more effectively. In Chapter Two, I will address the very important issue of stakeholders, and how their different interests in an alliance means that a variety of different metrics and standards must be created and managed in order to ensure the support of those who have the ability to make or destroy a good alliance.

The Five Stakeholders

The numbers of stakeholders who have interest in the alliance comprises more than your partner company and your own. The most important thing you can do in creating your metrics is to understand these different interests because they will ultimately define whether your alliance will be perceived as successful. You serve many masters in making sure these perceptions are as you want them to be.

The five stakeholder groups for partnering metrics are:

➤ Management. Results of relationships tied to perceptions of expected success as well as the promises made by internal sponsors and external partners.

➤ Other functions within all partners. Other functions will be asking, what's in it for me/us/them? How does the partnership add value to us?

➤ Alliance department and managers. How does this alliance fit into the alliances group? What are the effects on the alliance manager's job? What are the career/learning and risk/reward opportunities?

➤ External analysts, competitors, market. These people try to evaluate the competitive impact of the alliance.

➤ Partners. The company's partners will be interested in whether the results of the relationship meet contractual and verbal/nonverbal expectations.

A Special Kind of Partnership: Channel Partners

Before we dive into the details of the five stakeholders, it's important to mention a special kind of alliance known as channel partnerships. These are the distribution relationships that provide the channel for the supplier to their customers. Some channel partners offer many different products, even those of competitors. Also, some suppliers offer their products and services through many different channel partners, some of whom might be competing with each other. So there is a natural affinity and tension in many of these unique relationships which require special attention.

All the five stakeholder characteristics will apply also to this partnership, but it has some special characteristics that are worthy of mention.

Siebel Corporation is extremely adept at managing these kinds of relationships. At a recent conference of The Association for Strategic Alliance Professionals (ASAP), Scott Creighton, a Siebel Corporation executive, presented his insights on the stakeholders that feature in the channel arena. He saw them as follows:

➤ The stakeholders are four different channel business owners.

  ➤ Channel executive.

  ➤ Channel marketing manager.

  ➤ Channel account manager.

  ➤ Channel operations manager.

There are a number of different management challenges for each stakeholder group, which must be managed by the senior executive differently using the Mindshift approach.

Metrics to handle these challenges could include:

➤ Revenues—actual and influenced.

➤ Leads.

➤ New customers—numbers of new and renew/upsells.

➤ Projects in the pipeline.

➤ Customer satisfaction.

➤ Market awareness (from all alliances including channel).

➤ Market cap (if a big channel relationship, it could be all alliances).

➤ Revenue share.

FIGURE 2.1 **Channel Management Challenges (Siebel Case Illustration)**			
Channel Marketing Manager	**Channel Account Manager**	**Channel Operations Manager**	**Channel Executive**
Lack of coordinated marketing and inconsistent brand messaging through and with the partner	Limited sales effectiveness, low win rates and ability to ensure quality service	Limited partner readiness and lack of cost-efficient operations	Inaccurate forecasts or limited pipeline visibility
Misalignment with corporate objectives	Poor service request follow through and long service cycles	Inefficient process in providing timely sales tools, product information, and knowledge to partners	Misalignment of corporate and partnership objectives
Costly literature fulfillment and distribution	Poor lead follow through, poor sales collaboration, and channel lack of product knowledge	Incentives not aligned, silos of a partner and customer information, costly partner training	Inadequate customer information and no common 'face to partner' or 'face to customer'

Creighton presented Figure 2.1 in which he featured the various stakeholders and how they relate to each other. You can see from the interrelationship of the various stakeholders that there are a variety of opportunities for internal collaboration that could, if not facilitated, affect the customer relationship both in the short and long terms. Siebel pays particular attention to these issues and applies its service and software to these challenges for customers.

Now let's turn our attention to those five stakeholders that will be of importance to every alliance including the special ones called channel partnerships.

Management as a Stakeholder

The first stakeholder worthy of discussion is the general category of Management. As you can see from the list of metrics in Figure 2.2, many of them are the same in all five stakeholders, but the additional ones that are relevant for each group are highlighted at the bottom of each list.

As Figure 2.2 shows, there are substantive and specific needs that management has for particular metrics, many of which are important to the parties as well as other stakeholders. One need in particular which may be only of real importance to management, are the promises that have been made by subordinates or superiors and how well they are meeting their commitments. This may be career defining!

Another realization that will help you choose the appropriate measurements of your alliances for their ultimate success is that there are other functions within your company as well as the partner, which could have skin in the game, namely, something to benefit from or lose from your alliance. These could be those in finance, sales, research, and other line positions including other business units who will be directly or indirectly affected by your actions in the alliance. For example, they may have other alliances with the same partner, or a competitor of that partner. So this is where taking into account the concept of the internal customer (those within the organization whom you serve) will assist you to create a metric that will facilitate these parties' interests. Half the battle is just recognizing who is, and why they are concerned or interested in your alliance. The other half is, finding something to measure and a way to *compensate*, if necessary, so that credit is given where due, or special interests are taken into account and negotiated or facilitated, or you and your team don't go blindly into an alliance in a way that could cause a difficult situation for an internal colleague. This awareness will go a long way towards facilitating conflicts and will prevent the alliance implementation plan from coming to a standstill due to these internal or political problems.

If your partner is not managing their side of the situation with this awareness, you will do well to help educate them as to the possible leverage that could come from building this internal goodwill or the possible negative outcomes that internal sabotage could cause.

Management always has a strategic interest but also will have some awareness of competitive impact from external forces. However, don't underestimate the internal issues that often arise when one group of management is concerned about a *territorial grab* by another. Sometimes their

FIGURE 2.2 Management as Stakeholders

Alliance Development Metrics	Alliance Implementation Metrics
Mission/vision	Damage control
Time to market	Market education
Time to decision	Customer penetration
Time to implementation	Channel expansion
Competitive positioning	Channel management
Competitive preemption	Channel marketing
Capabilities enhancement	Marketing milestones
Corporate personality	Contract time limits
Individual personality	Lead conversion rates
Project personality	Customers new
Launch GANTT chart	Customers' up-sell
Partner criteria fit	Education and learning
Equity investment	Knowledge transfer
Financial management	Customer satisfaction/service
Accounts receivable	Cost savings in development, supply,
Return on investment	design, manufacturing, service, delivery
Return on equity	Outsourcing
Return on labor hours …	Quality improvement
Perception of value and definition of success	Risk mitigation
	Faster manufacturing cycle time
Promises made by internal sponsors	Faster market penetration
Strategic alignment	Risk mitigation through preemptive
Partner vs public perception of relationship	positioning …
	Revenue goals
	Faster sales cycles
	Faster inventory turns
	Faster development of ideas/products/services …
	Meeting of growth, cost savings, tech, market share, geographic, capabilities goals
	Promises fulfilled compared to those made
	Public perception of promises made and kept

particular interest in the alliance's success or failure may affect their sphere of influence and control, and the alliance will have the extra burden of that scrutiny to bear.

An additional concern of management is to compare the promises made to the performance and results. A number of CEOs and leaders ask their direct reports for their best estimate of production or results for the upcoming fiscal year and then hold them to it. In other words, they ask them for their commitments to achieve those results, rather than imposing the expectation that they will reach one result rather than another. This is particularly the style of former chairman and CEO of Motorola and of Eastman Kodak, George Fisher, who managed to get the very best that each of his direct reports could do because they always wanted to excel and pushed themselves further than he could have pushed them. This is a good management technique. In an alliance it works as well, however, it is important to remember that you do not have the control of your partner or of the market circumstances. Your results will be affected by both of those factors. It's a good philosophy under all circumstances to under-promise and over-deliver. Figure 2.2 is a good reference for the metrics that management is particularly interested in.

Other Functions within All Partners as Stakeholders

Figure 2.3 shows the complexity of taking into account all the other functions within the organization that could have an interest in the success (or failure) of the alliance. Figure 2.3 mentions the concept of the currency

---

FIGURE 2.3 Other Functions within All Partners as Stakeholders

Alliance Development Metrics	Alliance Implementation Metrics
What's in it for us?	The internal customer goals
What do we lose by this relationship?	The internal customer challenges met by the alliance
What can we leverage from these relationships?	Rewards
Leverage points	Credit (currency—see Chapter Four)
Cross-functional teams	
Performance reviews with alliance results included	
Agenda item on management calendar for other functions	
Customer or stakeholder added value from alliance	

vantagepartners

factor, discussed in more detail in Chapter Four, which is a method of rewarding contributions within an organization in ways other than monetary consideration but rather with internal recognition or branding. This is key to making internal groups willing to exchange and share information and knowledge.

The Alliance Department and Managers

The alliance department or group is another stakeholder in each of the partners. In some organizations, for example, Cisco Systems there are more than one hundred alliance managers worldwide, and the group manages their alliances with portfolio skills. I will address some of these skills as we move through the following chapters with examples like Starbucks and IBM. With a large number of people involved, as well as those in the business units who are affected by the alliance, especially if it's a customer or distribution relationship, there will be many eyes and minds watching the alliance group. Of course, if you are an alliance manager, this will impact upon your career, too.

Thus, it is helpful to do a SWOT analysis—strength, weakness, opportunity, and threat—to constantly see what issues could exist in the competency levels of the department, the alliance portfolio issues, if any, and the alliance processes that are used.

The metrics (Figure 2.4) suggested for the alliance department are further described in Chapter Four with a chart (Figure 4.3) that could be used for a portfolio approach to alliance management.

A responsibility of the alliance group is to perform alliance portfolio management. To do this, the creation of an alliance database is necessary so that all managers can link to or access relevant documents: strategic alliance plan, alliance contracts, data/metrics individual alliance report cards, relevant managers, ongoing meetings and work in progress, market positioning and external communications, learning captured, resource issues, conflict resolution in progress, expansion plans for individual alliances, and so on. The head of the alliances department and other members of senior management must be able to see at a glance what is going on in all the alliances; additionally, the alliance database will keep the record of all the alliances that the organization has entered into so that leverage in negotiation is possible, different business units don't bump into each other in the lobby of the same customer, and corporate memory and knowledge can be captured in a central depository.

FIGURE 2.4 **Alliance Department in All Partners**

Alliance Development Metrics	Alliance Implementation Metrics
What's in it for us?	The internal alliance group goals
What do we lose by this relationship?	The internal alliance group challenges met by the alliance
What can we leverage from this relationship?	Rewards for the group and for the managers and for you and your counterpart
Leverage points	
Cross-functional teams	Credit (currency)—who gets it?
Performance reviews with alliance results included	**Damage control**
Agenda item on management calendar for other functions	**Marketing of alliance success and learning from alliance failure**
Customer or stakeholder added value from alliance	**Public perceptions of alliance results and managing them**
Career opportunities or risks for you and other managers	
Marketing of the alliance within the organization	
Promotion of the alliance	
Capturing of knowledge developed by the alliance group	
Communication of the alliance success and learning	
Process refinement for *valuable* processes only	

External Analysts and Other External Stakeholders

One of the most ignored stakeholders in alliance management is the external stakeholder in the form of the analyst who, in many respects, both advises and represents the market. Unfortunately, many analysts only show interest in the alliance either when it is announced or when it fails. The external analyst is a critical commentator and contributor to the market perception of the company, and, more importantly, he or she must be educated about your alliances especially if they are strategic in nature. Of course, this is the place where under-promising and over-delivering will be critical because setting expectations too high would be unrealistic and ultimately damaging. Nevertheless, if alliances are important to your company's strategies and future valuation, analysts must become part of that evaluation process. Also, external analysts will not only talk to you, they will also talk to your partner—even more reason to hold partnering sessions where you can be sure to talk the same partnering language and have a similar or at least consensual basis for defining success for the alliance. Educating analysts regarding the metrics that are important for one alliance rather than another will prevent a cookie-cutter approach to alliance valuation, enabling the analyst community to become more sophisticated as you do.

I mention competitors as stakeholders, although that seems to be stretching the definition somewhat. But think about it this way: If you succeed, they may have something to be concerned about. If you fail, they could see an opportunity. So, they do have *skin in the game*. Competitors may be

FIGURE 2.5 External Analysts, Market, and Competitors as Stakeholders

Alliance Development Metrics	Alliance Implementation Metrics
Mission vision	Damage control
Time to market	Market education
Time to decision—time to decision	Customer penetration
Time to implementation	Channel expansion
Competitive positioning	Channel management
Competitive preemption	Revenue goals
Capabilities enhancement	Faster sales cycles
Equity investment	Faster inventory returns
Financial management	New customers
Accounts receivable	Customer satisfaction/service
Return on investment	Cost savings in development, supply, design, manufacturing, service, delivery
Return on equity	
Return on labor hours …	Outsourcing
Partner vs public perception of relationship	Faster manufacturing cycle time
	Faster penetration
Negotiation vs relationship creation (tire kicking)	**Risk mitigation through preemptive positioning …**
SWOT team approach for quick action and contracts	**Meeting of growth, cost savings, tech, market share, geographic, capabilities goals**
Legal and accounting team collaboration	

vantagepartners

bad mouthing you to your customers or suppliers in subtle ways, so it's important not to be naïve about your alliance. Be sure that your communication anticipates competitive negativity whether to your alliance partner directly or possibly to your joint customers or customers of the alliance itself, whether internal or external. Figure 2.5 lists the various metrics that might be of importance to those external stakeholders. As Figure 2.5 shows, some stakeholders seem far removed but, in fact, could affect the stock, the value of the company, and eventually the jobs of the company's leaders if they are not educated or informed about highly strategic alliances.

Partners as Stakeholders

The most obvious stakeholders are the ones I have left for last—the partners to the alliance. This subject will be covered in great detail in Chapters Three and Four which are devoted to these metrics. They fall into the alliance development metrics and the alliance implementation metrics.

CHAPTER THREE

Alliance Development Metrics: The Partners

Alliance metrics are divided into development and implementation metrics. The first group, called alliance development metrics are most commonly seen even before the alliance is launched. Remnants of these metrics will be seen again during the implementation metrics all the way from the startup of the alliance to the declining stages of the alliance. Remember—overlay the alliance life-cycle over all these metrics.

Creating an alliance is the fun part. This is where the adrenalin pumps, and accolades for *deal making* are given. It's also the time when future potential is plotted, discussed, and dreamed about. Alliances are all about realizing future potential. Many of the practices and expectations set in this seminal stage will be the basis of the alliance's success or failure, long after the creators have moved on to explore other opportunities. The metrics that support good alliances cannot stop at the creation stage. They must be designed and modified so as to give you and your partners a clear understanding of why the alliance is still worth doing, while gathering the results in such a way that can give meaningful insights on the alliance to those who are not actually involved in it.

The following steps in Figure I.3 will guide you through the development metrics, recommending where specific customization is appropriate for your particular alliance and organizational culture. Case illustrations will highlight how companies apply these metrics. Remember, although the process may appear lengthy, having a process can actually accelerate your alliance development rather than slow it. It is far preferable to have a template which is repeatable, proactive, and can be shared, than for the alliance development knowledge to reside in the heads of one or two members of the alliance team. After all, those who develop the alliance are rarely those who implement it. Development metrics will need to be communicated to all future members of the alliance implementation team to answer the often heard question: "What idiot got us into this mess?" Communication is a key success factor for smooth management of alliances; these tools and approaches will diminish the confusion and complexity of the handoff process if team members change over time. Here, for your convenience, is the chart from the Introduction (Figure I.3) which describes the large categories of alliance development metrics:

Conceptualization

Thinking about making an alliance? Contemplating a multipartner relationship to serve a customer more effectively? The time of conceptualization is a grand moment when all appears possible, and dreams are not yet reality. Similar to the courtship stage in personal relationships, partners appear without warts, blemishes, or history. Remember that every alliance has a life cycle and so conceptualization must include some reality checks about *what if* and *how* as well as the high level expectations and dreams of success.

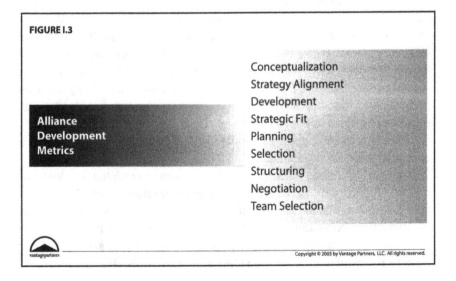

FIGURE I.3

Alliance Development Metrics

Conceptualization
Strategy Alignment
Development
Strategic Fit
Planning
Selection
Structuring
Negotiation
Team Selection

The subsets of conceptualization that could comprise metrics for you include:

➤ Creating a vision for the alliance. Much of the discussion in the early stages of the alliance goes to the potential of what can be done together. Recently, when working with a supplier client who had been approached by a retailer of huge proportions, I found the supplier's focus in the early stages of the discussions was to address the potential for growth in the alliance. They quantified the potential sales, talked a lot about margins, deliverables, and purchase commitments from the buyer.

However, the fundamental vision of the alliance for each party was very different. The supplier saw the relationship as strategic and long term with real concessions on price on their part, including the need to develop a customized private label product for the customer. The buyer saw the relationship as much more tactical, basically just a purchase agreement enabling the customer to be competitive in the market as the low cost provider of these products to the consumer. The vision of the relationship for each party was so divergent that had this become part of the threshold discussions, they would have seen that the alliance would face serious challenges, not only in the negotiation of an agreeable set of deal terms but also in the amount of attention the customer would pay to the supplier and the ensuing implementation challenges over the life cycle of the relationship. The customer saw the relationship as a vendor contract, namely, that there was no need for long-term strategic negotiation, no more than a one-year contract, and that the entire contractual relationship would be managed by procurement, rather than the strategic alliance or business development group.

In short, one party (the buyer) didn't have the same vision of a strategic relationship that the other party (the seller) had. Their visions were incompatible.

Could this be resolved? Of course—by discussion of the metrics that were important to each party. The time for discussion, however, was not at the end of the negotiation process but rather at the beginning. After all, why waste everyone's time if the margin reductions required by the supplier were not balanced with the longer term relationship and commitment of trust, follow-through, and relationship building that would be necessary to sustain such a relationship? The vision discussion would have been able to red-flag an area of potentially irreconcilable differences, put them on the table for discussion, and open the door to a different, more mutual type of relationship.

➤ Aligning the vision for the alliance to the strategy of the organization. This means understanding corporate vision and goals. Taking the same illustration regarding vision as a metric, one of the problems in the development stage partnering processes for these companies was that there was little to no discussion of strategy.

The entire discussion needs to move from the supplier, pricing, and volume arena to the vision and strategic discussion of "How can we both reach our long- and short-term strategic goals that we have decided, corporately, are part of our company's position and future in the market?"

➤ Identifying and testing the high level screens that make this particular alliance viable. Examples of some high level screens are:

➤ Strategic plan. Discussions in the implementation metrics take on a completely different tone when the strategic implications are taken into account.

➤ Business development plan. In many circumstances, a partner relationship is part of a business development effort either for future distribution, marketing, promotion, market share and geographic expansion, or possibly technology licensing or development and more. Before the relationship discussions go too far, the business development group, whether they were the ones that are reacting to a partner approach or are proactively pursuing a potential partner, will evaluate the opportunity by matching the partner's capabilities to the business development goals and plans. In many cases, organizations act in reactive mode—namely, they are so besieged by potential partners that they are constantly trying to screen and evaluate them, which is where business development and strategic plans can be helpful to direct and guide partner decisions.[1]

➤ Operating unit plan. This is a core principle for alliance management. Many of the most promising alliances do not reach their initial or even full potential because the operating unit that will have profit and loss responsibility for the relationship is either not vested in it, has no *skin in the game* in its early development stages, or sees the relationship

---

[1]See Chapter Eleven on how Starbucks does this.

as a wart on the nose of the division, rather than a part of its growing beauty! Do not separate alliance creation and development from alliance implementation—connect the teams who negotiate with those who will implement and collaborate early on so as to ensure buy-in, appropriate hand-off, and acceptable and realistic deal metrics.

➤ Corporate values. There is no way to overstate the importance of these criteria for alliance development. Whether the company is private, public, for profit or not, the value system is literally the DNA of the company, its learned and inherited behavior; therefore, it changes with great difficulty, often only after major trauma and rarely willingly. You will find a number of companies profiled in the rest of the book that have similar challenges and important cultural differentials that make them distinctive partners.[2] Here are a couple of key questions that you could answer for your company which will enable you to start looking into the strategic fit of the partner and alliance with your corporate DNA:

1. Would the results of the alliance be true to your values?

2. Would their potential partner have the same value system?

3. How could your company design a reward system for a partner that would be consistent with your goals?

4. How would you establish that the partner truly understands their intent in this area so that you will not find yourself in a relationship with a partner who focused on different goals (i.e., make sure that they didn't just say the words but lived them, too).

Each one of these concerns can become a metric, stated overtly, set up as part of the evaluation criteria for partners who could be approached or might approach you and could be given quantifiable values so that a numerical average of partner preference or eligibility could be reached in the early stages of evaluation.

Strategy Alignment

The second metric in alliance development is strategic alignment. Though this metric is mentioned in the conceptualization area, here I delve into it a little deeper. This step presumes that you have a strategy that either guides

---

[2]See Chapters Nine and Eleven on Staples and Starbucks, respectively.

your company, division, group, or your function. I have made an assumption that the alliance is going to be tied to some strategy and is in alignment with something that has been thought of before. In some companies, the situation actually works in reverse! That is, a partner shows up with a great idea, people get excited about it, they start working to influence others to their way of thinking, then they reverse-justify the partner opportunity into a strategy, i.e., they try to force-fit the opportunity or actually create a strategy to make the opportunity happen.

Now this could well be an appropriate approach once in a while, that is, a great innovative idea arrives on the scene that is so beneficial that it requires a change in strategy. However, running a company this way is risky. I am not suggesting that there is a need for a bureaucratic strategic planning process and lots of documentation to write it all in a nice thick manual which gathers dust on the shelf. Rather, I believe that strategic planning is an iterative, highly interactive learning process that should not take up more than two pages and be clear to everyone in the organization so as to push decision making to the lowest level, that is, to those closest to the customers. But it does have to happen—articulating a strategy, communicating it clearly, and getting commitment to it from the members of the organization will ensure that people are acting, for the most part, in concert, in focus, in the same direction, and with the same interests within the bounds of human error and market changes.

Simply put, creating strategic alignment creates the opportunity for a microanalysis of whether you know what you are trying to do, others understand it, too, and there is some level of agreement that what you are trying to do is within the range of what the organization as a whole wants to achieve.

Pre-launch Development

The third aspect of development metrics is the pre-launch development, a good generic term that can be applied to all the varied tasks that are part of assembling the alliance requirements before launch. It can be a long checklist, but its purpose is to help you organize and select the items that you consider important enough to become part of the measures that you want to track at this stage of the relationship. Here are suggested items that should be on that list. The character and specific nature of your proposed alliance will determine the nature of this list.

1. Communications protocol—external and internal.

2. Reporting and governance—accountability and responsibility.

3. Soft and hard metrics—e.g., soft are cultural fit and learning; e.g. hard are revenues generated or research projects in process.

4. Stakeholder changes—to whom is the alliance important now—compared to those who might have been interested at the inception of the relationship.

If the ultimate goal of the alliance strategy is to be able to manage all alliances within a context, then it is important to discover whether the alliance fits well into that context, which is part of the analysis we call *strategic fit.*

Strategic Fit

What a wonderful concept strategic fit is—two little words that make it sound so easy! When in the early stages of partnering, the analysis and discussions about partner opportunities take place and these concepts are part of the fun of imagining how things would be if . . .

It's certainly important to look at the strategies of all partners and how compatible they are, but strategic fit includes other issues that are not as clear, such as hidden agendas, internal cultural beliefs that are hard to find until the partnership is already operational. One of the threshold presumptions we have made herein is that each partner has a clear strategy, which is rather a large assumption. At The Lared Group (now Vantage Partners),[3] the alliance consulting firm I co-founded twenty years ago, we developed a couple of management tools that can test that assumption. My former Lared partner Emilio Fontana is particularly skilled in teasing out the real issues about strategic direction by using the tools in Figure 3.1.

Approaching the analysis from the left hand side of the chart in Figure 3.1, the discussion begins by examining the mission, vision, and values of

---

[3]On July 1, 2003, The Lared Group merged with Vantage Partners. The author is now a Partner at Vantage Partners, a consulting firm with expertise in building corporate relationship management capabilities. A spin off from the Harvard Project On Negotiation, Vantage Partners has provided thought leadership to executives and world leaders alike in the disciplines of relationship management, negotiation, supply chain, procurement and outsourcing management. Their website is www.vantagepartners.com

FIGURE 3.1 The Strategic Alliance Plan

In order to be effective, a Strategic Alliance Plan must be aligned with the Organizational Strategic and Operating Plan. This figure outlines the basic elements of such a plan and highlights the areas where it must share foundations and elements with the Organizational Strategic Plan.

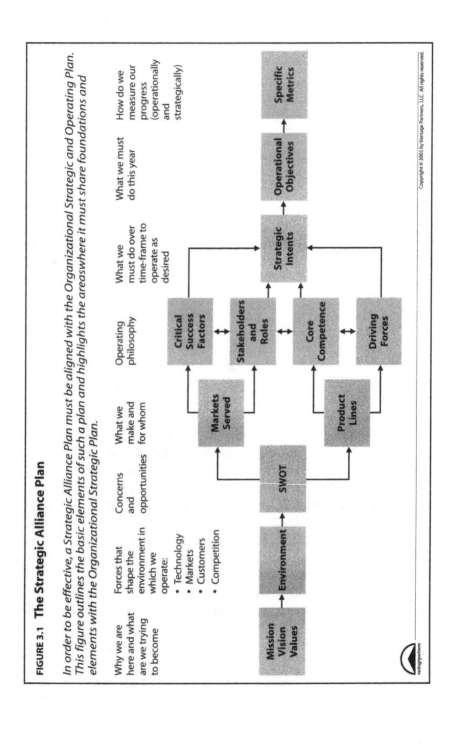

the organization, followed by answering the questions, "Why are we here and what are we trying to achieve?" This discussion must take into consideration the context of the environment of the company, including the technology, market conditions, customers, and competition. This discussion alone takes a number of sessions because it covers the entire strategic context of the organization. Once this information is well understood and communicated, the evolution of the strategic fit analysis will flow much more easily. After all, until you know yourself, it's difficult to know others.

Then have the group conduct a SWOT analysis of strengths, weaknesses, opportunities, and threats. This is a brainstorming-level discussion that should be carefully facilitated in order to include those voices that are not *singing the company song.* I mean that the people in the room who generally have a contrary perspective and get shouted down, should be included. Hear them out in this phase of the discussion; they could have a valuable, if unpopular, perspective. What should come out of this free-for-all is a list of the areas where we should focus, and those where we will get less return. Most importantly, we will see the gaps in which we could place strategic alliance relationships for the present and future.

The next stage of the internal discussion will address the more specific questions: "What do we do or make and what markets do we serve?" The answers require a market segmentation approach because what we do may change depending on those customers who buy our products or services. This approach has reached a micro level in the area of pharmaceutical products. There are now drugs that are targeted at the genetic level of disease. For example, Herceptin[4] focuses specifically on tumor cell proteins that flourish only in patients with a specific type of breast cancer in which there is an abundance of cells called HER2. For this company, the market segmentation process is extremely detailed.

The next step on the chart takes the outcome from the SWOT analysis and puts it through the scrutiny of the core competency test. This test asks: "What is it that we do better than anyone else and can sustain over time?" It also helps determine our fundamental strategy, the success factors we consider to be important, and the driving force by which we are propelled. An example of a core competency test for a company like Starbucks could be "enhancing a unique, coffee-related experience for the customer" that would cover their core activity in their retail stores, supermarkets, and food service environments, as well as their alliances with Pepsi Co for Frappa-

---

[4]A product of Genentech, a pharmaceutical company.

cino[R], Dreyers Grand Ice Cream Holdings, and more. One of the driving forces for them is that *everything matters*. No customer concern or exposure to the brand and experience is too insignificant to lack notice because everything about their customer matters to the people at Starbucks.

The right-hand side of Figure 3.1 links time frames with expectations of performance. It measures our strategic intention over a period of time, and what we have to do now to make it happen, and how we will measure all of this in the development stage.

Figure 3.1 demonstrates the significant overlap that should occur between planning the overall strategy for your organization and planning a strategic alliance. Organizations that think about their alliances in a strategic context (i.e., while considering or reviewing their strategic plans) tend to be far more successful than those who do not.

We asked the following question in a research survey of one hundred global companies in 2001: "Was alignment with the strategic plan a contributing factor to the success of your alliance? To what extent (very important, quite important, not important)?"

We found that alignment with the strategic plan was one of the key success factors for alliances (very important). The reasons for this are fairly transparent; the more strategic and integrated into the strategic thinking and planning of the organization, the more likely it is that the alliance will have appropriate resources in terms of both human and capital resources.[5]

It's clear that the strategic fit analysis (the left-hand side of Figure 3.1) take place in the early stages of the decision to partner. Using this approach will help answer critical questions about our rationale for partnering, the ideal characteristics for a partner, the reality check of our ideal to what's available, and the evaluation of partner candidates.

What is not often considered is that strategic fit is a moving target. Perfectly appropriate partners may become inadequate due to internal changes, external market pressures, or the different strategic directions that either or both partners may take. That is why I look at Figure 3.1 as a guide for continuing consideration. The outcome of the components of this figure is not a nicely bound manual or plan but rather a set of considerations that are continually visited and updated as conditions require. The

---

[5]Research survey by Larraine Segil in 2001 of one hundred global companies; this research survey also examined other key success factors including leadership and the Larraine Segil Matrix (LSM) presented in *Dynamic Leader, Adaptive Organization* by Larraine Segil (New York: John Wiley and Sons, 2002).

main benefit of using the chart is as a guide for discussion so that interim decisions can be set off against some sort of guidebook or plan. The figure is a guide that should be re-evaluated and assessed, along with all its underlying assumptions, continually, regularly and certainly when market or corporate changes occur.

Planning

The fifth area of development metrics is planning. I love to plan, but I love to do things more than I love to plan. So I like making lists and then checking off items as goals are accomplished. This gives me the perception that I am bringing some order to life. I have learned, however, that planning may be a way to organize my thinking, but it certainly isn't a way to guarantee the world will go along with that organization! Planning is no more than a bureaucratic act or avoidance mechanism if it doesn't lead to action. So planning for and then acting is the key set of skills that are needed for effective alliances.

Planning in alliances and the metrics that go along with them should be seen in this context. Metrics are a good guide. They help you organize your activities and thoughts, but they certainly will not control the behavior of your partner nor, indeed, of those in your organization and most certainly not those in the market. Does that mean that planning is useless? No. At Vantage Partners we have excellent processes, guides, planning protocols, and implementation scenarios appropriate for every application related to relationship management. So we believe planning is a good thing. Flexibility is more important.

Planning metrics is the message throughout this book, but flexibility around those metrics will be necessary in all your alliances to ensure partner management and compatibility. Ask the following questions:

1. What is the stage of alliance life cycle we are in?

2. What are the metrics that are critical for us in this stage?

3. Are they different from the metrics that are important to our partner? Development or implementation metrics?

4. How do we reconcile these differentials in our metrics—and if we cannot:

    a. Is this the right partnering strategy for us (maybe the problem is not with our metrics but with our strategy—see Figure 3.1 for the discussion that will give us that answer or decision)?

b. Or, is this the wrong partner—because their strategic goals are so different from ours and may be irreconcilable?

c. Or, will all partners in this industry have the same problems as this one? That means that we are back to the Figure 3.1 discussion again of what the right strategy is once we have done the reality check with our ideal partner and the actual partner candidates that are out there in the market?

d. Or, do we have the wrong metrics? Are we looking for the wrong things at this stage of the alliance? Maybe we should bifurcate our expectations and divide our metrics into early stage and late stage to give the relationship more time to evolve and the partner more time to meet our needs?

If the metrics of each company are, at first look, irreconcilable, this needs to be confronted as soon as possible. Unless some serious and straight talk takes place about the expectations on short and long terms for each partner, both will end up disappointed. Ways to help this conversation are to use the following metrics as conversation stimuli:

1. Time to decision making.

2. Resources to be committed.

3. Alignment with the strategic plan and intent.

4. Executive sponsor in each company and level of importance.

Then evaluate the positions of each partner and try to find a compromise between them. Not everything can be compromised. Some alliances, for all their strategic opportunity and potential fit, are better abandoned. The reason is that the cost in capital and human terms as well as the market opportunity cost could outweigh the potential upsides, and walking away (respectfully and appropriately) may be the best alternative.

Selection

The sixth area of development metrics is partner selection. Partner selection is the fun part of this dating game. It's the reality show of alliance development. Here the partners show themselves off, and everyone gets to evaluate everyone. Is it the most eligible bachelor or bachelorette who makes the best partner, or the one that is less arrogant but excellent nevertheless? Selection processes are all about the work you did up front to develop the criteria of your choice. The selection becomes more obvious once you know what you want.

Another aspect of partner selection that is critical is to do a stakeholder analysis of all those who will be touched or affected by this alliance as it is implemented. This is a key issue because a potential partner may compete with an existing partner of yours. In addition, this can be disruptive internally. Another division of the company may partner with a competitor of your selected candidate which could cause interdivisional conflict. Then there is the internal nature of stakeholder analysis, which is to dig out the political landmines that exist in most companies where people feel that their turf has been invaded or their jobs are threatened.

For example, this happens often when technology companies have a professional service component that they offer their customers and they partner with systems integrators who are all about professional services. The key issue is to find out who and where within their own organizations will there be overlap, how that can be mitigated by making the pie larger for all parties concerned, and whether this anticipated conflict can be headed off at the pass (to use the John Wayne approach). Stakeholder analysis will assist in finding who will have a turf issue or be concerned that they will lose market share or will confuse the customer. The results of the analysis are not easy to achieve and many companies continue in an ongoing process of in part alienating their internal groups and in part engaging them.

We will continue talking about stakeholder analysis when we look at the implementation scenarios in Chapter Four.

Below are some selection metrics which various clients of ours have used. Among all the metrics that we discuss, the selection metrics will be primarily about the business reasons for partnering with one partner over another. You know those better than I do, and they might fall into the following categories:

SELECTION METRICS FOR BUSINESS AND ECONOMIC REASONS

1. Geographic reach or market share.

2. Product knowledge or line of products to contribute.

3. Customer knowledge.

4. Service knowledge.

5. Distribution network and know-how.

6. Research and development knowledge and capability.

7. Brand.

8. Market segmentation (e.g., Spanish-speaking market in the United States).

There are other metrics that are also important for the ultimate success of the alliance. I raise them here so that you don't focus all your attention just on the business justifications and economic reasons for partnering with one particular partner over another.

SELECTION METRICS OTHER THAN THE BUSINESS OR ECONOMIC REASONS

1. Culture. Country culture involves looking at the elements of culture that are common in every country. Examples are the ways each country culture addresses the issues of power and hierarchy, time, and verbal or nonverbal communication styles.[6]

2. Ethics. This is a tough one to explicitly spell out as a metric because it has to do with perceptions of honesty. It also is culturally dependent. Ethics as a metric could present itself in the development stage of an alliance as follows: Starbucks partners with many companies and individuals worldwide. Their commitment to the coffee experience is their primary driver. As they are expanding worldwide, they are partnering with companies some of which already have a presence in the food service or coffee market. Their initial discussions with those partners involves some tests. These tests are their early stage metrics, which take the form of questions. In casual conversation, they might set up a couple of scenarios like this:

   "You are busy in your Starbucks retail store, and the main category of orders is lattes. You look at the clock and discover that it's been two hours since you have made a pot of coffee for those few people

---

[6]*Intelligent Business Alliances* (New York: Times Books, Random House, 1996) by Larraine Segil devotes Chapter 6, Cross Cultural Alliances, to this subject.

who seem to just want regular coffee without the latte or other options. The coffee pot is practically full. In comes a customer and asks for a regular coffee. You are pleased that you are well prepared and serve them the coffee."

The potential partner agrees. Wrong answer.

No pot of coffee should sit for longer than an hour. The right answer is to toss that coffee and brew a fresh pot. Starbucks' commitment to quality goes along with every single cup, and a bad customer experience affects the brand. They consider that coffee which has been sitting for longer than an hour is a bad coffee experience. "But the customer wouldn't really know—few people are that discerning," the potential partner might say. And that's the point. The ethical thing to do is to take the standards of excellence and not compromise them no matter what the customer may or may not know. Is this a formal metric? Maybe it's not written, put in a chart, and formalized, but it's part of the partner evaluation process at Starbucks by everyone that the potential partner meets. It's a rigorous process all the way up and down the organization. The Starbucks employees who meet the potential partner in the evaluation process will eventually be asked to *grade* them on multiple issues. This one will fall under the area of the selection criteria for a partner that is culturally and ethically compatible with Starbucks. We will take a closer look at Starbucks and their alliances in Chapter Eleven.

Structuring

Another key aspect of development metrics is structuring the alliance. Clearly, the early development metrics of the alliance will have to address the way the partnership will be structured. We use one particular management tool that we designed over twenty years ago at The Lared Group, which is now part of the extensive tool kit of Vantage Partners. It remains valid to this day. We call it the pyramid of alliances (Figure 3.2). It was well described in my first book *Intelligent Business Alliances* (New York: Times Books, Random House, 1996). It is reproduced here for you. I will take a different analytical approach to it that was not covered in my first book to show the application of this tool to the area of metrics.

The most important aspect about this tool is the statement as a heading—*philosophy before structure*. This means that the various legal structures that are reflected on the pyramid should *not* be considered as the appropriate legal structure until the decision has been made about the

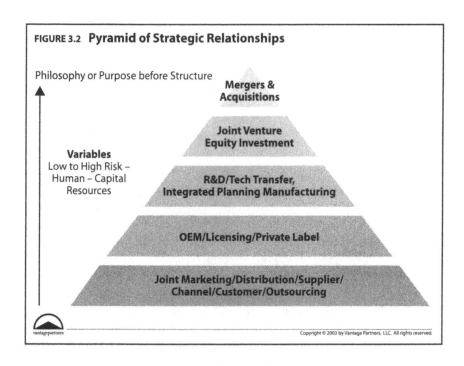

FIGURE 3.2 **Pyramid of Strategic Relationships**

Philosophy or Purpose before Structure

Mergers & Acquisitions

Joint Venture Equity Investment

R&D/Tech Transfer, Integrated Planning Manufacturing

OEM/Licensing/Private Label

Joint Marketing/Distribution/Supplier/ Channel/Customer/Outsourcing

Variables
Low to High Risk – Human – Capital Resources

philosophical goals of the partners. The philosophical goals could also be seen as the purpose of the alliance. This means asking and answering these questions:

1. Why are we going into this alliance?

2. What do we hope to achieve after a year? Two years? Five years (if relevant)?

3. How do we want the partner to think of us? On what level of the pyramid would we like to be considered, regardless of the legal structure that we actually choose?

4. Have our partners considered their philosophical answers to these questions, and if not, how can we make sure that they do so to align with our expectations?

Here is an example of how to use the pyramid of strategic relationships as a metric for expectations of partners. Ask the following questions:

1. Philosophically, on what level of the pyramid would you like to be in this partnership? Here it is important not to let the partner define where you should be nor to let legal counsel define it for you. It's all about your dreams, goals, and intents. Once you can define this, move to the next question. If it is not clear, this is worthy of debate and study. For example, the DaimlerChrysler past and recent discussions with their suppliers is a great example of how understanding the philosophical changes in positioning on the pyramid can lead to a clearer understanding of what is really going on. Whereas Chrysler had an integrated intimate relationship higher on the pyramid with their suppliers, seeing them as collaborators, DaimlerChrysler has pushed the relationship to the lowest level of the pyramid, almost commoditizing it, and pressuring the suppliers on price and performance rather than involving them in a collaborative relationship. I will discuss this example more below.

2. Philosophically, on what level of the pyramid would your partner like to be in your understanding and in theirs? Is it the same level? If not, this is important information for you to manage, that is, increasing or decreasing their level of expectations.

3. The next question is: What should be the appropriate structure for this alliance, taking into account the different philosophical intents of each party?

4. And finally, how can the alliance be structured now so as to take into account the changing and evolving expectations for a future outcome? For example, if one party has in mind to create a supply and distribution agreement but could later want to sell their company to the other party, should equity investment, acquisition value, and other valuation issues now be part of the structuring? The answer should be yes!

CASE ILLUSTRATION: APPLYING PYRAMID ANALYSIS TO DAIMLERCHRYSLER'S SUPPLIERS

When Chrysler was still Chrysler, their relationships with their suppliers looked like the Japanese *keiretsu*, taking into account that they had to be aware of and not violate United States antitrust law. Integrated supplier arrangements in Japan were similar to those in Korea and involved suppliers as partners in a networked family of companies that did business exclusively with each other. In many of the Asian arrangements, there are cross ownerships, majority equity ownership of some top-tiered suppliers and a great deal of information and knowledge transferred among the parties. Chrysler achieved a lot with these integrated relationships. What they said to their suppliers then was, "We have a cost problem, we need your help, we won't tell you how much and where because we are not sure we actually know, so help us cut costs, and we will all benefit from that together." There was a high degree of trust that developed between Chrysler and its important *tier one* suppliers which was then communicated to the *tier two* suppliers, and so on down the supply chain.

Along came Daimler and in the acquisition that followed, much of the trust was fractured as DaimlerChrysler started to drum down prices, broke up the trusted integrated arrangements, and considered suppliers as arms'-length subcontractors who had to help them cut costs and increase quality. To say that the relationships were fragile would be an understatement. However, DaimlerChrysler management changed, and their new chief executive, understated Dieter Zetsche, re-examined the supplier situation. In the summer of 2002, the company began discussions with United States suppliers and met with a lot of resistance. Their new idea was to create a factory that was 60 percent owned by the suppliers, specifically in the body and paint shop. Finally, agreement was reached in Canada, with the unions agreeing to the deal because at least they would get one thousand new factory jobs and fifteen hundred new supplier jobs. This was not a great arrangement for the suppliers, and the United States suppliers are still not happy. What has happened here, using pyramid analysis?

In the first instance, Chrysler took their suppliers who were on the lowest level of the pyramid as ordinary suppliers and philosophically elevated them to the third level which is that of research, development, integrated planning, and manufacturing. This meant that they were talking to each other earlier in the relationship before the deal terms and pricing were decided, problem-solving collaboratively rather than waiting until discussions became conflict resolution.

After the acquisition, DaimlerChrysler actually pushed their suppliers so far down on the pyramid that they were barely considered partners at all but were treated like arms'-length contractors who were expected to do higher quality work at lower cost with more customized components. Naturally, this arrangement was in opposition to what the company was actually saying to their suppliers. But calling someone a partner doesn't make them one, and the suppliers knew how they were being treated.

Now DaimlerChrysler is not messing around with fancy words and concepts. They are being blunt about what they want. By moving now to the second from the top level of the pyramid, equity investment or joint venture, which is majority (60 percent) owned by the suppliers, they are stating what they philosophically believe in.

a. They can't stay in business, be profitable, gain market share, and take all the risk.

b. They want the suppliers to take most of the risk in these specific areas.

c. By this arrangement they will guarantee that these suppliers get most of the business; after all, this will be a long-term arrangement.

d. They want the latest technology from their partners, which makes sense for the suppliers, too, because technology could help them run these new operations more efficiently. Now they don't have to worry that Daimler-Chrysler will take their technology and transfer it to their competitors.

So by migrating up the pyramid and using this analytical framework, you can see how the metrics have changed. No longer is the supplier putting into the development metrics the amount of business they will get because they now own the factory and will get it all. However, the metrics that they *do* want to use in this development stage now are associated with running their own business—so they will need to answer the question for themselves as to how efficient they can become because they have control. This is exactly what Daimler Chrysler wants to happen. So it is conceivable that auto companies could become virtual organizations with networks of suppliers, large powerful suppliers who do all their design, manufacturing, assembly, shipping, and services. In this scenario, the auto company becomes a shareholder in these myriad service suppliers and controller of the brand (and maybe the sales organization) worldwide. This could be an interesting business model which shifts the risks, changes the dependencies, and creates a new set of metrics for these relationships. By using the pyramid analysis tool, you can apply the right metrics for each level of the pyramid.

Negotiation

The next stage in development metrics is negotiation. I am a partner of Vantage Partners who are considered the world experts in Negotiation and Relationship Management processes. Evolved from the Harvard Project on Negotiation, Vantage Partners are co-authors of the book *Getting to Yes* by

Roger Fisher et al. Our belief is that negotiation is a corporate capability that is worthy of installation in organizations as a competitive advantage along with relationship management. This is not a competence that should reside only in a few individuals who are considered to be "good at negotiation." Rather, negotiation should be seen as a process that is prepared for, implemented and measured, just as relationships should be. Indeed negotiation is an essential element of relationship creation and management— ensuring internal alignment among the various interests of internal stakeholders, as well as external deal making and partner development. The negotiation infrastructure is a process that ensures that parties' interests are uncovered and implementation is, as a result, more effective. Within the context of alliance metrics, the metrics of negotiation are essential to success. These metrics are important, and I cannot do them justice here since they are so extensive that they could be the topic of another entire book so I have selected a few that are both "hard" (drafting of the letter of intent by a specific time) and others that can be seen as "soft" (ability to work together) yet all are part of the capability that will lead to well managed and valuable relationships.[7] Negotiation metrics could include:

1. Time to decision making.
2. Assessment of internal alignment.
3. Assessment of cultural and personality fit and ability to work together —variance from norm or similarity.
4. Ensuring that the way the negotiation is conducted serves as a model for future interactions by setting standards for negotiation and communication.
5. Drafting Letter of Intent.
6. Signing Letter of Intent.
7. Time to closure.
8. Passing on knowledge of deal development history.
9. Clarifying commitments—establishing understanding.
10. Internal approval process through legal and other corporate functions.
11. Senior management education and buy-in.

---

[7]Bruce Patton, founding partner, Vantage Partners offer a complete range of negotiation competency consulting, infrastructure implementation and tools as well as training. See www.vantagepartners.com

Vantage Partners' course on negotiation is the gold standard developed at Harvard University which was used by Cyrus Vance for the Camp David accords, as well as for facilitation of the constitutional transition in South Africa, and other international crises including the Israel/Palestinian peace negotiations happening as this book goes to press in 2003.

Professional education of this nature is essential to assist you to decide on a negotiation approach that works best for your organizational culture and goals. It's important to have a negotiation strategy and not to just show up, waiting either to see what the other side will do, or to imagine that you already know what to do. It is extremely difficult to negotiate with those who have a strategy and a negotiation plan. The outcome will be less than satisfactory. Learning more about negotiating is worth the time and investment. Negotiating is a set of skills just like anything else, and most people can do it. Applying the approach to the metrics of alliances means plugging in the deliverables (some of which I mentioned above) into the process of negotiating. Any good course on negotiating will cover the following:

a. Understanding the partner culture, context, and business interests.

b. Understanding your culture, context and business interests.

c. Preparing for the negotiation; getting your data, facts, background on the team, selecting your team, and knowing the partners team.

d. Using negotiation as an iterative process.

e. Coming to agreement.

f. Setting the terms and documents to evidence agreement.

g. Implementing, which will be covered in Chapter Four.

Team Selection

This last aspect of development metrics is a significant part of the alliance development stage. What most people miss is that team selection is not static. It is a repetitive act that continues throughout the life of the alliance. The team that might create the idea for the alliance may be different from those who negotiate it and different again from those who document it, and, finally, from those who implement it. Different expectations and capabilities are necessary for all those team members, and one size does not fit all.

This means that the measures or metrics that you would apply to these various team members at the varying stages of their roles will be different.

Alliance Development Team

Often this group includes those in corporate or staff positions, such as business development, and the alliances group either at corporate or in the operating units. The team is often best served, however, by including those in the business unit who will ultimately have profit and loss responsibility for the relationship because their insight and knowledge will contribute reality checks and consistency to this stage of relationship development. Often those in the functional role such as sales and marketing or research related to the subject matter of the alliance, will play a role here. An early life cycle stage is also where the executive sponsor may start to play a role. The executive sponsor is the person in the senior executive team who is selected (or volunteers) to be the major influencer in the relationship. I will discuss this role in more detail below.

Alliance Negotiating Team

This team will include others, such as those from legal and finance, and a relationship manager. Sometimes another person is added to the team who is considered to be *good at negotiating* but is then removed before the later implementation role. This approach is not a good idea because negotiating skills are most effective when they do not reside in a single individual but rather are seen as a competency that is critical across an entire organization. It is important to remember that the modus operandi of the negotiating team (and the *taste* that they leave in everyone's mouth post-negotiation) will affect the mood and expectations around the implementation of that relationship. In this way, it is critical to see negotiation as a part of the continuum of relationship development, not as a separate activity for those who then have no responsibility or involvement with the relationship. A better approach would be for the entire negotiating and implementation teams to have negotiation training so that they can see the continuum of relationship development as part of their mutual responsibilities.

The relationship manager is a key player and should have the following characteristics:

1. Able to embrace action as well as process.

2. Willing and able to manage ambiguity.

3. Manage contradictions.

4. Conflict resolution is something he or she enjoys.

5. Good salesperson for internal issues.

6. Able to communicate with and understand many functions: finance, sales, research, legal.

7. With excellent personal skills in communication and cross-cultural understanding.

Alliance Documentation Team

The alliance documentation team often includes the legal counsel inside and outside of each party and can get quite complicated depending on how many lawyers and firms are involved. The main responsibility of the relationship manager and key sponsor internally of the relationship is to manage this process. Legal counsel should be advisors and the business terms should remain the purview of the business team members. I always try to include internal legal counsel in the education sessions that we hold for senior and middle management as part of our consulting process for alliance competency. The more that legal counsel knows about the nonlegal aspects of the alliance, the more contributive they can be.

Alliance Implementation Team

The alliance implementation team is the key group that must include the now-knowledgeable relationship manager (knowledgeable because he or she has been involved since the inception of the idea to align) as well as subject matter experts if they were not already involved (e.g., salespeople if it's a distribution or sales alliance, research if research and development, and so forth), as well as the executive sponsor who has been well defined as the highest level relationship manager.

The Executive Sponsor

The executive sponsor is at a senior executive level and must have the following key characteristics in order to qualify:

1. Be senior enough with sufficient position-power to make decisions, be a port of last call, and influence the allocation of resources.

2. Have good relationships with other key stakeholders within the organization in order to bring about political influence if necessary to achieve buy-in of the concept and alliance as it is being implemented.

3. Have good communication skills.

4. Be willing to be available for advice, input, and acceleration of conflict to resolve issues and make recommendations via phone calls, e-mails, and meetings within reason.

5. Have a real interest in the project and be enthusiastic about it!

6. Preferably know the relationship managers and the team leaders for the alliance and have some sort of positive history in working with them—this is not essential but it certainly helps.

The executive sponsor needs to know how much time, within reason, he or she needs to have available for this project and what would or could be involved. To that end, a short summary, short instructions, and a brief meeting regarding your expectations for the executive sponsor would be greatly appreciated by him or her.

I have covered a lot of specific principles thus far in Part I. These are not just quantitative formulas but include some qualitative issues and outcomes as well. The language of metrics is not complicated but it is comprehensive. Here are some of the lessons from the past three chapters:

1. A clear process, which includes the alliance life cycle, is essential for metrics. The process is set out in this chapter. The life-cycle is Chapter One.

2. Not all metrics have the same meaning to various stakeholder characteristics so each of them must be identified and their interests discovered and addressed throughout the alliance. The stakeholders are specified in Chapter Two and included in this chapter.

3. The alliance development metrics will set you up for success or failure. Do it well and you have laid the foundation for the important implementation challenges. The various parts of the development metrics are laid out and discussed with illustrations to underscore their importance and impact in this chapter.

From Chapter Five until the end of the book, I will explore specific companies like Avnet, IBM, HP, Starbucks, Staples, to see alliance metrics in action. First, in Chapter Four we will cover the implementation metrics. Now we get to some action!

Implementation Metrics: The Partners

The second largest group of activities that occur within an alliance are the implementation metrics. You are more prepared for this group if you have gone through the details we covered in Chapter Three on the development metrics, but even if you find yourself inheriting an alliance that has already been implemented, the metrics in this chapter will be helpful.

Figure 4.1 lists the large categories into which I divide implementation metrics. These metrics address what happens when the alliance actually has to start delivering results. The nature of these metrics will also change over the course of the alliance life cycle.

Alliance Implementation Metrics: Operationalization

The operationalization metrics, a cumbersome term, relates to the multitude of activities that put flesh around the skeleton of the alliance. This is also the moment of alliance hand-off from those who developed and negotiated the alliance to those who must implement it. There are a number of steps in the operationalization of alliances. We use Figure 4.2, for the activity flow at The Lared Group, now Vantage Partners.

The left-hand side of Figure 4.2 shows the movement of activities at this point in the alliance from those who might have negotiated it (possibly at corporate headquarters or in the business unit) to those who will start the implementation and create the operating plan and structure for the alliance. A transition team might include some individuals from the early stage of alliance conceptualization as well as those who will be responsible for the

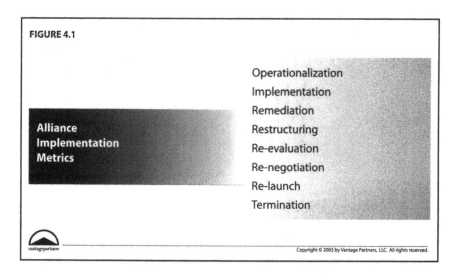

FIGURE 4.1

Alliance Implementation Metrics

Operationalization
Implementation
Remediation
Restructuring
Re-evaluation
Re-negotiation
Re-launch
Termination

alliance in the future and are now looking at maintaining continuity of concept as well as the nitty-gritty details of who reports to whom and the structure for the alliance. The middle column lists the considerations to be noted such as existing plans and how the alliance fits with them, schedules, and personnel policies. The right-hand column lists the people who will most likely be involved in doing the activities.

The alliance negotiator or the project manager for the relationship can do the hand-off process if the manager of the alliance will not be the same person who was involved in early relationship development. Here are a number of items for your checklist to assist you in your operationalization process and help you move through the various activities mentioned in Figure 4.2.

1. Creating the team that is responsible for implementation. This can be started, if not completed, in the development metrics (see "Team Selection" in Chapter Three). Now the selection must include those who have accountability for the alliance as well as those who are responsible for its implementation, *not* just staff people. This is the time when many staff members who were involved in the alliance creation and formulation will take a backseat to the operators, those in line positions, and those who must operate the alliance. The transition team must both contribute to the functional planning, the financial, operational, technological, and communication protocols and activities that will make the alliance work. These activities cannot be done in a vacuum. They have to be socialized

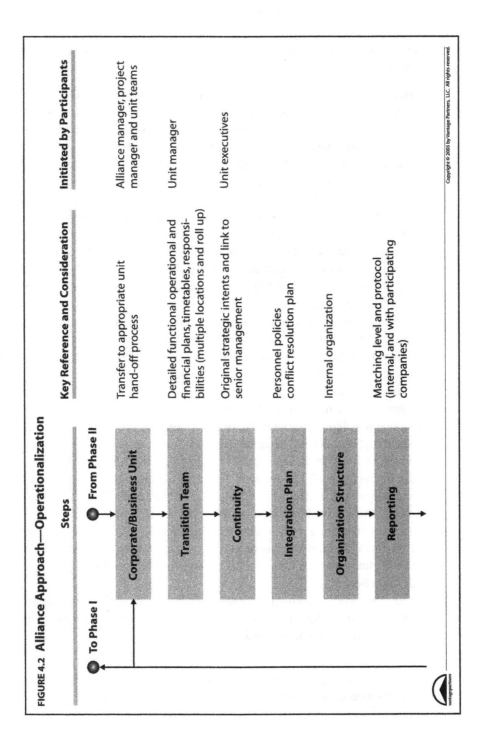

FIGURE 4.2 Alliance Approach—Operationalization

Steps	Key Reference and Consideration	Initiated by Participants
From Phase II		
Corporate/Business Unit	Transfer to appropriate unit hand-off process	Alliance manager, project manager and unit teams
Transition Team	Detailed functional operational and financial plans, timetables, responsibilities (multiple locations and roll up)	Unit manager
Continuity	Original strategic intents and link to senior management	Unit executives
Integration Plan	Personnel policies conflict resolution plan	
Organization Structure	Internal organization	
Reporting	Matching level and protocol (internal, and with participating companies)	
To Phase I		

with those in the organization who will be affected or touched by the alliance.

2. Ensuring continuity through socialization. This means transferring the alliance into the culture of the organization. It is part of the buy-in process. This should also be started in the development metrics but continued into the implementation process. It means a clear statement of what the goals are of the alliance, communicated with an understanding of the potential concerns and contributions of the audience for the communication. In the development of the alliance, we conduct a stakeholder analysis. Now is the time to approach all those stakeholders with the information they need, to understand the impact the alliance will have on them, and their role in it. They need to be part of this process from the beginning with regard to getting their buy-in, but now is the time to be sure that no roadblocks are put up to prevent alliance implementation.

   In large, complex organizations, this process will carry on at the same time as the alliance is being launched. In smaller companies, it can be accelerated into smaller feedback sessions or one-on-one meetings prior to or simultaneous with the launch process.

   In one alliance, the operationalization and socialization discussions began at the same time as the vice president of business development initiated the alliance process. There were many groups within the organization that had skin in the game. Because it was an alliance that would include technology transfer and eventually distribution as well as joint manufacturing, each key decision maker and influencer (not necessarily the same person in each instance) had to be informed. Their comments and opinions had to be included in the alliance team considerations, and, wherever possible, a representative of that functional group became part of the team. Then, it was his or her job to *socialize* the concept within their job function over time to ensure buy-in when the alliance was actually launched.

   In other words, it would have been too late to leave the socialization process to the implementation metrics. The way to make this a metric is to make quantitative that which is a qualitative process. The questions to ask are:

   a. Do we have representatives of each functional group in the alliance implementation team? If not, let's find the right ones and include them!

b. Do we have a clear statement (the vision and mission) of our alliance so that we can clearly communicate it to the team and the larger audience of the organization?

c. Have we identified all the stakeholders who could have skin in the game of this alliance and are we moving along in the education and socialization process about the alliance with them?

   For all the above questions, give the answers a numeric value from *no* to *yes* in terms of the degree of implementation or completion of the task, and you will be able to see how much you have done or have still to do in the socialization process.

3. Strategic alignment check. This is part of the handoff process and a good way to anticipate any problems that may come up later regarding the provision of resources to the alliance. Some time may have passed since the alliance idea was developed. It may no longer be as important to each of the partners as it once was. It's good to run this short analytical test (a metric of sorts) to see if things have changed since you did the strategic analysis and, if so, take steps to fill the gaps of information.

   This step requires answers to the following questions:

   a. Do you have the same executive sponsor in place or do you need to find another one for this alliance? Has the executive sponsor changed for the partner? This person will ensure that you get what you need to make this relationship work whether it is resources or high level intercession when conflict arises and more.

   b. Is this alliance still in line with the strategic intent and fit of the companies?

   c. Has the partner's attention and focus moved elsewhere?

   d. What impact will this have on allocating resources for this relationship because this is the time for the development of the resources that will staff, capitalize, and fund the operations of the alliance?

   e. Are the resources coming from the business unit? Or from corporate headquarters? If so, whose budget is it coming out of? If there are partial contributions where and when are they being made?

   f. What is the reporting structure? Is there matrix reporting? Is it clear to the alliance team? Is it clear who is accountable to whom and is there a difference between accountability and responsibility? (Those who are responsible for the day-to-day activities of the alliance may only be partially accountable—accountability could be at a higher level or multiple levels of the organization.)

g. What is the communication protocol for the alliance? This will also indicate the alignment with the interests of various groups in the company. It means understanding who contacts whom about what issue and when. It's critical that the partner understand the protocol for communication. This will help avoid the clash of multiple copies of unnecessary e-mails as well as misdirected information and grandstanding of copies to senior executives by those at lower levels. The hard work done on sorting these issues out here at the initial stage of the implementation process will stand you in good stead later on when the alliance is in full swing and multiple parties and team members are exchanging information.

Alliance Implementation Metrics: Implementation Launch

The implementation launch is a large area of activities that will vary greatly depending on the chosen legal structure. Clearly, a joint venture will be implemented very differently than a distribution agreement would. A joint venture is a separate legal entity that is set up by multiple (sometimes more than two) parties and will need to have a formal governance process such as board members, shareholders, and employees separate from the partners. A distribution agreement could just be a contract between the partners. A distribution agreement may also be one of the agreements that a joint venture could hold with the other partner being one of the shareholders of the joint venture. So you can see how complicated the metrics can become in alliance implementation. Additionally, this is an area where most operating managers have very distinctive goals—like numbers of products shipped, manufactured, capital contributed, technology, or products developed.

My goal in the next few pages will be to highlight some of the particular metrics that you might not have thought of, that are in addition to the business considerations that you are so familiar with (e.g., licensing, distribution, equity investment, joint ventures, co-promotion, outsourcing, supply chain management, research and development, and even mergers and acquisitions).

Metric 1: The Change in Mutuality

The first metric that you may not have paid much attention to is the change in mutuality. Namely, are you measuring the benefit in the alliance to your partner (as well as to yourself)? This measurement is critical because reduction in the benefit to your partner will be a leading indicator of alliance failure. If you are not measuring it, you will not see this until the failure process is already in place. The failure process will make remediation, which is the next stage of discussion, a lot more difficult. When you make mutuality a metric, you give yourself and your partner the best opportunity to discover problems before they dissolve trust and create conflict. How do you do this?

➤ Set a quantitative baseline for the issue of mutuality.

➤ Measure the level of agreement at the inception of the relationship by noting the significant terms of agreement at varying times during the implementation process and the percentage of fulfillment responsibility on each term.

Here is a sample mutuality template:

Terms of Agreement:

Time 1:
January 14, 2004: Term 1:   *Party 1: 80% of fulfillment of expectations*
                                    Party 2: 20% of fulfillment of expectations
Time 2:
July 14, 2004: Term 1:   *Party 1: 60% of fulfillment of expectations*
                                    Party 2: 40% of fulfillment of expectations
Time 3:
September 14, 2004: Term 1:   *Party 1: 10% of fulfillment of expectations*
                                    Party 2: 90% of fulfillment of expectations

ANALYSIS

The parties started the relationship with an understanding of who would do what and when about this particular agreement term. They gave certain values to each activity or area of commitment. For example, one party would manufacture and the other would distribute. Values were given by the distributor for quality levels that the manufacturer would deliver to the distributor, for example, timely delivery, among other issues. Values were then given by the manufacturer for the market share expected to be achieved by the distributor and the timeliness of the achievement of a certain percentage of that share. These were the values given by both parties at the beginning of the alliance which we call *Time 1*. This way, because situations are always changing, when the parties measure again at *Time 2*, there should have been warning flags alerting them that, unless they planned to see the level of expectation and satisfaction between their organizations change this way, something fundamental is happening that is changing the dynamics of this relationship. This difference needs to be managed.

By using this approach, the changing situation will be noticed and can be brought to the attention of the relationship managers at a level higher than the managers who may be in the middle of the organization who are managing day-to-day issues. This is a time when you would try to sort out the situation yourself but in the event you cannot, you might want to call on some goodwill with your executive sponsor who could assist in managing this issue.

I will discuss remediation further in the next section.

Metric 2: Portfolio Management of Alliances

The second metric that you might not have thought of is in addition to all the operational metrics that relate to the substance of your business whether distribution or manufacturing or research and so on. It is the important issue of how the alliance fits within the large portfolio of alliances that your organization or your division has because it adds perspective to your present alliance. There is no guarantee of success for alliances because you cannot control the behavior of your partner. One should not lightly enter into them. Acquisitions are no different in that respect as you will see from Chapter Eight, which addresses the incredible HP/Compaq integration process. It's all about people, discipline, and buy-in. Seeing your particular alliance as part of a portfolio will lead to the understanding that some are long or short term, some are more strategic than others, some fill product or technology gaps, and others are for market gaps. Overall, this perspective will also give alliance teams, who may be working on different relationships, a reason to communicate, to share best practices, and to learn collectively from success and failure. Basically, it is a way to realize that even though your alliance may or may not be reaching or exceeding its goals, it is part of a portfolio and that even alliance competency sometimes cannot save an alliance that is failing.

Following is an example (Figure 4.3) of a tool that I use in our two-day course at Caltech on alliances, in the section devoted to alliance metrics.

Figure 4.3 is helpful in that it shows you at one glance, the various alliances, the teams and their relation to each other. Also, each cell connects the data archives that you can access to get the information you need about each alliance. Accessibility is good for senior management and will be helpful for those managers running various alliances.

Let's go through Figure 4.3 together. The information on this chart is entirely fictional. The names and companies are used for illustrative purposes only and do not represent any expertise or lack thereof in those named. In the left-hand column, you see a theoretical partner name, Oraculosis.

The alliance manager has designated that the strategic interest and market focus that this company has in partnering with Oracle is because of the application of their software and know-how to the automobile and financial services industries. The next cell over to the right shows that the alliance manager has considered this to be a preemptive alliance because the other partners that were eligible are competitors of Oracle—SNAP, and Capillini, Gerneste and Old. The alliance manager has decided that this alliance links to the corporate strategic plan through the business unit operating plan so he has established both strategic alignment and fit in part by his decisions for the names in these cells.

He has put into the chart the placement on the company database of the contract for this alliance and also the use of a software search tool created by a (real not fictional) company called Knowledgebase.net.[1]

The alliance manager who filled out this form for the alliance group put in some metrics. They are the right ones for the business proposition, but he has left out some of the metrics we have discussed such as mutuality, knowledge transfer, pyramid analysis, and others such as compatibility review, and more. The rest of the chart outlines the resources, the contact people, the meetings that are currently moving forward, and the present status of the implementation of the alliance. These data are stored in the alliance database and are available for those who need to know it. Each cell links to the relevant documents—for example, strategic alliance plan, alliance contracts, data and metric individual alliance report cards, relevant

---

[1] I am familiar with this company and its software, a low-cost alternative search engine for customer call centers: www.knowledgebase.net.

FIGURE 4.3 Alliance Portfolio Management—For Senior Management Reviews (Sample Analysis)

Each cell links to the relevant documents— strategic alliance plan, alliance contracts, data/metrics individual alliance report cards, relevant managers, ongoing meetings and work in progress, market positioning, and external communications, learning captured, resource issues, conflict resolution in progress, expansion plans for individual alliances, and so on.

Strategic Partner	Market Segments	Preemptive	Link to Strategic Alliance Plan	Alliance Contract Archive Location	Metrics	Alliance Report Cards	Relevant Manager	Ongoing Meetings	Resource Issues
Oraculosis	Financial Auto	SNAP CGEO	Business Unit operations plan Q4	Use Knowledge base.net for archive retrieval	Sales Upsells Rev by Q	www.our intranet .com/3/4	Joe and Maria email addresses	Conflict resolution See memo of 2-2-2002; all hands meeting June 5	In budget cycle planning for 2003/4

 Vantage Partners

managers, ongoing meetings, work in progress, market positioning, external communications, learning captured, resource issues, conflict resolution in progress, and expansion plans for individual alliances.

Many companies are considering portfolio approaches to alliance management. They integrate this into their processes for alliance creation, segmentation, and management.

In Chapter Seven about IBM, I describe in detail how, in their software group, they have refined a process of more than 147 points through which their alliance teams move in order to assure that when they partner with independent software vendors, that the process is fair, clear, and repeatable. It is this kind of metrics standard that multiple companies should learn. Part II of this book will move you through a series of examples enabling you to create a metrics schematic that works for your company and your corporate and country culture. I will focus on the details of a variety of development and implementation issues so that you can place them into the life-cycle analysis seen in Figure I.1 in the Introduction. This perspective will help to simplify the task of forging an alliance so that it becomes achievable and fun!

The next section will address what happens when your alliance is running into some problems. This approach will look at post-deal remediation, rather than pre-deal remediation. Pre-deal remediation is covered in negotiation.

Alliance Implementation Metrics: Remediation

The large category of remediation includes issues concerning how to fix an alliance that is in distress. Or, it could apply to an alliance that is not in distress but is chugging along without much incremental value being added after its initial launch and early stages. The remediation strategy that you will use will be dependent on the life-cycle stage of the alliance in terms of its urgency, team composition, and resources needed. In other words, how much history is there, how bad or good it is, and what needs to be done to do a mini re-launch of the alliance to increase its value.

These are the most important steps when considering remediation:

a. Status of alliance at present. This is where the concept of alliance manager documentation can be so helpful. The history of the alliance is easily accessed regarding conflict resolution, meetings held, documents shown, and all the other considerations that build the picture of the alliance. This is important because otherwise one depends on anecdotal stories about the travails of the players. Gather the data about the alliance in as much detail as possible and with as much objectivity as feasible.

b. Consider the interests of the parties involved and that means the internal issues, the external issues, the stakeholder analysis, the resources and their source, the executive sponsors on each side, and the politics of who is trying to position themselves where, how, and why. I developed a metric I believe to be important that will help you greatly to understand the internal issues that sometimes are the hardest to resolve. It is called the *currency factor.* Figure 4.4 illustrates the currency factor and how it works within an organization.

The currency factor is the name for an internal recognition process that enables a kind of payment (although no money may change hands) from one part of the organization to another or from one individual to another. It takes the form of recognition, or acknowledgment, of giving credit where credit is due, and making sure that those who feel that they were responsible for or contributed to the creation of something valuable are given recognition for that contribution. For example, one business unit provides ideas or intellectual property or its unique skills and capabilities to another busi-

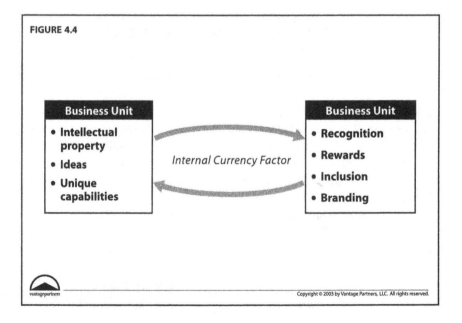

FIGURE 4.4

ness unit within the same organization. How is that normally managed without taking this idea of the currency factor into account? Normally, the other business unit may receive that information and use it, incorporating it into their activities and, thereby, ultimately taking credit for it. That is what most organizations do. However, when the business unit does that, the one that sent the information is reluctant to do so again. After all, why should they not be recognized for their brilliant work?

Certainly, you could argue that everyone in the company should be working together for the good of the shareholders and the company as a whole, but that's not the real world in most organizations. People are by nature territorial and this is the kind of internal conversation that may occur in the heads of those who gave you the information.

> "If you take some of my stuff and use it and don't give me something in return, unless I work very hard at giving, I will feel somewhat taken advantage of."

I wish this attitude were different, but working with large companies for three decades has taught me it isn't. Smaller companies are not quite as territorial as those in the silos of divisions or functional groups in large companies because they can often consider the well-being of the entire company to be their territory. Rewards are more visible and immediate. It's the larger or more complex organizations which suffer from this disease.

As stated, the currency factor takes the form of recognition of the contribution, something like an award ceremony, or inclusion of the sub-brand of the group in the final product or service. Thus, recognition is the currency exchanged in a reciprocal relationship where monetary currency is not appropriate.

For example, "With grateful thanks to Global Services for their contribution to the Dumpy Toy." Or, an actual award ceremony with all the accompanying hoopla and mention in the company magazine, on the Intranet, or even Web site. Or, something written on the internal documents that says: "A joint project of the Shared Services and Finance Departments," and so on. This internal currency of goodwill will take you a long way toward breaking down the silos of internal groups and competitiveness. It's simple, but it works!

In the steps of remediation, we have covered review of the status of the alliance, the interests of the parties and stakeholders, and now we move to do the same analysis for the partner, which follows as 'c'.

c. Go through 'a' (review of the status of the alliance) and 'b' (identify the partner's interests in the alliance and that of their stakeholders) using an outside facilitator or resource, if necessary, to get their point of view.

d. Discuss various options with the parties separately to achieve a plan of action, a series of activities which can then be prioritized, and do the same with each individual party to a level of satisfaction before bringing the parties together.

e. Come to an understanding of the issues.

I cannot emphasize enough how important and valuable it can be to engage a conflict resolution expert in this stage of discussions. This expert need *not* necessarily be a lawyer, but someone who has the skills, the knowledge, and the objectivity to play this role. You will get your money's worth back many times if the alliance is important for your company and strategic. In many cases, failure is not an option, and engaging a facilitator is not a statement of failure or acceleration to litigation. Rather it is a statement that objectivity is easier to find in a hired hand than in two teams who have a history of working together (without huge success).

So remediation is an attempt to find the sweet spot, the area in which the parties can re-negotiate and re-launch the alliance. Skillful remediation can actually do some of the redesign of the alliance, which now takes a different form compared to the new and exciting relationship that was launched earlier. Indeed, remediation may require that the team is changed on both sides, the executive sponsors are different, the resources come from an alternate source, and even that the business goals are redefined.

Because remediation will address whether the alliance is actually now still viable, a number of considerations should be evaluated before entering into remediation. They are:

1. Is continuing with the alliance a risk mitigation strategy? For example, is this partner one that you cannot afford to terminate because you have transferred so much of your knowledge to them that you might have educated a competitor?

2. Is trying to do this alliance putting your team and resources into an area that is far away from your core competency? If so, would you be better served to make an outsourcing make-or-buy decision?

3. Is the problem the selection of the leaders or the team members? Can team performance be increased by training? In your evaluation of their

performance, is ignorance or lack of maturity or experience the problem or is it a lack of tools to manage a complex, often contradictory set of relationships?

4. In your redefinition of success for this alliance, does it now appear that even if the alliance succeeded, that your company would have less interest in the result—namely, the priority of achieving the alliance mission has dropped for your company, lowering the desire to make this work?

I am sure you can think of other considerations that would precede the remediation process. But you get the idea—it's not a foregone conclusion that remediation should be applied to every alliance. Some are just better off dying, but don't leave them to linger because they drain your resources. If the alliance is not worth keeping, end it as respectfully and gracefully as you can. There is no need to make an enemy if you can avoid it. You never know when you might want to return to that partner.

Alliance Implementation Metrics: Restructuring

Restructuring of the alliance will involve an actual process and legal or structural change in the alliance. Restructuring is a term used for the legal maneuvering and operational changes that take place in organizations that are looking to improve whether in efficiency, costs or growth. It affects both organizational groupings and human and capital resource allocations.

Restructuring an alliance is not that different from restructuring an organization. It may mean changing the team of people who were committed to the relationship, changing the reporting responsibilities of those who remain, bringing in a new leader of both the partners teams, and redefining why the alliance should be continued. The restructuring process will depend largely on whether the continuation of the alliance with these partners is seen as the right thing to do—strategic or tactical, economically viable, or preemptive in that it cannot afford to be terminated because the partners know too much about each other's business, or, in some cases, one partner has become so knowledgeable about the other's business that they could compete with them should they wish.

Here are restructuring metrics that could be of assistance to you:

1. Risk mitigation through preemptive positioning. This addresses the diminishment of your risk by partnering with a partner who helps you

preempt or prevent other competitors moving into the situation. Even if the returns from the actual partnership are not as healthy as you might like them to be, this metric could still make the alliance a viable and useful one. Many companies don't consider this issue and look at the alliance on its own recognizance and terminate it as a nonperforming alliance thereby losing the preemptive win that this placeholder relationship could achieve for them.

2. Check the return on labor hours worked. Accounts receivable, return on investment, return on equity—these are all well-recognized metrics. However, the return on labor hours worked is not. In a world of global labor where companies like Wipro, an Indian outsourcing provider of software-related services, can provide labor that is highly skilled and competent at a fraction of the labor cost to the United States and Western Europe, it is becoming important to evaluate alliances that are labor intensive such as research, development, manufacturing, and more from the point of view of return on labor hours worked.

3. Return on market opportunity cost (ROMOC™). This is the cost to you of doing the relationship. The alliance ties up resources for other activities, so the return you receive must at least equal your market opportunity cost, and should exceed it.

4. Return on intellectual property invested (ROIPI™) means that whatever intellectual property you have invested into this relationship should have given you at least the same return that you would have received had you invested it elsewhere. The real return would be if you got more from this alliance than you could have gotten from an alternate investment of use of that intellectual property.

Alliance Implementation Metrics: Re-evaluation

Many of the metrics that we have applied to the former stages of remediation and restructuring apply also here to re-evaluation. The difference is that the alliance in this instance needs to be seen as a relative relationship—one that is part of a mix of corporate activities so that the evaluation of the alliance is not on its stand-alone viability which remediation and restructuring consider, but rather as part of the activities into which the organization is going to pour attention and resources. This is called the validity test and rather than testing the viability of the relationship—namely, can we restructure this so as to make it succeed—the questions that now have to be answered will include those below:

1. Is this partnership still the right one for us when we consider the other activities we are involved in that may have changed in priority since we launched it?

2. Is this the right partner now that we look at what's really involved and understand the skill set and look around the industry at other partner options?

3. Is the subject matter of this alliance still valid? Has the market changed or a competitor come in so that we find ourselves in the position of replacing the ribbon on the typewriter (when no one is using typewriters)?

4. Has this alliance become the baby of one or more evangelists, but no one else really cares much about it in our company? If that is the case, will our partner be prepared to pick up the slack and do all the work to make this happen because we have lost interest?

5. Has this alliance grown in importance so much that we need to remove it from this division/business unit/group/team/individual in order to roll it out with appropriate resources and capabilities?

Re-evaluation of the alliance will lead to action items in the short term that could either be: re-negotiation, re-launch or termination.

Re-negotiation

This will be very similar to the negotiation process except for the fact that there is now some history between the parties, which may be supportive or destructive of the relationship. If it is negative history, it must be put on the table again. I suggest strongly that an outside facilitator with skills in this arena will be very helpful to diffuse the tension and ill will if any still persists. Even though people say there is none, those hurt feelings can stay around for years. One client with whom we were working whose product development cycle is fifteen to twenty years omitted to mention the contributions of an internal working group when the first iteration of the product was launched over a decade ago. As the second product launch was coming up, those long-timers who were still with the project, remembered how they were passed over and lamented this in front of the entire project team, many of whom were still in high school when it happened. However, this poisoned the well, so to speak, and the project team did not get off to a good start due to the described distrust.

Re-launch

Everything that I mentioned about the first launch of the alliance applies here. However, now you have lots of information about the partner, yourself, your cultures, the modus operandi, and ways of doing business. Much of the partner selection process can be deleted, but do keep in place the criteria development portion that looks at what your ideal partner characteristics are as well as the reality of the marketplace. This will help you remain realistic about what the definition of success should be in this revised relationship. Your advantage here is the following:

1. You have experience with this partner and can realistically project the performance and relationship direction from past experience.

2. You understand your re-adjusted goals and that your new definition of success may be very different from the earlier one.

3. You may have a new team to work with on all sides of the alliance. They need to be educated, and it would be a good thing to establish their level of alliance competency with internal education on alliance skills and templates.

4. Be sure to perform joint implementation planning and create that operational plan with your partner. You have a wonderful opportunity *not* to make the same mistakes again.

5. Whatever metrics you use here should ideally be short term, that is, give the relationship short milestones to reach, so that the team can feel success early on, which will go a long way toward dispelling any bad tastes that are left from past history.

6. Document the relaunch well. Have templates for the alliance process (who does what when and the results of their actions), which will serve as a present history and a clear road map for the parties. In the re-launch, there should be as little confusion as possible. It is far preferable to clarify the approach beforehand so that there can be some agreement on action steps and responsibility for them.

7. Communicate, communicate, and then communicate again. Share lots of information. Tell your partner when things go well and when they don't. Overcoming the distrust of the earlier conflict or less than successful relationship can only be done by:

   a. Performance—nothing resolves issues like growth and success.

   b. Communication—open sharing of information.

   c. Team competency—making sure that ignorance, arrogance, and nonsense don't mar team performance and partner compatibility.

Alliance Implementation Metrics: Termination

Termination is an area where legal counsel will have a lot of input. Most, if not all, alliances will have some provisions in the contract for termination. In some cases, the alliance reaches an end that has been agreed upon and the parties stay on good terms. Sometimes, if termination is premature and not according to the expectations of the parties, it can be a painful process, as in the divestiture and breakup of an acquisition. The rancor that has been developed, for example, among the various groups and factions within AOL Time Warner will linger long after the organizational structures are reorganized for the umpteenth time.

If you are involved in an alliance termination, some negotiations will focus on damage control as well as, potentially, litigation regarding rights and obligations. The alliance contract and the terms of agreement will now be discussed. Possibly this is the first time they will surface since inception, that is, if it was a good relationship. Termination occurs naturally in alliances that are defined by time or circumstances—the best way to end. The parties have achieved their goals and are moving on.

However, most terminations are not that clear, especially if they have occurred before the term of the arrangement or as an outcome of conflict resolution.

Here is a checklist of some termination metrics that your lawyers will certainly have considered:

1. Material breach of agreement.

2. Breach of law.

3. Repeated (two or more) deadlocks among the board of directors.

4. Changes in the laws or regulations of home or host country or industry.

6. Failure to meet specific targets.

7. After a time period has lapsed, should the contract be renewed?

8. Disposition of assets (liquidation or sharing).

9. Both partners should specify methods to be used in evaluation, for example:

   a. Mutual buyout agreements.

   b. Asset valuation based on actual amounts invested.

   c. Independent appraisal.

   d. An offer from one partner or an external buyer.

10. Disposition of liabilities. How will partners deal with liabilities and contingent liabilities? For example, if there is an issue of international employment, you will need to address termination costs which could be one to three years of full salary and benefits.

11. Dispute resolution:

   a. Are disputes resolved through arbitration or traditional intervention? Which law should apply?

   b. Dispute resolution mechanisms: mediation, arbitration, and litigation are some of those most commonly used.

12. Distributorship arrangements:

   a. Intellectual property arrangements and licensing agreements.

   b. Rights over sales and territories and obligations to customers.

13. If you have defined success, this will make your decision to remain or exit easier.

14. Consider when you enter into the alliance what will happen to the employees of the alliance after it is dissolved.

15. Consider whether employees will be absorbed by one of the parties or terminated.

The fifteen-point checklist above is the start to get you prepared for the various tasks and obligations that will be yours if you are involved in the termination process. Termination is not a lot of laughs.

FIGURE 4.5 Alliance Metrics Relate to:

Alliance Development Metrics	Optional Sub-Metrics	Alliance Implementation Metrics
• Conceptualization	Time to market	• Operationalization
• Strategy	Time to decision	• Implementation
• Alignment	Time to implementation	• Remediation
• Development	Competitive positioning	• Restructuring
• Strategic Fit	Competitive preemption	• Re-evaluation
• Planning	Damage control	• Re-negotiation
• Selection	Capabilities enhancement	• Re-launch
• Structuring	Market education	• Termination
• Negotiation	Customer penetration	
• Team Selection	Channel expansion	

Optional Sub-Metrics (middle column):

Faster sales cycles
Faster inventory turns
Faster deployment of ideas/products/service
Lead conversion rates
Equity Investment
Customers new
Customer's up-sell
Education and learning
Knowledge transfer
Customer satisfaction/service
Financial management
AR/ROI/ROE/RO
Labor hours
Cost savings in development, supply, design, manufacturing, service, delivery
Outsourcing
Quality improvement
Risk mitigation

Alliance Development Metrics (continued):

Channel management
Channel marketing
Mission/vision
Marketing milestones
Corporate personality
Individual personality
Project personality
Launch Gantt chart
Partner criteria fit
Contract time limits
Revenues goals

Third column metrics:

Faster manufacturing cycle time
Faster market penetration
Risk mitigation through preemptive positioning
Market share increase
Market share acquisition
Market penetration
Brand enhancement
Brand dilution
Customer referrals
Market share milestones
Geographic milestones
IP limitations
Territory limitations
Knowledge capture
Knowledge management
Market share increase
Technology development
Technology transfer

Figure 4.5 has the two groups of alliance metrics with many of the specifics that I suggest you consider. All of them may not apply to you, so select from this list. Optional sub-metrics could be used in both groups or only one. The subject matter of your alliance will determine that. I am sure there are some metrics that I have left out, but you will get the idea of what you should measure.

Prioritize the list of metrics found in Figure 4.5 and add any that you feel are intrinsic to your alliance. The metrics you choose must then be matched with the partner expectations, and just by having that discussion, you will find out lots of areas in which you agree or disagree, which then can be ironed out before the alliance runs into conflict.

The placement of the metrics is debatable; it's not set in stone, and you can place them as you will. The main issue is that Figure 4.5 will guide you to think about metrics you might not have considered items worth measuring. Make sure you overlay these into the alliance life-cycle stages.

If you have completed reviewing this chart and thinking about which metrics apply to your alliance and in what group (development and/or implementation), you have put most of the work together to ensure that your alliance has the structure and the operational details to succeed.

Congratulations!

By the way, there are no right answers or wrong ones for this analysis. What does matter is that you apply this discipline and your partner does as well. You cannot be better prepared than this. When you combine this knowledge with the life cycle stages of the alliance and the five stakeholder perspectives of metrics (the angles from which they each see the issues), you will have a solid base of alliance metrics knowledge and overall alliance competency.

Now we are going to dive into some of the fun part—seeing how various companies do it. The rest of the book will describe how specific companies develop and measure their alliances. Most of you are familiar with companies like Starbucks, as a provider of a favorite service, while others may not recognize a company like Stronghold Engineering. What I promise you, however, is that in each of these situations, you will see the management tools and processes that we have covered together in the past four chapters as applied by some of the best companies. Most important, you will be able to adapt what they do to your own business situation.

PART II

Exceptional Examples of Partnering

CHAPTER FIVE

Avnet:
The Master
Distributor

For eighty years, Avnet has been a leading force in the technology industry. As a Fortune 500 company with over 10,000 employees serving customers in 63 countries, their business is multifaceted, complex, challenging—and all about alliances. Few businesses have the emphasis on relationships at the core of their very essence in the way that Avnet does. They stand squarely in the middle of the continuum of supplier to customer, and their mission is to add value to each of those relationships in the short and long term. To say that alliance metrics were important would be to underscore that everything they measure is related to these fundamental relationships. In the past three to five years, they have embarked on a major acquisition program of 16 acquisitions; of those, only 6 were in North America with the balance in Europe (6), Asia (3), and the Middle East (1).

"We are all about alliances—relationships are fundamental to what we do and we measure them in order to constantly ensure that we are increasing shareholder value." (Roy Vallee, CEO, Avnet)

The metrics by which the whole business is driven are not optional—every business unit is expected to drive these metrics. They are: profitable growth and return on capital. When they achieve these goals, everything else falls into place. Vallee made this statement recently to his team at their senior leadership conference:

"Functionality migrates to the most efficient provider, which means that we, at Avnet, *must* react if another provider is better, and we must constantly be improving on and adding to our core competencies."

Vallee has a simple formula that is complex in its execution. Here it is:

➤ Value = Benefits – Cost

➤ Results = Strategy × Execution

Avnet's business is described in Figure 5.1, which shows the various businesses on a continuum, the value chain as it moves from supplier to customer, and the role that Avnet plays in each instance. It is helpful in the quest to find out how Avnet runs its business of alliances and the metrics that count for them to look at each business group separately. We will begin with Avnet Electronics Marketing, which is run by Andy Bryant.

Electronics Marketing (EM)

Avnet Electronics Marketing is an authorized distributor of leading technology products manufactured by more than one hundred key suppliers. Ten key supplier lines represent 80 percent of their revenues. Their industry has consolidated rapidly, and Avnet has been a key consolidator. Between their major competitor Arrow Electronics and themselves, they represent 30 percent to 40 percent of the total available distributor market. The past few years have been devastating to this industry and the market is down 30 percent. But Avnet has taken the opportunity to review all its expenses and cut costs aggressively, while looking at new markets and products for future positioning, and making consolidating acquisitions to grow their volume.

So how do they measure success? They measure customer satisfaction and market share for each supplier. After all, they ask themselves, why would the suppliers use them if Avnet can't build market share in the market for those suppliers? The suppliers are constantly measuring Avnet to see if the supplier is becoming a bigger part of Avnet's business. So the key metrics are on both sides, measuring market share. There are times when the supplier will sell directly to the customer. The direct sell occurs when the purchase is of a substantial size, the customer doesn't want a lot of flexibility, and the customer will take the product *as is* without a lot of added services. In those circumstances, the supplier will set out the rules of engagement, maybe even payment in 30 days, and so on. However, as soon

FIGURE 5.1 **Supply Chain Solutions by Avnet which Address Four Essential Elements: Information Flow, Physical Flow, Financial Flow, and Knowledge Flow**

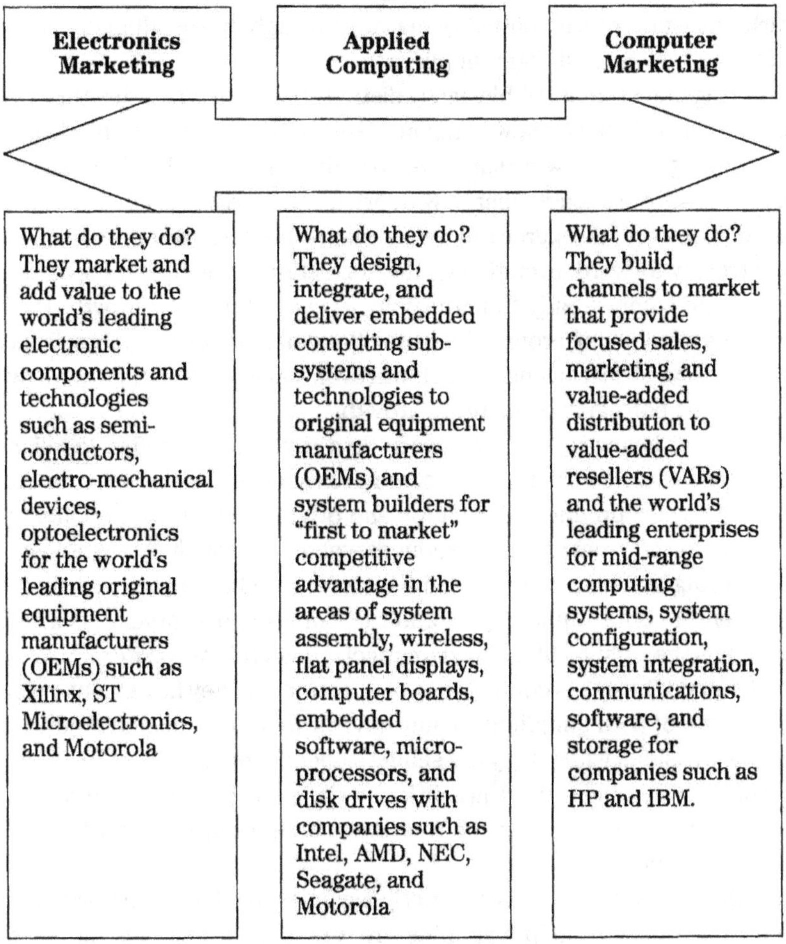

Electronics Marketing	Applied Computing	Computer Marketing
What do they do? They market and add value to the world's leading electronic components and technologies such as semi-conductors, electro-mechanical devices, optoelectronics for the world's leading original equipment manufacturers (OEMs) such as Xilinx, ST Microelectronics, and Motorola	What do they do? They design, integrate, and deliver embedded computing sub-systems and technologies to original equipment manufacturers (OEMs) and system builders for "first to market" competitive advantage in the areas of system assembly, wireless, flat panel displays, computer boards, embedded software, micro-processors, and disk drives with companies such as Intel, AMD, NEC, Seagate, and Motorola	What do they do? They build channels to market that provide focused sales, marketing, and value-added distribution to value-added resellers (VARs) and the world's leading enterprises for mid-range computing systems, system configuration, system integration, communications, software, and storage for companies such as HP and IBM.

as the customer wants certain services, or if it is a tier-two customer that is not so large, the supplier will require that the customer work through a distributor like Avnet. These are the real issues that set the stage for a good alliance, the setting of expectations, who will do what, for what value, when, and where. Avnet and their suppliers and partners define the issues clearly in alliance development and continue to monitor and tweak them during alliance implementation. The alliance between Avnet and their suppliers is seen as a life-cycle issue because the relationship must be viewed in the context of a changing market and economy. At one time the relationship will grow and at another time be under stress from market changes. Thus, keeping the metrics of communication clear and focused will be a bulwark of sustaining the mutuality metrics throughout the alliance life-cycle stages with Avnet and their suppliers.

During the Internet bubble, many distributors were afraid that they would be dis-intermediated by new companies on the Internet on-line markets who were aggregators and were supposed to make value-added additions to information and were unencumbered with brick and mortar. However, Avnet prevailed. Many on line aggregators went out of business, where Avnet continues strongly forward, even though the correction in the technology industry has affected them greatly from the point of view of top-line growth. They do see some silver lining around the storm cloud of the past few years, from the point of view of cost savings, which will eventually position the company for outstanding bottom-line and profit growth.

So Avnet has weathered the storm and even made profitable alliances with some of the surviving Internet winners such as China ECNet in China, which provides product information and offers electronic components for sale over the Internet and also produces webcasts providing technology and engineering seminars around semiconductor technology. Avnet forged a joint venture with China ECNet and the Chinese government; as a result, Avnet has the right to fill the orders received via this Web site.

Their core business continues to be their focus. They have many masters in the form of their suppliers so they have broken their business down into various divisions where they are selling a specific product type to a specific customer. Sometimes, there are different divisions calling on the same customer, but mainly they have sorted out which groups should be serving which customers.

In the early days, they were strictly a wholesaler. Over time, Avnet were seen as a vehicle to help a supplier create demand, which is the heart of their supplier alliances today. Bryant recalled that when he entered the business in 1978, Intel Corporation made a move that changed the industry. They required their distributors to have a field applications engineer trained and dedicated on their product, or they would not get as much margin or sell as many products. That changed the nature of the industry for the next thirty years.

Steve Church, senior vice president of services business development at Avnet, who has had responsibility for the strategic planning process as well has having been an operating group president, shared a visual description (Figure 5.2) of what Avnet does now that aptly describes the multifaceted nature of their business and how far they have come from the early twentieth century company that started on Radio Row in New York City.

Figure 5.2 describes the role of Avnet in the life cycle of the products it sells and buys. Electronics Marketing buys products from electronic component manufacturers and sells them to subsystem manufacturers, contract manufacturers, and electronic and computer original equipment manufacturers (OEMs). The subsystem manufacturers also sell to the contract manufacturers and to Avnet Applied Computing, one of Avnet's operating groups, which adds value to the products such as disk drives and computer boards, and then sells those to electronic and computer OEM's but also to the contract manufacturers who also could be selling to those same OEMs. The OEMs then sell to Avnet Computer Marketing who sells products and provides services to value-added resellers (VARs) and also to the

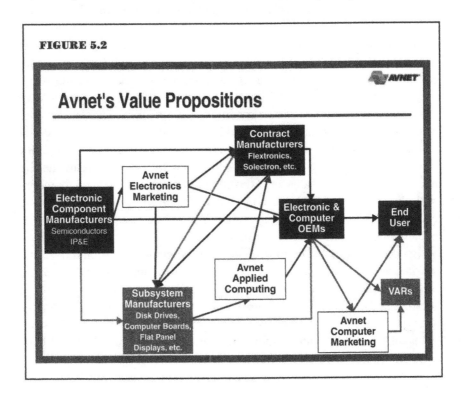

FIGURE 5.2

Avnet's Value Propositions

end users. So if you look at the chart from the upper left-hand corner to the lower right-hand corner, you can see the space that Avnet plays in—squarely in the sights of the connection between supplier and customer where value can be added.

This means that Avnet gets to play a significant role in the life-cycle launch, maintenance, and extension of various products. Their value is not, then, only of a distributor or customizer of services and products, but is a key element in establishing and extending market viability of a variety of different products and their categories. This expanded role has a significant effect on the life cycle of the alliance with their suppliers.

Bryant explains:

"Certain products are introduced into the market, and they reach acceptance over time. But in the interim, Avnet gets to play a huge role in the demand generation role of the supplier with their technical expertise and field service and engineers. Then, as the product moves over time to general purpose products in which they don't need their engineers involved, the relationship and the margins change."

So, in this way, Avnet helps their suppliers to create demand for their products and the suppliers use them to help them through their own product life cycle. In the up-and-down cycle of product and market changes, the suppliers take advantage of Avnet's position in emerging markets to give them insights, ideas for product modifications, and innovation at one end, and new market penetration and entirely new product lines at the other end. At one time, they are pulling their suppliers into the market and at another time they are pushing the suppliers into new markets. This means the alliance drivers may change, and the efforts and skills of the team members will change. Because Avnet keeps close watch on and manages those changes as the alliance life-cycle mutates from high-growth to maturity and back to high growth again, the supplier commitment to them stays stable.

Bryant tells of helping Intel penetrate the emerging communications market, which was a huge boom (and, later, a huge implosion!) There is no doubt that the supplier sees the value and is willing to pay well for these services and insights. But once the market matures or changes, the supplier sees that the added value and services are no longer needed. So Avnet is constantly under pressure to help their suppliers, a mutual desire of both partners, to always find new customers and new markets.

It is a sobering thought that most of the customers of Avnet today in the top ten were not part of their top ten a decade ago. The market and product life cycles and changes have accelerated dramatically and will continue to do so.

The supplier goes to the distributor when they need them to create demand generation or add valuable services; then they leave them because the market matured, or the customer grew, or they found another way to procure the product through a contract manufacturer, or the worst of all situations, the supplier failed. So Avnet is always on the hunt for new suppliers, new customers, and new markets. The supplier knows that distribution will do the banging on the doors and finding the new opportunities—these are the expectations that are created, managed, and monitored as the main metrics throughout the relationship and contribute to the quantitative metrics that measure the market share acquisition, loss, and the percentage of Avnet's business that the supplier contributes over time.

Fortunately, a few customers and suppliers don't change. One of the constants in the business are those verticals that constitute the aerospace market and their components. These companies stay with Avnet because Avnet doesn't outsource their manufacturing offshore due to security reasons. Then, there are industrial control markets where companies make medical equipment, which is a steady and repeatable business, and those customers, too, have stayed with them. So, along with these steady customers, Avnet has taken an overall strategic look at the market and realized that their three-pronged strategy is as follows:

1. Grow through acquisition so that they can gain as the large volume distributor and use that critical mass to cut costs and get all the economies of scale that come with supply chain consolidation and rationalization.

2. Constantly be in the forefront of discovering new markets and products, working with venture capitalists, emerging companies, and new industries to forge relationships from which their suppliers can benefit by creating the new demand generation curve.

3. For Avnet Electronics Marketing's Americas region: Continue to grow the steady reliable vertical markets that will stay on shore and need secure, quality, and superb value-added services such as the medical industry (where failure and anything below Six Sigma—which is perfection quality without flaws—is unacceptable—Avnet meets this test) and

the aerospace industry where security and supply chain skills and excellence are critical success factors (Avnet meets this test, too).

Avnet competes in a maturing market, but it is a survivor. Even in maturing markets, Avnet still gets to add value in the demand generation arena, and as a survivor, they also get to enjoy the volume aspects of that maturing market. The next big wave they believe is wireless. Much of their technical expertise is pointed at that market. In order to protect themselves in electronic marketing against off-shore manufacturing, they have put their stakes into China to play a role in that market. They see that high-product mix with low volume is focused on the United States, but high volume with low-product mix will not be in the United States but rather in Asia. And Avnet is there.

Bryant is convinced that one of the key elements that has caused them to succeed in their alliances has been the company culture and track record of professional people with integrity, ethics, and trust. Their CEO Vallee has built a company around supplier and customer satisfaction.

The key mutuality metric is that their supplier believes that Avnet must win as the supplier must win in order for their alliance to succeed. If Avnet does not win, then the supplier doesn't believe they can win either.

This realization and metric is one of those that I consider to be Avnet's competitive advantage and essential in the alliance implementation metrics described in Chapter Four. As Vallee says:

"It's all about making the right decisions, choosing the right people and executing well. But more important now, I have recently come to believe that organizational and human resource development is akin to research in a technology company, so the way to do this is first to identify the needs for education and knowledge development of our people, then develop programs to address them. So now we have senior executives teaching classes to ensure knowledge transfer. I teach a class on the 'Alchemy of Running a Successful Business.' Our chief financial officer, Ray Sadowski, teaches a class on 'Finance,' Ed Kamins from Avnet Applied Computing teaches a class on 'Decision Making,' and more. We are doing knowledge transfer in a massive way from a dozen senior executives to hundreds of level 2 and 3 executives worldwide. And we are also doing it the other way—recently, we had a senior leadership conference and before it we went worldwide and interviewed many employees and asked them what they wanted from their leaders."

How do you measure professionalism? This is difficult to measure, but it is how the partnership translates promises into commitment. It's all about how the company treats people and the internal and external relationships over time. It's not only about on-time delivery. The way that Avnet trains its people is by setting a standard of what is proper behavior, observation of how people behave, and how they treat their customers and their suppliers. There is no magic. Bryant put it well:

> "People do what you do, not what you say, and it's unemotional, professional, and on a business level with the relevant facts."

Also, the value propositions that have evolved out of Electronics Marketing are industry leading. The company believes that they have to be really different to come up with outcomes that are beyond the normal metrics of shipping it faster, better, and so on. Electronics Marketing has done that with the value-added services that they offer, such as Integrated Material services where they help customers lower their total acquisition costs around manufacturing products and speed up their time to market, as well as the Avnet Design Services which is the engineering "value-add."

The largest group in the company is led by someone who understands the value that Avnet must bring to its partners both internally and externally every day. Bryant communicates this message clearly to his people worldwide: "Do as I do." It's professional, accessible, and honest. It's a good formula, and it works.

Phil Gallagher is senior vice president of Global Business development for Avnet Electronics Marketing. The metrics that he is looking at for the group are global in scope:

> "We have to drive 'linkage' and coordination of efforts globally to meet the changing needs of our customers and suppliers. The truth is that they are moving their manufacturing to different regions of the world and outsourcing will continue which means that our supply chain has become more complex."

Gallagher provided me with Figure 5.3 that lays out the three interlocking focus areas of Avnet Electronics Marketing in a world of commoditization and global offshore outsourcing.

Figure 5.3 shows the continuum of products and services that Avnet Electronics Marketing provides from supplier to customer with their expert

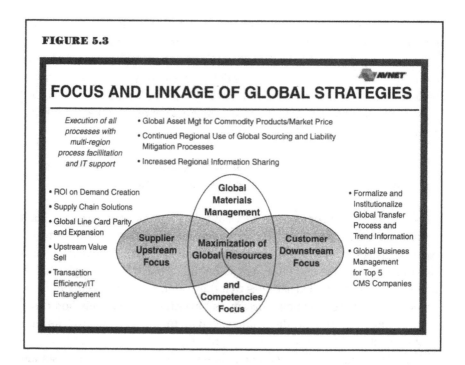

FIGURE 5.3

FOCUS AND LINKAGE OF GLOBAL STRATEGIES

global materials management, and their ability to maximize the global resources and competencies needed to help both supplier and customer reach excellence and exceed their own expectations for costs saving and more profitability from their Avnet relationship. In addition, the various activities in the three blocks of text that surround the three circles describe the company division focus as they integrate themselves with supplier or customer needs and provide them with cultural knowledge worldwide. The concept of *entanglement* is how Vallee and Bryant as well as the entire Avnet team see themselves vis-à-vis both customers and suppliers, so that they can positively affect their businesses.

AVNET Applied Computing

Ed Kamins is president of Avnet Applied Computing. The company was in this business for some time before they created a separate group. Both Computer Marketing and Electronics Marketing each sold part of the products and services in Applied Computing. Computer Marketing saw it as *half a computer* and Electronics Marketing saw it as *a large component.* Now Avnet has placed these activities into the Applied Computing group.

The business has many segments. When they sell a microprocessor, it is a single digit margin business, but when it needs to be built onto a board and put into a system, it is in the high margin business. Then, the margin doubles again if they are just selling services. The services-alone margin is six times that of just selling the product.

Kamins moved the entire Applied Computing operations into one building. His goal has been achieved. He wanted lots of knowledge transferred and developed with the integration of the different aspects of the business. There is a real sense of excitement generated by the fact that their warehouse and assembly center can be seen through a glass wall. Although they protect very carefully the sensitivity of their customers to security and potential competitors, nevertheless, the corporate and administrative people can see the people on the line and in management.

In their integration center, they use a modular or cellular system. They could, in the same part of the warehouse in the morning where they load disk drives with software, arrange huge racks of equipment in that same space in the afternoon. So they have complete flexibility to move carts of equipment about as well as people with different expertise to meet the needs of the customer.

It is important to remember that as a distributor and value-added service provider, they are always squeezed in the middle between the customer and supplier. Applied Computing is employed by their suppliers and set out with the objective of selling the suppliers' products. That is why they build a line card with complementary devices and products. On that card wherever there is a flat panel, there will be a microprocessor and a storage device with a system to support it; there will be software, too, which is why they have an alliance with Microsoft Corporation for its embedded operating systems where they resell their product as part of their solutions to their customer problems.

Applied Computing is a highly customized service business and is the group within Avnet that has been growing.

Their alliances include joint marketing arrangements, and, in most instances, they have joint campaigns with suppliers. They just finished launching Avnet Fast Build. It's an on-line Web-based configurator. If the customer wants to build their own server, they could do it on the on-line configurator and all Avnet would require is that the customer build it on their standard system, then Avnet will commit to ship it within seventy-two hours (this could be an existing customer or a new customer who likes a design and wants to either buy it on-line or reconfigure it). The software is pretty smart; it won't allow a customer to design the system incorrectly. In the relationship with Intel, for example, because the configurator is focused on Intel designs, Intel distributed it to their 10,000 Intel product dealers. The result of this campaign was that there was a spike on the Avnet system that generated customers' interest.

In addition to these joint campaigns, Kamins builds intimate customer alliances. He has one hundred sixty people internally and externally in his North American sales force calling on customers and trying to understand the project needs while helping them through the early stages of design. Applied Computing uses the field people to get customers interested and to bring them in to see and start using the product showcase. Then, many customers go to the laboratory. Avnet will build them a first prototype. Their engineers build a specific model that the customer requests and once it is built and shipped to them, the customer is asked to sign off on it. Avnet then builds the model into an Avnet Manufacturing Spec that reflects the specific needs, materials, and ways of building the product put into the system. The whole spec is put on-line on their FasTrac[R] Web portal, and they can order as much or little as they want (asking only that the customer give them a heads-up if there will be a large volume order so they can get the materials in time).

Applied Computing does not compete with the contract manufacturers because most contract manufacturers are low flexibility, high volume, and low cost. Avnet is high flexibility, low volume, and a fair cost. The contract manufacturers would go out of business trying to do what Avnet Applied Computing does. They have big factories set up to build large volume. The set-up costs that they would have to charge for changes and customized orders would be too great, generating a perfect niche for Avnet. Through the trough of the recession when everyone was going down, they held flat and then grew slightly in 2002. With the downturn in 2002, even small growth is a major accomplishment. They are picking up market share all over the place in 2003. The customer alliance is focused on alliance development metrics initially to be sure that the value that Applied Computing brings to the table is appreciated by the customer, and that they understand the strategic fit between the two companies. Then, it's all about implementation—Applied Computing's ability to be flexible, deliver on time, and at the quality level expected by the customer.

Regarding competitors, the issues are not so much about Applied Computing and Arrow Electronics. Rather, the market is highly fragmented. This means that there are lots of small companies in the market that are local to a specific customer which will be reasonably priced yet may not have the breadth, depth, and financial staying power to meet the customer's long-term needs. The outcome is more business for Applied Computing as the customer's specifications and demands increase.

Kamins prefers to think about the Applied Computing business as product integration but does not call it manufacturing because they are not building raw parts. Regardless, it is a manufacturing of sorts because they are assembling, testing, and certifying.

The integrated aspect of these alliances that Applied Computing has with its suppliers and customers is one of the more intricate, customized, and service-oriented areas of Avnet's business, particularly when communication of needs, expectations, and outcomes is important. Kamins, with his wry sense of humor, relies heavily on his good business instincts. Certainly, he has the process people doing the data analysis and measurements and giving him the answers to quantitative issues when he needs them.

Following is a sample of their Annual Strategic Long Range Planning Session and their expectations associated with it. This information was provided by David Rapier, senior vice president of strategic planning in Avnet Applied Computing. The example is a process builder tool for which he is responsible and is illustrative of the alliance metrics and expectation documentation that they collect and use in management.

100.0 Annual Avnet Applied Computing (AAC) Strategic Long-Range Planning Session.
Review vision and mission statements and compare prior
    year's results.
Establish strategic imperatives and scorecard.
Establish key performance metrics (KPMs) at the division and
    business unit level.
Communicate to AAC globally.
Budget planning to support AAC strategies.

200.0 Data Gathering and Reporting.
Collect facts and feedback.
Compile KPMs and communicate to appropriate parties.

Identify issues, problems, or concerns.
Validate data and inputs; review for exceptions.

300.0   Corrective Process—Define and Document.
Analyze information and root cause.
Identify outcomes and tasks.
Develop solutions and/or processes to support outcomes.
Document; ensuring compliance with ISO 9001:2000 where
     appropriate.

400.0   Daily Discipline Support Activities.
Review process flow, procedures, and/or activities to determine if
the primary outcome requires: enforcement of a process, process
needs re-engineering, training assessment is needed and/or human
resource effectiveness.

Training needs assessment.
    Evaluate training for performance, re-engineering, or skills.
    Assess training effectiveness.
    Develop/modify training as needed.

Process performance enforcement.
    Determine how to assess if individuals need to adhere to the
    process.
    Communicate and train.
    Role clarification and accountability within critical performance
    factors (CPFs).

Re-engineer the process.
    Determine what of the process requires modification.
    Determine metrics for success.
    Communicate and train.

Human resource effectiveness.
    Assess job-person fit for ensuring appropriate outcomes are met.
    Employee development and succession planning as appropriate.
    Organization/structure changes as appropriate.

500.0   Implement and Discipline.
Re-evaluate to confirm process, training, and resources are meeting expectations.

Develop implementation plan; communicate.
Continue reinforcement of discipline.

600.0 Establish Measurements.
Obtain executive confirmation.
Validate against KPMs.
Establish and measure CPFs.
Frequency of measurement.
Daily
Quality measures (Avnet and suppliers)/ employee quarterly
progress reviews.
Annual review and compare to business strategies (see 100.0).

The above steps are fairly self-explanatory. They could fit into any company's internal strategic planning and evaluation process. The difference here is that Avnet is all about alliances. Key performance metrics (KPMs) and critical performance factors (CPFs) are all related to its alliances with suppliers and as a result how they measure themselves and their business with reference to their customers. Figure 5.4, which illustrates the process builder tool, is considered a daily discipline tool for Avnet Applied Computing.

The process builder tool works as follows:

Moving from left to right on Figure 5.4, the tool is used as both a diagnostic of the processes that are in play, as well as a guidebook for how to change and fix them. As the process that is being addressed is identified, the team or individuals who are implementing them are also identified. Corrective action is applied either through awareness, training, and education or maybe transferring the person who may not be capable of executing (or is unwilling to execute) the task(s). The feedback loop of learning, diagnosis, and remediation continues. It is a scheme to manage processes better, which, for those readers who love processes, is very useful. For those for whom process is a bad word, realize that the good thing about this approach is that action soon follows once you know where to put it—which is the point of the tool! The idea is not to analyze forever but rather to get to the problem quickly, fix it, and move on. Avnet Applied Computing has the growth rate to prove that this method works for them.

Kamins likes to know the outcomes and results of these tools and processes. But he is more interested in getting face time with the customers and suppliers rather than reviewing multiple processes and detailed spreadsheets. He can be detailed when he needs to and gets to brag about the fact

FIGURE 5.4

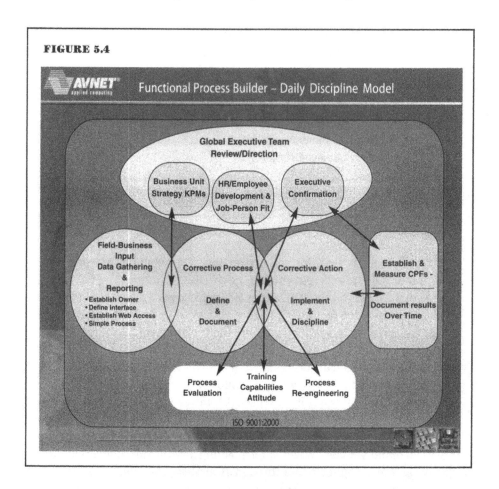

that his group is now at 5.3 sigma (six sigma is perfection—so that is pretty impressive!). His personal skills are engaging. His employees drive themselves to profitable growth and return on capital. Kamins's group manages based on those metrics, which helps him avoid bloated warehouses and products that they cannot sell.

Kamins holds to the philosophy that if customers don't value what Avnet offers and are constantly trying to drum them down on price that probably this isn't a customer worth his time. If they cannot see the value even after many visits and education, then Avnet is better off not serving them. Most of the time, that customer comes back after having been burned by a lower cost distributor who could not deliver what was promised. It is here that return on market opportunity cost plays a part. They analyze what it would cost Applied Computing to stick with this customer and not be able to make any profit compared to putting those sales and service resources elsewhere where their value is appreciated, paid for, and makes money for both the customer and themselves. That kind of basic wisdom is working for Kamins in Avnet Applied Computing.

In my conversations with Fane Friberg, vice president of operations of Avnet Applied Computing, it was clear that he and his team work hard with a detailed focus on quality activities by correlating process sigma to process yield. The outcome of this kind of specific set of metrics used in quality management is the 5.3 sigma that made Kamins proud.

Avnet Computer Marketing

This important group is led by ebullient Rick Hamada whose energy levitates those around him into action! He has visionary views on his business unit and huge plans. Yet, his focus regarding the supplier is to remain humble, no matter how big the role is that Avnet plays for that supplier in the market. For example, Avnet is one of IBM's largest *customers* as the number one value-added distributor of IBM enterprise computer products, with total IBM sales of over $1.2 billion of these products in 2002. They also added a Cisco Systems relationship when they acquired Kent Datacomm in 2001 and have had a long-standing relationship with HP dating back to 1978 and the former Digital Equipment. Avnet Computer Marketing is number one in market share for enterprise products with HP and has significant market share with a select group of other premier technology companies. They have thousands of value-added resellers (VARs) to service as customers to whom they parcel out over $2.0 billion in enterprise products in North America and Europe. The company also provides networking, infrastructure, and enterprise storage technology to end-user companies in the United States through its systems integrator division. This poses not only a logistical challenge but also requires a steady hand at the tiller with clear leadership and areas of focus for the business.

Avnet Computer Marketing became a reality at Avnet in 1988. Computer products distribution emerged to provide manufacturers with a means to deliver products to a broader spectrum of customers than manufacturers could effectively reach by themselves. The company's first major supplier relationship was with Digital Equipment, which later evolved into a relationship with Compaq and HP. At that time, distributors served as intermediaries for the manufacturer who lacked the market reach to deliver products to multiple end points rapidly and efficiently. Resellers also appeared on the scene to help businesses select and procure technology. In 1993 the acquisition of Hall-Mark Electronics laid the foundation for the company's one- and two-tier business models. Avnet Computer Marketing focused on the end user sales and Hall-Mark Electronics' products focused exclusively on value-added resellers.

Later acquisitions in North America, the Europe, Middle East and African Region (EMEA) and Australia extended both the company's reach and its expertise. The company now has three customer-facing divisions: Avnet Hall-Mark, a value-added distributor serving North America; Avnet Partner Solutions, a value-added distributor serving EMEA; and Avnet Enterprise Solutions, a solutions integrator serving end-user businesses in the United States.

Volume-oriented or commercial distributors focus on reducing costs for suppliers by leveraging the volume of transactions processed across hundreds, sometimes thousands, of product line. These are the important metrics for Avnet Computer Marketing in their alliances with their suppliers. They combine cost-effective order acquisition and solution provisioning with services that deliver return on investment for partners based on the value of new customer acquisition, opportunity identification, competitive wins, and true sales advocacy. By focusing on a select group of premier technology brands, Computer Marketing offers suppliers greater technical expertise and market understanding in order to drive sales. If the issue is strategic fit as an alliance metric, the factors just mentioned become Avnet's competitive and strategic advantage for their suppliers.

Hamada is very specific on how he wants the team to build a relationship with the customer and the steps that they must take. He wants the outcome to be *global reach with personal touch,* and he describes that as leveraging the global scope and size of Avnet to deliver products and services through local operation to meet the needs and preferences of local markets. In this respect, this group is a classic example of multiple alliances along the value chain of supplier to distributor to customer.

Hamada's business is built on customer intimacy, comprised of a number of metrics. What he wants the team to focus on is to be the problem solver, to know the customer's customer. His value proposition to his customers and suppliers is to accelerate their success. Hamada sets expectations that there are no shortcuts. He feels employees have to have the following characteristics, which translate into metrics of how he wants his people to measure their performance with their customers and suppliers, that is, their alliance partners:

1. Do you do what you promise you will do, consistently? If so, you can then differentiate yourself and build trust (the fundamental basis of all successful relationships) and the customer and supplier will look to you to help solve other problems.

2. Being a problem solver is the next step that assists the customer to deal with existing challenges so you become so valuable, respected, and competent in this arena that you may then be asked to advise on future or expected challenges.

3. As a *problem anticipator*, you may be consulted on problems that could arise and assist the customer or supplier in avoiding them. Getting in the loop before the problem will ensure you achieve the relationship of trusted advisor and implementer.

So how do you achieve this? Hamada explained that his business is built, as a technology distributor, with logistics, sales, marketing, financial, and technical services that benefit both reseller and end-user customers. They provide these services effectively and also with real understanding because they serve both end users and resellers of technology. Below are some of the internal metrics that are used to differentiate Avnet externally with their suppliers and customers.

The following are three major strategic areas of metrics for Computer Marketing:

1. Assets flow. They currently drop-ship over 70 percent of their products and are involved in the asset flow because their activity actually triggers the flow. The metrics are built around this issue with their suppliers and customers—they track on-time delivery, quality, logistics efficiency, and so on. Other metrics are cost of shipment, cost of handling and warehousing, days of inventory, days of payables, and days of sales outstanding, and all the metrics familiar to those in the sales, marketing, and distribution arena.

2. Financial flow is built around working capital. For their suppliers, it's consolidated into one credit risk—for IBM and HP they only have to deal

with Avnet in this purchase, whereas Avnet has thousands of VARs to deal with so this metric has to be well managed.

3. The information flow ties directly to customer satisfaction measurement. The actual VAR contract is directly with the supplier and the relationship is also facilitated by Avnet. IBM, as an example, conducts a VAR partner satisfaction survey of Avnet-affiliated VARs every year and shares the results with Avnet to help them appreciate and understand the metrics and expectations as well as they can. Avnet also helps target and deliver a lot of the information flow from the supplier to the VAR. The information flow area is a newer area and now their own information technology (IT) and e-business development is allowing portal development and success metrics. Much of the information flow has been traditionally in the arena of "Where is my invoice?" but now it is going into the area of true knowledge sharing so that the customers can learn and access timely and relevant information. They measure the adoption rate of the portal and ask whether it is taking time from value-added (i.e., sales) activity or increasing productivity and adding value. Their relationship with the VARs is uniquely intimate. I spoke with Catherine Serie who is vice president for divisional marketing at the Avnet Hall-Mark division of Computer Marketing. She shared with me their specialty of building channels to market and helping the VARs look and act like professional, larger, and established companies. In many instances, the marketing support that Avnet provides in terms of market positioning, materials, and promotion is well beyond what a VAR could ever hope to create and so positions them strongly in their marketplace. Avnet has learned how to take the suppliers requirements and help build the channel to support them.

Hamada shared with me that they now have a sophisticated customer information management system that has merged some sixteen customer databases into one operating customer database. This has an activity record regarding all customer information, including such issues as how many times they call the technology services group or whether they currently have a return or perhaps a credit problem. All of this information is now in one place reducing unproductive internal communication loops. As their internal user adoption continues to increase, it adds more value to what they are doing every day. This database can also act as a valuable archive and resource for those managing these critical supplier and customer relationships because they get quick access to information.

A CHALLENGING SITUATION: A NEW SUPPLIER MODEL

This challenge relates to one of the three critical strategies that form the foundation of Hamada's business: asset flow. About two years ago, HP came to a conclusion that they wanted to handle all the logistics and integration for their Unix server line and wanted to bring all of it back to their own facilities. Before this, Avnet had committed to their suppliers, and HP was one of them, that Avnet would be their final stop on their assembly line. Avnet could respond faster and could take and process an order and ship it out in the most cost-effective and efficient way. That value proposition worked very well for quite some time. Then quite suddenly (Avnet's perception), HP indicated:

> "We want to bring this activity back inside and we want to do it internally. We don't want the contingent liability of multiple inventories and we believe that we can gain economy of scale by doing it ourselves."

This indication was before and not related to the Compaq acquisition. The announcement by HP occurred in 1999 and became a reality in October of 2000.

As in all businesses, it's not just the hand you are dealt, but the way you play it that can make the difference. The hand that Avnet was dealt now had a few cards less than they were used to holding. Instead of being an integral part of the asset flow, they were now challenged with focusing primarily on the financial and information flows to create and articulate their value. Not *touching* and transforming (final assembly) most of the product along the way was quite a foreign concept to them because they considered one of their core competencies to be material handling and asset velocity. Avnet Computer Marketing management was faced with answering the fundamental question: "How can we be a partner under these circumstances?"

If you review some of the considerations we talked about in Chapters One through Four, it's clear that this alliance is going through an entirely different stage of its life cycle, the strategic design of the relationship has changed, the fundamental expectation for performance has changed and, in short, the alliance required a re-launch. Avnet realized that they had to look at the world differently. So they started to outline the interests and value-add that they could still offer to HP.

HP agreed that Avnet was a good partner to create and develop demand, that is, a partner demand manager. This agreement was certainly an added value as Avnet managed the downstream network of resellers. In addition, Avnet also contributed in the sales, marketing, and technology support arenas to the large and sometimes disparate group of VARs. This was a good evaluation of value, but the problem was that the conversation on the channel of the future for HP was not happening between Avnet and HP.

The conversation was happening between HP and an outside consultant group and between themselves they talked about, strategized, analyzed, and decided the future of the partnership without including the existing (and affected) partner in the discussion. By the time Avnet entered the discussion, decisions had pretty much been made. Here is a classic example of one side of the partnership seeing itself as a value-added partner (Avnet) while the other side said, "Yes, you are, but we are still going to consult others to help solve our problems." In the realms of managing expectations, building trust, adding value to the relationship, this lack of communication was the reason for the failure of mutuality.

But Avnet was not dissuaded. It is a core part of their culture not to cry over spilled milk but to find the nugget of gold in the mine of dust.

Avnet saw that a consultant was able to more strongly influence HP about what to do instead of the partners working it out with each other and that was of great concern to them. They went forward with a redesign and re-launch of the relationship.

They continued with the RosettaNet link between HP and themselves and also aggregated the resellers so that HP, instead of billing three hundred smaller companies, now bills only one, Avnet.

They started the journey on this new model and the need for changes began soon thereafter. The resellers presumably said, "but I need this marketing support" and Avnet said, "it's not priced into our contract, but let us discuss this with our partner." The value was needed so they put it back into the new model. Over the past three years, both HP and Avnet have continued to tweak and refine the model to fit the needs of the market and the financial targets of both companies. In essence, they have returned to a *mutuality* model after all.

Computer Marketing started to look at what their activities actually cost them and how to price and value them if they wanted to increase their return on working capital. This got them thinking about other relationships and how to quantify, value add, and change them. There has since been a fundamental change in their market and that of their suppliers in the last few years. Everyone shared in the great buildup in the 1990s and are now sharing in the contraction in this period of time.

Avnet still sees its importance in the financial and information flow arenas even though they are not as much in the asset flow. They have also learned to articulate their value better in the financial and information flow arenas so that they can connect and communicate at all times with their suppliers and customers.

When the new model announcement was made, the Avnet Hall-Mark division of Computer Marketing split into focused business units: one to focus on the IBM business and another to focus on the HP business. Whenever a supplier reached the $100-million mark, they would be a candidate to consider for a new business unit. This way, the sales, marketing, and technical people could focus completely on what was going on with each company who were their suppliers. IBM doesn't care that Computer Marketing has fourteen hundred people in North America; they want to know which four hundred of them get up each and every day to make IBM successful. The same goes for HP and for any large supplier. The newest re-organization of Avnet Hall-Mark now has a dedicated, focused, and valuable proposition for that supplier. Now there are three groups: IBM, HP, and Enterprise Storage and Software. Currently, IBM and HP, who are their two biggest partners, comprise 65 percent of their sales. They can identify and articulate exactly which people and which resources make each one of those suppliers successful. A major takeaway from the HP lesson for Hamada and Avnet was that they didn't want to be in a position again in which the supplier tells them about the new model after the decisions are made. They want them to be willing to come and talk about the relationship and treat Computer Marketing as a *trusted advisor.* As Hamada put it:

> "Please allow us to get our point of view into the mix (and, of course, feel free to calibrate it and possibly even check with a consultant), but please be sure I am part of the mix and discussion. I do look to enhance your success because I do want to ensure you are around for a long time. For me to succeed, you must succeed."

IBM: A VALUED SUPPLIER

Of Avnet's IBM VAR customer base, over 50 percent sell IBM exclusively so the sales people generally deal with VARs that are very focused on IBM. They also have resellers who sell only HP and their own dedicated sales people. A dedicated team is essential and enables Avnet to grow while meeting and balancing specific supplier challenges.

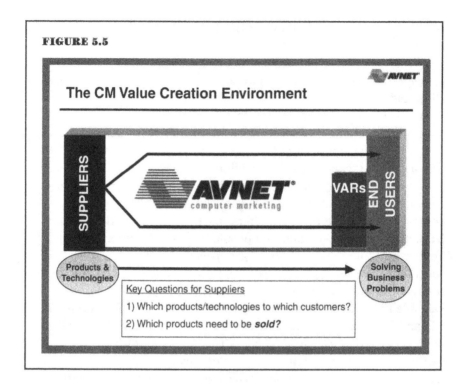

FIGURE 5.5

Figure 5.5 lays out how Hamada and his team like to think about their customers and suppliers and how they add value to both groups. The questions at the base of the chart connect the reality of the customer need and that of the VAR to solve business problems with the products and technologies that Avnet obtains from their suppliers on the left-hand side of the chart. Hamada feels strongly that it is important to know the supplier well. They need to know what it is that is a religious battle for the supplier in that it is something that they really care a lot about, or maybe it's something that is not worth arguing about. It is important to know which lines you can and cannot cross. Trust in the relationship is key. Hamada's major goal for all his people is to get to the position of the trusted advisor role.

The IBM relationship has grown since its inception in 1996 and became a $1-billion reality in 2001 when there was consolidation in the channel since Avnet finalized a couple of acquisitions. As the relationship has grown, so has the trust. IBM values and takes the time to say "here is what we are thinking" or "we are not happy about this particular result and we want the channel to focus on this."

Fred Cuen is general manager of the Avnet Hall-Mark IBM business unit. He constantly shares his metrics about what he has accomplished, what the pipeline and the opportunity list are, and what the confidence factor is, all in alignment with IBM's metrics and goals.

An important cultural issue has been making sure that everyone has the same meaning of all the metrics and words used and to ensure that when they implement an idea that everyone has the same idea. This means spelling out the sales methodologies that make up their metrics, strategically as well as tactically on a monthly basis, and reviewing their progress financially based on achievement of sales results versus the plan they laid out for the year. Then they are also measured in terms of looking ahead at what's coming, sharing information on how many deals are being worked on downstream so that the myriad suppliers and customer relationships are aligned and focused.

Hamada personally reviews Avnet's performance with Bill Zeitler from IBM (Bill is Avnet's executive partner) who has worldwide responsibility for IBM's servers and storage. Every three months they talk and then meet face to face two or three times a year. They review the numbers and current areas of development and revisit their expectations of each other as partners.

They have, in the past, reviewed operating plans and financial plans that are out of sync with the supplier expectations. Sometimes, discrepancy is found in the financial plan. But when they talk to the supplier, the only thing that matters to them is their financial plan. No matter how important the relationship appears to be to the supplier, Hamada has the same approach:

> "My philosophy is to be humble. The most disastrous relationship is when a channel player tries to tell a supplier how to run their business. I will not do that. I consider myself privileged to be included in a strategic discussion and I feel like a trusted partner."

Computer Marketing, indeed the whole of Avnet, is managed with humility, not hubris, which accounts for its success.

Shared Services

David Birk was given the opportunity of a lifetime. In 2003, he was given the responsibility for creating shared services out of the disparate corporate services that used to reside at the corporate level of the company. He left his role as general counsel and took to his new role with vigor and excitement. The idea had been launched describing the business units like speedboats with their profit and loss responsibilities and that the corporate services which were formerly uncontrolled costs (i.e., they were not optional but actually were seen as kinds of taxes that the business units had to pay) would now be put into a profit center run by Birk. This would mean that there would be certain services that even the Shared Services group would not provide directly but that working with the business units they would decide which of those services to outsource. Then they would have the responsibility to monitor those services as they were provided to the business units. This way the business unit could choose the services they wanted except for a basic few that they were required to have, such as human resources and finance. Figure 5.6 describes the flow of services well.

A number of companies are doing this with some success, and Birk is determined to make this happen. I have no doubt that he will because he has the support of all the operating group presidents and is changing the mix of those within the shared services group to those employees who

FIGURE 5.6

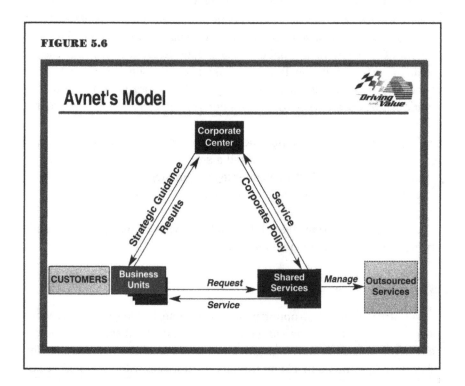

understand the need to be a profit center rather than a cost center. This group has buy-in, talent, and an enthusiastic leader who sees the need for metrics to measure their activities and the quality of what they offer to the internal customer as an alliance which is as important as supplier and external customer alliances. The Avnet shared services group will succeed.

Finance and Investor Relations

It is in this arena that Avnet is particularly impressive. Ray Sadowski, CFO, is communicative and creative. He teaches a course on finance to the managers at Avnet as does John Hovis, who is vice president and director of investor relations, making difficult concepts easy to understand. Their influence and knowledge transfer has, however, enabled the division and business unit presidents and their teams not only to manage with a financial perspective but also with clear operational, supplier, and customer orientations.

Sadowski made me feel quite vindicated. The reason is that for many years I have been preaching that CFOs should and must become involved in the areas of strategic alliances and should not leave the metrics on the all important relationships only to those in marketing, research, or general operations. Sadowski confirmed that for me:

> "Alliance metrics are very much part of what I do. Measuring the effectiveness of alliances that we have with our customers is a critical financial metric for us. For example, we keep track of all the sales, costs to maintain the account to come up with a ratio of customer profitability, and then we also keep track of those customers where either the customer will not pay more due to a perception of lower value or is willing to pay more but was not aware of the added value that we provide. These metrics help us improve and increase our business since we can look at whether we are making enough money for the resources that we have invested."

About 30 percent of Sadowski's time is spent with outside stakeholders, sell-side analysts as well as major shareholders for the company. Most of the analysts who follow the company are very thorough, but it is still necessary to keep up good communication to prevent untoward concern.

Sadowski was upbeat, as were all the executives at Avnet with whom I spoke:

"Jan Jurcy in public relations and John Hovis in investor relations are always trying to get our message out and assist analysts and the public to understand our story and the cycles of our business. But one thing I know for certain—the cycle always ends, the business conditions will improve."

Hovis endorsed this view:

"When times are bad in this industry, as in any industry, the real issue is how you manage your financial scenarios in the downturn. It's a delicate balance to get the right capital structure. These are the metrics that we must attend to when we manage our alliance relationships with the analyst and shareholder communities."

Hovis is a former academician and an economist. He has a macro as well as a micro view of the business:

"You manage the balance sheet in the downturn and in the upturn you manage the profit and loss statement," he explained. "You cannot divorce yourselves from the financial metrics—there always has to be a wonderful dynamic tension that you will never be comfortable with, and frankly, you need to have the tension and then you know you are in the right operating spot. In difficult times, it's all about liquidity. The credit rating agencies are looking at every company's ability to generate enough cash flow to take care of all the obligations that are coming due. In October of 2002, Moody's Ratings took us by surprise. They had analyzed that we would not have enough cash flow to satisfy our debt and bond obligations that were coming due. They downgraded us and at the same time, put a negative watch on us as well as a comment about the cash flow issue, and our stock plunged. The next three weeks were an experience of a lifetime. I personally spent three weeks on the phone with hundreds of callers and Roy (Vallee) and Ray (Sadowski) were on the phone with the institutional investors. We mobilized to ensure our investor base and over the next few months, the stock has doubled. What an experience!"

Avnet has replaced the bond obligations with those that mature in five years and have over $1 billion in liquidity today, so they are in an excellent cash position. This is not an experience they want to repeat. Their communication with the investor community is a major focus of their alliances with external stakeholders today.

Avnet is a company that well deserves a reputation for strategic, operational, and cultural excellence. Although Vallee assures me there is lots more to do, when it comes to alliances, they are among those with the best practices.

CHAPTER SIX

Women and Big Brother: Strange Companions

No, this chapter is not an off-color story about sibling rivalry. Rather, it is a series of inspirational stories about women-owned businesses that have succeeded against all the odds and who have done so because of the alliances that they have created and the ways they manage them using metrics. The similarity between and among them is that both businesses count as their major customers—in one case, their only customer—various groups within the federal or state governments.

Stronghold Engineering Inc

Started by Beverly Bailey in 1991, Stronghold Engineering (Stronghold's) has grown by leaps and bounds. At the core of their success is Stronghold's knowledge that it must create and maintain solid partnerships with their customers who are governmental entities. Literally every job puts the reputation of the company over its 12-year history on the line again. When Stronghold's was established ten years ago, Bailey had the self-propelling vision and unwavering commitment to start a different kind of construction company—one based on the belief that quality should surpass any other project goal and when achieved, everything else important would fall in line. That is exactly what has happened, and Bailey, working with her husband Scott, has made their dreams come true. On October 1, 1991, the company (then called Stronghold Electric) was founded. What began as a small, home-based business has blossomed into a full-fledged general, civil, and electrical design-build construction company. The first three years (with three full-time employees), Stronghold focused on small, mainly electrical contracts that helped the company practice important procedures that set the stage for further growth. In 1994 Stronghold began prime contracting, and through 1999 saw increasing and diverse projects from multiple government agencies such as the United States Army Corps of Engineers, the United States Department of the Navy, and the Department of Veterans Affairs, to name a few. In 1994 Stronghold Electric earned its 8(a) certification from the United States Small Business Administration (SBA) which opened the door to contracting opportunities that were previously not accessible. Working closely with the SBA, Stronghold has gained experience and has grown its business and customer base to include many government agencies, while maintaining the same high-quality standards on which the company was founded.

At the heart of Stronghold's purpose is a strong sense of faith that centers the company goals and missions on the meaningful and lasting success that comes from diligence, ethical standards, and high moral conduct. They don't just talk the talk, they walk the walk. With the detail, attention to quality, various difficult personalities, and cultures with which they have to work, this is no small feat. This ability is what led me to examine their ability to develop alliances with governmental entities in large complex projects. They do an outstanding job. It's important to understand the scope of the projects that the company works on to understand the alliance metrics challenges, so here are a few examples:

Design-build. This crosses a broad range of capabilities from design through construction.

Construction. This means having technically proficient in-house personnel to meet all types of construction needs.

Civil and heavy/highway construction. We all see these people when we are stuck in traffic; it involves specialized heavy/highway and infrastructure experience with significant equipment resources.

Electrical and mechanical construction. Again, another area which is not for the inexperienced or faint of heart; they have in-house high voltage and electrical capabilities for any size or scope of project.

Environmental remediation. From ecosystems to abatement, Stronghold's gets involved in providing a full range of environmental solutions.

Repair and renovation. They have been called upon to fix government real estate, which is occupied with tenants in place including medical, dental, and food service facilities.

High voltage and utilities distribution remote. Again, not for the faint of heart, they bring distribution capabilities to the high voltage area as well as the ability to service remote areas, especially in the southwestern United States.

Anti-terrorism force protection. Experienced with mission sensitive, highly secure military installations and proven track record of meeting ATFP goals, the company has been extremely busy in this area especially in the past year.

The variety of projects that Stronghold's involved in and the diversity of customers shows the flexibility of the company and how they have learned to understand the customer in many different applications. For example, their projects include repairing the Hansen Dam Swim Lake for the United States Army Corps of Engineers and renovating Sherman Indian High School for the US Army Corps of Engineers/BIA. Other projects include: Kino (Ajo) Detention Basin Ecosystem Restoration for the United States Army Corps of Engineers, Los Angeles District, and building Dental Clinics at United States Marine Corps Camp Pendleton for the Department of the Navy. A diverse project was the creation of a Wastewater Treatment Plant in Barstow, California, for the Navy and, one familiar to some readers, the improvements for the Ontario Airport Runway for the City of Los Angeles Airport Authority. This is not a business where failures in customer alliances are permissible. In fact, the only evaluation that is acceptable from any customer, as far as Bailey and her team are concerned, is outstanding. And they get a lot of those. The customer rates them in terms of their experience and then makes their selection along with price in choosing a contractor. For example, yet another project is building a barracks. It's not only necessary to put in a bid but also to show the experience the company has had in building other barracks, how they were rated, and points of contact as well as any difficulties. Again, this is not an alliance where they can fail in any of the projects that make up a long-standing relationship with any of the divisions of the federal, state, or city government.

In the past, the federal government chose the lowest bidders on many projects. Those contractors failed through poor quality and financial difficulties. Similar to Avnet's experience, it is clear that service providers can only do good work when they make a financial return on their effort—so dumbing them down to the lowest bid will eventually get the customer what they pay for—poor products, poor quality, and lousy performance. Neither Avnet nor Stronghold's is willing to sacrifice the project for the bottom line.

Now the federal government has smartened up. They now look for the best value, and contractors have to be both strong in technology as well as their services and skills. It is now necessary to show the government who will be the project or alliance manager. Resumes and organization charts are expected to be included in the bid and proposal, as well as everyone's function within the project. Namely, the customer or alliance partner expects a schedule and an operating plan. [These elements of basic alliances 101 are detailed in great depth in my first book *Intelligent Business Alliances* (New York: Times Books, Random House, 1996)]

In construction, Bailey's approach is to determine the customer's needs up front, develop a plan to achieve them and manage her team and resources in that direction. Of course, then she has to deliver. The result? They consistently receive the evaluation of *outstanding*, sometimes *above average*, rarely, *average* and never *below average* or *poor*.

This is an important generic metric for all alliances—under-promise and over-deliver. Building trust, commitment, reliability, and sustainability will all evolve from partner behavior that consistently delivers better results than were anticipated. This metric can be applied throughout the alliance life cycle, in both the alliance development and the alliance implementation metrics.

The federal government developed the *outstanding to poor* metrics as their standards for all government contractors. Stronghold's internal metrics are tougher. Bailey always asks what can she do to make it outstanding and if it is realistic, they will push for that. The company has created a set of internal processes that have propelled it to a high level of respect and a substantial growth rate even in tough times.

Bailey's team is impressive. One of her internal experts who works on the partnering activities is Jennifer Fogg. She puts together the technical charts and documents and understands and develops the process.

I spoke with Fogg about the alliance metrics that are most important to the company. She explained the dramatic shift that happened in the industries that contracted with the federal government before the last decade when the federal contracts were procured through the lowest bid and whoever had the lowest price got the work. The new way which is now based on performance is called a *best value* approach which is the government's way to ascertain they are getting the best value regardless of prices. The government requires that a performance evaluation form is completed which is similar from agency to agency, although not all government agencies are required to use it. The form contains adjectives that rate the contract's performance, and it is supported with a grid-rating system with specific items relating to the project. The Army Corps of Engineers issues it at the conclusion of the job or in the middle.

Stronghold's is given opportunities to be rated in certain terms and clearly prefer *outstanding*. Their company mandate is to work toward achieving this at all times, which means meeting certain metrics:

1. Meeting the project budget.

2. Schedule.

3. Keeping the customer happy by doing more than is expected.

They also have to meet safety and quality issues. It's a catch-22 situation. If the evaluation is *outstanding*, this will encourage the granting of further business and contracts. If it's less than that, it will deter the allocation of more work. So your performance will determine if you win the next project. Which is exactly as it should be. For once, it seems as if the government has actually gotten it right—very right. Value is the essence of the reward. Give good value, you will be rewarded. If only all businesses could be that simple!

The good news is that the alliance with their major customers just gets stronger and stronger the better the work that they do. There is nowhere to hide. The proof of every project is published by the government to the company, it's on the résumé, and it serves as reference for past and future work. This is sure to keep every contractor's attention.

This is akin to the selection criteria we referred to in the alliance development metrics, which require that if you are looking for the optimum partner, part of your due diligence will be looking at the metrics of how they performed with other partners, that is, their track record on implementation and not only their strategic fit with your company. Finding this information is not as hard as you might think. Most alliances are announced, therefore, a search on the Internet will dig up the public information; also, asking questions of those in the industry, or even of the partner, will bring up many of the issues and metrics. This knowledge will be even more relevant when the implementation metrics are reached.

Bailey and her team do many things that make them an excellent alliance partner. These are metrics which they add to the project that customers do not request. But these metrics have been their differentiating competitive advantage over the past twelve years. Stronghold's develops a set of partnering criteria which they make part of the expectations for the relationship. They bring into a one- or two-day facilitated session, the key stakeholders—representatives of their customer as well as users of the end product. These are the same or different people. They also include all the members of the Stronghold's team and, additionally, any potential subcontractors. All of these people are discovered in their stakeholder analysis, called *project stakeholders*. They bring them into a meeting, which is facilitated, to discuss the goals and project partnering objectives which are then incorporated into a measured matrix to be sent out so partners can rate the project.

This way, from the beginning of the project, they have the measuring benchmarks. At the conclusion, they are pretty well assured of receiving the evaluation that they want, namely, *outstanding*.

The partnering objectives are unique to every project and customized to each piece of work. Projects are never the same. Sometimes, the project needs lots of interaction with the public, which could be very different from a small project, possibly only a room inside a building and not visible from outside.

An example of a project with one of the departments of their best customers was a recent project of approximately $4.5 million. This was completed in a very challenging government environment in one year. The point person for the customer said he had never and would never give an evaluation of *outstanding*. But he did for Stronghold's. The evaluation was based on two real, measurable factors:

1. A high degree of support from corporate for project. This involved frequent meetings with the stakeholders and lots of communication.

2. Conflict resolution skills. The project was not without obstacles. There were relationship issues with Stronghold's and one of their subcontractors that required a special partner meeting; as a result, the issues were resolved.

Another project was one that was incompetently undertaken by another contractor. The project was deemed unsafe and had to be closed to the public. The local corps of engineers were notified by the city about the problem. The public was upset. Then, the local congressman became involved and threatened to take further action unless the city fixed the problem and reopened the facility to the public. So the corps came to Stronghold's in dire straits and said: "We really need your help. You have to get this fixed for us now. In fact, we will hire you on a time and material basis with an open-ended contract to fix the problem." This kind of request never happens, but it showed the high trust level that this department of the corps of engineers had for Stronghold's, that is, they would not gauge them and would do it right. They asked for a time and materials proposal to conduct the survey, the submission of an assessment proposal for repair, and request to do the actual repair in less than 90 days. The corps asked Stronghold's to undertake this at the beginning of April, to complete the work, and have the area open and serviceable for the public by the Fourth of July. They did it.

Stronghold's ability to perform on other contracts and get *outstanding* evaluations resulted in the valued customer becoming an alliance partner who went to them when they had a politically sensitive, difficult, and time-dependent project which they knew had to be done right with trustworthy partners. It doesn't get much better than that!

Following is the agenda of Stronghold's approach developed by Fogg, which shows the level of detail that this company is committed to in being a solid, dependable, high-quality alliance partner.

Partnering workshop with alliance stakeholders: agenda

1. Team building.

2. Project overview—key features of the year-long project.

3. Planning process—to avoid disruption to personnel on the military base.

4. Master project schedule.

5. Safety issues.

6. Lines of communication—protocols, accountability, who should or shouldn't be speaking to whom.

7. Three-week, look-ahead schedules and weekly key points and agenda items including:

   a. Quality control updates.

   b. Review phases.

   c. Review impacts and outage requirements.

   d. Communication of commitments.

8. Conflict resolution issue escalation ladder (names and contact information for every level given); conflict was defined; safety goes to the top immediately:

   a. Executive level.

   b. Upper management.

   c. Project manager.

   d. Site level.

9. Worst case scenarios:

   a. Each team worked to develop the worst case scenarios that could be faced during contract performance.

   b. Solutions were planned.

   c. Preventative actions were planned to avoid the situation from occurring and the group decided whether the action could be prevented or not.

   d. Scenarios included miscommunications, incompetence of team members, inadequate supervision, personality conflicts, schedule delays, cutting through unmarked utilities, installation of wrong equipment and improper design.

10. The entire partnering group of representative and stakeholders from all sides created and signed a project charter stating their mission, vision, and planned and achievable goals as well as internal and external objectives.

So that you don't think that Stronghold's is the only government contractor owned and run by a woman who gets the *outstanding* evaluation, let me turn now to another company started and run by Lurita Doan, the CEO of New Technology Management.

New Technology Management

New Technology Management, Inc. (NTMI) is an information technology provider specializing in nonintrusive remote inspection devices; remote data transfer technologies, and complex NT integration. Founded in 1990 by Lurita Doan, NTMI is a provider of cutting-edge IT operations management, acquisition, maintenance, and integration services for a variety of civilian and military agencies, including the US Department of the Navy, the US Army, the US Air Force, the Nuclear Regulatory Group, the US Department of Agriculture, US Treasury, and the Immigration and Naturalization Service. This means that they have only one customer—the federal government. Even when they do business outside the United States, it is for an American Embassy or Consulate.

It's helpful to understand why and how Doan started her company in order to see why alliance metrics such as commitment to quality, completion on time, and remaining within budget are part of the culture and belief system of the company.

Doan was formerly employed by Unisys. Just a short thirteen years ago, she had a great idea for a new product for Unisys. She was so excited that she couldn't wait to get to work that day. The moment she arrived, she ran to her supervisor to tell him all about her great idea. He basically told her to go back to her cubicle and continue programming. She was so furious and disappointed that she left the company that day and never returned. She got some letterhead printed, started consulting from her home with $25 in capital, and was in business. She was the only employee of her business for three years. Doan is no slouch. In fact, it soon became known that she was the programmer that the government or company called when their system had crashed, and no one had the foggiest idea how to get it back up again. When they had given up on trying, they called Doan. She would come in, recover the system, and provide the networking support to large organizations with crashed systems.

Then one day she got her first really big break. This is now something of an urban legend in her company. She was forty weeks pregnant. Yes, if you do the math that means the baby was actually overdue by a week. She was a subcontractor on an $89-million contract with the US Navy where she was not the prime contractor, but the company that had actually won the award could not make the system work. They would lose the job and contract if they couldn't do a live test demonstration and no matter what they did, they could not get the Unix system to work properly.

Doan got the call as she was sitting uncomfortably at her desk, just wishing the baby would come so that she could stand up straight again:

"Don't make me drive all the way to your site if you are not going to give me the job," she told them, "so I want to know if you are going to give it to me or not."

So the group on the phone call spent the next hour discussing whether they should use a woman on the job, and even more problematic for them, whether they should use a pregnant woman on the job. Finally, they decided that they had no option because Doan was the only person who had any idea of what to do and they were, frankly, desperate. So Doan was told, "Do it!"

She did.

She worked for forty-eight hours without a break and solved their problem.

The US Navy said, "Great—you've got the contract." Doan was overjoyed and started to hang up the phone which, by that time, was practically grafted to her ear. "But," said the Navy guy, "this is going to go onto an aircraft carrier. And we have to see it installed and want a walkthrough, too." Doan gulped. What was she going to do? Her husband was on business in Russia, and she had a toddler at home. So she packed up the baby and the nanny and heaved herself into the car. She drove to Norfolk, Virginia, knowing that she had to get through the next three days until the walkthrough was over, praying that the baby would not come. She knew that this could be the turning point of her business life. If she had to do anything, it was this. After the walkthrough, she insisted on driving back to Washington, DC, to her doctor, even though she was clearly in labor. She made it to the emergency room where, fourteen minutes later, she delivered her baby.

Now, if that isn't commitment, I don't know what is! And it so happened that the major metrics that the government was looking for in a contractor was the ability to undertake a project, complete it in time, at the level of quality expected, and within budget. Consequently, Doan wasn't the only one to notice her commitment. The US Navy did, too. Now she and her company are the prime contractors, and the Navy is still her customer, one of her largest. They have never forgotten her devotion and delivery on her promise to them and her country at the same time as she was delivering another special package for herself and her family. Doan has incorporated this level of commitment and determination as part of the measurable deliverables of her company with their major partner, who is also their only customer, the federal government.

Doan's company is into its second decade. That Navy contract was the springboard for the rest of the business. She learned she wanted to be a government contractor for the simple reason that she didn't want to have to plead to be paid. As a government contractor, she could have control over cash flow, and that has happened. She hired her first four employees and is still extremely involved in the company. She owns 100 percent of the company. Because Doan started her life as an English major, the company prides itself on writing readable and great (grammatically correct and interesting) bids!

NTMI started in the encrypted wireless arena in 1997 to 1998. They were on the Internet before it was cool. Once they entered the encrypted world, they were squarely into the intelligence world. So when September 11 2001 happened, all of a sudden the company was catapulted into prominence because they were able to do nationwide surveillance systems at the ports of entry. Now the metrics of commitment, ability to complete projects in time, and within budget became the company's differentiating competitive advantage in the market.

The company has grown, but they are still project-oriented and see the companies they work with as teaming partners. In this way they partner not only with the federal government but also with other contractors. Nevertheless, they are primarily and morally responsible for all the contracts on which they are the prime party and take that very seriously. After all, it's not just a contract—it's national security that is involved.

In October 2002, they received a Presidential Award for one of President George Bush's Management Initiatives from the US Department of Housing and Urban Development (HUD). The award was for developing enterprise solutions for Upfront Income Verification of Public Housing subsidies.

Now they have 173 full-time employees and more than 100 part-time, flexible employees. They employ many people who are retired from the military and are cleared for high levels of security and do maintenance. They also have many people coming and going who are on extended maternity leave.

NTMI thinks of all the companies that they work with as teaming partners, even though they are often called *subcontractors* by other companies. Doan believes that you can't be successful as a prime contractor if your subcontractors aren't successful and that you can't afford to have your subcontractors go out of business or leave you. She makes sure with intensive due diligence that her subcontractors have similar goals and the right skills set. In this way, Doan spends a lot of time in the alliance development metrics making sure that she is not sorry later to have that subcontractor as a partner in the alliance implementation metrics. You can see a similar theme here compared to what we saw in Chapter Five on Avnet—if both partners can't be successful (albeit in varying degrees and with variation along the life cycle of the alliance), the relationship will not work.

Doan will ask a subcontractor to send her their costs, and she pays them without haggling about it. She expressed it this way:

"You can't sit and squeeze them and then expect them to give 100 percent."

Sometimes, a subcontractor will come back to NTMI with a low bid because they are desperate for the work. If NTMI feels that the bid is too low, it will refuse the offer. NTMI knows the subcontractor will have financial struggles later on if they sell their services too short. If NTMI is working with a small startup company on the leading edge who has little or no experience in these kinds of contracts, Doan works with them to ensure they have reasonable prices.

One of the recurring themes that we have found in the best practices companies which I have featured in this book is their commitment to the alliance (internal) that they have with their employees. I mention this later on in the chapter again, but it's worthy of mention that you will see this internal relationship with IBM, Starbucks, and with NTMI. Doan has an alliance philosophy applied to various aspects of employee management. The company is a collaborative company with a high level of respect for the individual. Doan wants to work only with companies and partners who have the same approach toward their employees. She treats her people very well with high levels of fringe benefits. If her subcontractor partners don't, that is, if they give their people poor wages and no time off, this makes for lots of tension. The last thing Doan wants is for the employees of her subcontractors to defect to her company, because this creates tension and difficulties and undermines her overall goal of her subcontractor partners trusting her.

> "I feel that employees are like money in the bank. You can't have people breaking into your bank account, so you can't have the poaching of other company's employees. Certainly, we do have legal documents that address stealing employees, but that's not the point. There needs to be a fundamental philosophy that you won't take other companies' employees from them."

This philosophy of the organization also moves to the ethical issues associated with the general management of people as well as honest pricing with transparent and ethical financial management.

NTMI works like a small business. They want to like the people with whom they work. They will not sign up a subcontractor partner unless they see who they are. So they will fly to see them if the subcontractor can't afford to fly to see NTMI. There is a general feeling that unless you know your partners, you cannot resolve conflicts and problems with them later during the contract stage or implementation. (See also the philosophy of Starbucks. Howard Schultz believes strongly that unless partners of Starbucks and their families and philosophies of life are known to him and his team, there can be no partnership.)

Doan's company has expanded greatly in the past few years and now they have competitors, especially because $3 billion has been dedicated by the federal government to Homeland Security. Although many companies have a Homeland Security department with lots of people running around, few of them have the expertise, track record and abilities that Doan's company has.

One of the more interesting aspects of Doan's company is that they spend a lot of time on research and development, which is what they call their *emerging test-bed*. This is any emerging technology that could have value. They look at over one hundred hardware and software products every day. They feel they have an obligation to do technology refreshes, which is critical to making sure they are ahead of the curve. So they always look at new products and evaluate whether they will integrate with what they already have in place. They send multiple white papers to the government, and if they think a certain technology is truly superior, they will lobby for it. In this way, they have added another metric to the partnership that they have with their customer, the federal government—innovation. It's added value for the partner because Doan's company provides access to this information and evaluation of the technology for the government without being asked for it, thus making the relationship more valuable. This is an important metric in any partnership: added value achieved from the relationship.

Doan has established a series of ground rules. She and her employees don't invest in other technology companies so they are more objective. She tells people in the evaluation area of her company the following:

"You don't want to color your judgment."

If the product works, they use it. If it doesn't, they will tell the emerging company how to add value to it. Some of them embed those changes and others don't. NTMI tries to be objective about it. They see lots of new technology daily and are constantly on the lookout for the next new thing.

One of the relationships that is mentioned as a stakeholder in Chapter Two is worthy of note here because Doan's company does an excellent job in that regard. It is where management is a stakeholder and how they work with the ensuing internal partnerships which they have with their employees. We discussed management and their relationship to the partners in an alliance, but here the reference is to management and their employees in general as the actual alliance. Doan values her employees greatly. Because NTMI is a privately held company, there are many benefits that she can add to the employee relationship as she is the controlling and major shareholder. For example, Doan has instituted a form, which she calls the capital investment form. Anyone in her company who has an idea applies for funding and argues why the idea would be useful for the company. She remembers all too well her great idea days while she was an employee at Unisys and how that company lost an innovative contributor when she left. How many others had they lost before and after her! In this way, she has created a methodology for partnering with her employees when the opportunity fits the budget and the market situation.

For example, someone in her company said three years ago, "We would like to look into facial recognition." So she said, "OK, here is $24,000," and the project took off!

The company does this all the time within the technology area, which allows aspiring developers or researchers to get a product, play with it, and integrate it into one of their product lines if appropriate.

Metrics for measuring those who manage the external alliance with the customer through different projects include bonuses which are based on performance on existing contracts. The company is based on teamwork, team reward, and team orientation. They do a lot of cross-training with the metrics and measurements of people used to augment their skills so that they can do more activities on more jobs with better partnering and fundamental substantive skills.

"I look at it as if it were starter dough for sour dough bread. Whenever there is a new project, we take someone and offer the opportunity within the company first since when you are starting a new effort the last thing you want is to have to explain the basics on how the company works when the focus should be on the issues associated with the project," Doan adds. "We call it working on the project, not the infrastructure."

Doan is still the senior level relationship person or the *closer*, involved in the alliance development, and is integrally involved in the conceptualization and marketing of new projects as well as the development of relationships with teaming partners. She is also involved in the alliance implementation as the resolver of conflict and re-launcher of the relationship, if necessary. She is always looking for new things and new areas. Doan makes sure that she is also subject to the same metrics as everyone else in the company. Last year she instituted her own 360-degree review process.

One of the new commitments that they have made is to have at least one new high visibility project every year because they do well in these, and it makes the employees proud and excited. That is why the President's Management Initiative, which is the award she got in October 2002 from HUD, was number seven on the President's list of priorities for the nation. They are very proud of this and so they should be.

Even though this business has far exceeded her wildest dreams, there is still so much of the business that is small business, like her financial statements. She looks at her numbers weekly and must be sure that they are profitable all the time. Although Doan thinks this is small business, I assured her it's just plain good business and the fact that she has her hand so closely on the controls of the company is a good sign that they will continue to thrive. Her conservatism will stand her in good stead as the company continues to play a critical role in the United States and supports the families of the employees of New Technology Management Inc.

In summary, here are the aspects of Alliance metrics that are particular and worthy of emulation in the NTMI example:

1. Alliance development. Doan's company has conceptualized their relationship with the US government in such a way that it fits strategically with their intent, goals, and expectations. This is core to her success because she understands the metrics that are expected of her. Doan has been able to communicate these metrics to her team suppliers who assist her in delivering her promise to the customer. These are the main metrics that the government expects and measures:

   a. Ability to complete.

   b. Ability to deliver quality.

   c. Ability to deliver within budget.

   d. Ability to deliver on time.

e. Commitment to all the above.

f. Security and trustworthiness.

2. Alliance implementation metrics. Doan's company has excelled at delivering those abilities and promises made in the development stage of the company's relationship and partnership with their customer. Here are a number of the metrics that they have included in the government relationship that add value:

a. Innovation.

b. Operationalization. Doan, through her unusual commitment to her team suppliers, supports that they must make money and not undervalue their services to get the contract, operationalizes her promises with quality and on-time performance. Other aspects of her ability to operationalize (as described in Chapter Four) include:

i. Creating the right team to implement: long-time employees, good teaming members.

ii. Ensuring continuity through socialization: meaning that Doan's story of how she created the company and her belief system is legendary in the company; the story is told often and is used as a way to ensure that there is continuity of commitment and quality of service.

iii. Strategic alignment: the government's goals and NTMI's goals are well aligned; national security is at stake.

iv. Tracking of mutuality as a metric: Doan's public and corporate accolades keep her company's profile high within the view of the right people within her customer. Part of every subagreement with the government includes a clear understanding of the benefits that go to all parties and how those benefits need to be realized at various milestones in the contract—who is to be informed, who is to be involved, who and what are to be delivered, and what the procedures and processes are for quality products, services, and payments.

Bailey and Doan have set metrics that are particular to their style of doing business with large federal and state customers. Their approaches have application across the board to those doing business in the commercial space and show the effectiveness of both development and implementation metrics that are quantified, clear, and communicated well.

Chapter Seven gives us a look at a company that has repositioned itself over the past decade in a remarkable turnaround and has used alliances as a core part of their strategy to make that happen—IBM.

IBM and Alliances

If you had the ideal situation, with major resources, huge stakes, and a CEO-level driven commitment to make alliances part of the corporate DNA, then you would want to do it the IBM way.

It is well known that IBM is the world's largest information technology company with an eighty-year history. What is not as well known is that they have created an approach to alliance creation, management, and metrics with multiple processes that is well planned, thought through, and includes a massive company-wide buy-in approach in which alliance metrics are linked to compensation and reward systems.

We will look at how IBM has used alliance metrics in their everyday operations starting with the major strategic decision they made at the highest level of the organization, which changed the rules of the game for them in partnering, particularly with their independent software vendors (ISVs). We will then look at the particular processes that IBM has applied, what has worked for them, and what may or may not work for you. Moving beyond IBM, we will then apply the lessons learned from their experience to your situation.

IBM has made a dramatic turnabout in the past five years, with Lou Gerstner (former CEO) lighting the fire under a demoralized group of employees and Sam Palmisano (CEO) taking up the gauntlet in an industry environment that John Chambers (CEO) of Cisco Systems called the "toughest industry environment he has ever seen." Yet regardless of the tough times, IBM is doing a lot right. Their professional services group has been growing by leaps and bounds. Even though the company has seen its stock hammered by the same forces that have affected the entire technology sector, IBM has made some important philosophical and strategic moves in the past few years that have affected the way they do alliances. We will focus our attention primarily on their software group because that area is particularly one in which partnering is critical because there is a need to partner with small and large companies.

The software group has had its own partnering group for over 7 years since IBM had a partnering program in the developer space. This required that they have in place many of the special services that are necessary to support developers in their relationship with IBM. This included technical support as well as enablement assistance in their distribution and channel areas. The group was a strong one, but in 1996 the decision was made to evolve the group into what became The Partnerworld program. It was a program set up for developers, many of whom are called developer partners, with unique requirements for doing business with IBM. However, many of these developers also competed with IBM in the development of applications that were used in the marketplace. Therefore, the dilemma that permeated these relationships was the one that we referred to in the alliance development metrics in Chapter One—the issues of knowledge transfer, competitive and strategic alignment.

In 1999 IBM made a pivotal strategic decision that would affect their partnerships with the ISVs for the foreseeable future, while repositioning them competitively vis-à-vis companies such as HP. They decided that they would no longer compete with their partners, meaning that certain ISVs would be better at various applications than they were and that they would yield that application to them rather than compete with them, on the one hand, and expect full collaboration from them on the other.

The alliance with Siebel Corporation serves as a good example of how IBM changed the rules of the game for itself and in many ways, for the industry with its about-face in 1999. Following is the sequence of events:

The strategic change was announced in November 1999. In fact, IBM had signed a strategic alliance with Siebel Corporation prior to the announcement on 10 November 1999, so they allowed Siebel Corporation to make a joint announcement with them ten days prior to that. The idea was that Siebel Corporation would lead with some of their tech platforms and IBM would make them their main customer relationship management (CRM) partner. Siebel Corporation and IBM alerted the business and trade media. CEO Tom Siebel and senior IBM people came together in New York. They had a big press conference where IBM announced that they would not compete with Siebel Corporation and would go to market jointly. The press asked what would happen to the IBM CRM applications that they had been selling. IBM said that they were in the process of phasing them out because

Siebel Corporation was their CRM partner, which had been announced prior to the initiative.

The rationale was that IBM, working together with its partners, would have the best creative functionality because IBM has the best infrastructure and their partners have better knowledge of vertical industries. By working together with their applications providers in those specific industries where alone they were small players, IBM felt that they could do better. At the press event announcing this change, Siebel announced that his corporation's deal was the first relationship of this kind for IBM.

The press day was a big splash with lots of excitement because IBM representatives were saying that they had reversed course and would no longer compete with their partners. This attracted market attention since a statement of *we weren't winning in this area* is dramatically different from what the market had expected to hear from IBM. In addition, in the industry and certainly among their existing partners, there were significant doubts that IBM could present themselves as a democratic partner and not revert to telling their partners how things should be and taking control of the relationship again.

As it happened, the doubters were proven to be wrong. IBM did make the change, they did move out of competing with their ISVs and they have not browbeaten their partners into submission as was feared.

IBM also created a drumbeat of continuing interest in the industry by signing new partners and announcing partners individually. They created a detailed process for alliances and, wherever possible, they combined different partners into one relationship. There was an ongoing belief that every partner deserved its own press release. Certainly, IBM informed the press about their ISV alliances. Sometimes, IBM announced to certain reporters that they had just signed three ISVs in the financial services sector or in other sectors in which particular press sources were interested. In some cases, they might have signed multiple partners who were focused on mid-market rather than on a particular industry. The IBM relationship development arenas could be by solution area, geography, or industry. IBM looked for every angle to tell a story of how they were changing into the new IBM and how differently they were conducting business.

A landmark event in January 2001 was on the front page of *The New York Times* business section featuring a photo of Bob Timson, then head of alliances for the software group. The article was titled "The Strategic Alliance Initiative 101" and was described as "Retrenchment Not Retreat at IBM."

The story said that IBM was getting out of the applications business where it competed with their partners, that IBM was proceeding with ISVs, and that they supported what IBM had been saying to the industry and their partners. This was a huge story. From then on, the program got a lot of recognition. Internally, the company was being converted into the new partnering mentality. There were lots of meetings and internal communications, but the more external success and coverage they experienced, the more those within IBM started paying closer attention.

The New York Times story was a turning point internally and externally. Before that story, internally, senior IBM executives were interested but not convinced. The alliances group had had some success working their way into the chairman's office with this philosophy as speaking points, but because of the publicity, the new alliance approach became integrated into the management system at IBM.

This is a good example of using the stakeholder approach in order to create internal buy-in. The software group realized that external press (an external stakeholder of sorts in that the press is often a vehicle to the market) could be helpful in getting the message out not only to the external market but in raising internal awareness to the partner program. So understanding the power that the internal stakeholder of management could play in the alliances program, in conjunction with the external stakeholder of the market (through the press), they were able to increase the level of acceptance of the partnering program as a whole. This is a good strategy for you to consider when internal buy-in is a challenge, not because your internal colleagues don't accept or want what you are doing, but rather, that there is so much *noise* about people doing wonderful or interesting things for and within the company, that it is hard to be heard. Otherwise, using press to convince naysayers inside the company that what you are doing is a good idea could backfire and cause even more acrimonious feelings.

So in spring 1999, IBM left the applications business, created a new partnering group, and from spring to November, the way was clear to build and construct the strategic alliances program. The formal announcement of moving out of the applications business made in November enabled the group to move very fast into the market as a major partner for some of the world's leading application developers.

What was different about this initiative compared to all the other initiatives that IBM undertook?

The program was adopted company-wide.

As a single company, they decided that every unit within IBM would come to the table to build the alliance program. They agreed across the company that they would do market management work, that is, select the markets that they wanted to compete in and develop jointly the selection process for the application providers that were the best. This meant that IBM had to develop consensus on which application providers would be selected.

IBM is, as a company structure, very matrixed, meaning that they have lots of flexibility across business units. Decision-making is not hierarchical and takes some consensus building and time.

It took 30 days at both the senior executive level as well as with the line executives to build consensus. This meant co-opting and explaining the opportunity to people who had profit and loss responsibility and had to agree on how to build a cross-divisional, cross-functional team that would comprise the alliance group and ultimately be responsible for the development and implementation across the company of alliance processes.

The execution and implementation issues were critical.

No really great plan has any meaning until it executes.

For ease of understanding and implementation, IBM created an approach to management of the company with five major categories:

How to Measure Success

These metrics have to do with what is going to be measured and how they would collect and report results. They then analyze these data in such a way that they could evaluate it and, if necessary, escalate any concerns.

What to track and report

- ➤ External tracking. They decided to track revenue targets and market share, that is, how much share each of the partners (IBM and the ISV) were gaining.

- ➤ Technology tracking. They also established and measured specific technology objectives. For example, the integration of IBM middleware technical products or service was one of the metrics that was important to IBM. They decided to track that level of detail because unless they could get that done, they could not sell effectively without the understanding of the effects and impacts of what was being sold.

➤ Inside tracking and reporting. They analyzed results. This meant that they measured the opportunity pipeline that had been developed with their partners before the sales were closed, that is they answered questions about whether they were generating enough leads together at that time all the way to the details of city and industry where the products and services were being sold. They put action plans together with their partners.

In this way, using a joint planning approach, they had a root *cause analysis* as to what they were going to do. As a result, IBM and their partners developed multiple sets of tools and metrics, which could be put in place. The approach was to build on the fundamentals of the sales management system, which was used globally across IBM.

After all, there was no point in creating an entirely new sales management system, which would then not only conflict with the existing one but would cause unnecessary work and effort. By using a partnering methodology and metrics that were compatible with and followed the same principles as their sales management system, they were ahead of the time-line for implementation and would find limited resistance to adoption. Their field forces would be able to identify the ISV more easily when an opportunity arose. Additionally, they would also know where the opportunity came from and how well the leads were going. This very detailed level of information even seeped down to the transaction level which gave the sales team the ability to do weekly reviews and address problems in the territory or with an account.

The IBM matrix management system and development divisions included those in the organization who build products as well as those who sell and distribute them. Their systems are connected together so that they interlock on where to sell the product or service.

Due to this initiative, the partnering, sales management, and the development systems were connected. The development division could also view the partnering group's systems.

IBM places a great emphasis on the management of the execution of the alliance. They feel that as long as an alliance or a partnering approach is fundamental to the strategy, it will work. This means, in IBM-speak, that a transition to any new program like an alliance with an ISV had to have strategic fit with the IBM overall strategy. In order to establish that, the alliances team put in additional measurements enabling them to be able to constantly review the program and to resolve nonaligned issues.

This is probably one of the most important and critical metrics that has led to IBM's success in this arena. Too many organizations are not aligned regarding their alliances with senior management across all divisions and *silos*. For IBM, the strategic fit of their partners is appreciated company-wide and supported within each business unit as well as by corporate.

The concept of market management is what other companies call strategic segmentation or partner selection. I include it in Chapter Three under the section on Alliance Development metrics.

The questions that must be answered are centered around these two primary concerns:

➤ How do you know you have the right partners?

➤ How do you keep the partnering portfolio fresh and timely, which could require positioning one partner against the other?

To answer these questions, IBM uses a solution map. The most important place on the map is where the company identifies the right players. Following in Figure 7.1 is an example of the solution map, which has been adapted from IBM's and is generic in its application. None of the company names are taken from IBM's solution map and are used for illustration only. The Solution map starts the intense conversation that assists in the strategic positioning and development of the segmentation that will ultimately lead to a partnering portfolio that makes sense for the company.

FIGURE 7.1 Solution Maps for Virtual Organization

Deliver to the customer the lowest cost, highest value product from the whole-value chain through alliances. Solution Maps could be for distribution, small to midsized businesses, the government, and public sector.

Industry and Solution	Auto	Electronics	Energy	Financial
CRM	Siebel	Oracle	SAP	BAAN
EFT	HHH	ZZZ	TTT	SSS
Service	EDS	FFF	DDD	YYY
Certification	GGG	RRR	BBB	MMM

The next thing to agree on is:

➤ What is the right positioning of those players for both the present and future?

A solution map must be a living process; it is a combination of corporate intelligence and insights from those in IBM who are in industry vertical solutions as well as those within groups who build product. This means that executives at corporate say what should be in the IBM portfolio. They contribute their insights as to which leading providers are in the industry and add information regarding brand intelligence and strategic considerations, which point to various corporate assumptions of what IBM should be doing. These insights coming from corporate and the intelligence community that IBM reviews for its industries is a collaborative process. They work together holding regular meetings and are known in IBM as their various *communities*. The solution map and the team that works to create it are also those that work hard implementing the processes that bring the entire organization to consensus and ultimately to an alliance. This team is known as the *one IBM team*.

One IBM team

Here are some of the communities that comprise the one IBM team and how they work together.

a. The intelligence community (described above as a mix of people from branding, corporate, and external and internal intelligence groups).

b. The executive team who sponsor the relationships. These are the senior executives who support and lead the top level of relationship management and sponsor the alliance.

   These two communities regularly review the selection of the partner and evaluate on an ongoing basis what they are doing. The reasons are the same as those we discussed in Chapters Three and Four in that the repeating questions are:

➤ Is that partner the same strong strategic fit that they were when they were selected?

➤ How is the fit related to an overall view of how the alliance is going?

IBM regularly reviews the position of all their partners because their mutual businesses are changing. This occurs quarterly, monthly, or even weekly.

c. The negotiating team is another community that must be taken into account. If the intelligence community finds out that they are moving into another market, the negotiating team has to come back to the solution map, which will involve all the IBM business units and adapt it accordingly.

Across IBM, the tracking process starts with the customer. Then every business unit votes on who the best partner should be. They use a nomination process. This way, every unit gets to weigh in on who the best partner should be to solve the customer's problem. They don't always agree, but they all sit at the table; the person who leads the team which created the IBM alliance management process, Cynthia (Cindy) Erdman, managed the discussions and debates during her tenure in this group. Everyone gets his or her moment in the sun and an opportunity to put forth reasons why one partner is preferable to another. This means that the interest groups represented cannot later say that either their opinions or their concerns were not heard. This kind of consensus building takes time, but in the IBM culture, it is expected. It also makes good sense because it ensures that commitment will exist for the selected partner later, when the critical moments arrive for implementation.

The next step is that the partner is selected and the person who will play the role of the lead IBM sponsor, who has the most to gain as well as others who think that they have something to gain, stay as a team. Then they build the negotiation criteria with the team who actually does the negotiation. These people join with Erdman's group along with the IBM single executive sponsor and provide a forum to discuss all the concerns of every business unit.

There is careful planning that goes on before they all sit down at the table to discuss each opportunity as follows:

Before they sit down at the partnering table, they know the needs of each of the business units at the company who feel they could be affected by the alliance.

➤ Before they sit down with the partner, the process roles and responsibility roles are defined.

➤ Before they decide on their positioning with the partner, they assess the capabilities of the firm and the company with whom they will partner, and have a good assessment of where their leverage will be, how the negotiation should go, what the yield areas are, the points for emphasis, and the value for both them and the partner from the relationship.

The beauty of the IBM process is that before going into internal or external negotiations, they do their homework.

The executive sponsor is the senior executive who will take a leadership role in mentoring and sponsoring the team as well as be the highest point of contact with the partner company at IBM. Before the partner negotiation begins, this sponsor will know the discussions thus far, and where and how he or she will play a role in the negotiation and beginning relationship.

For example, in the communications industry should the ISV have an opportunity for the IBM Web-sphere product, the executive sponsor will know how to have that discussion and can include other executives from his or her groups or other business units if and when necessary.

d. Business development is another community. This group is part of the management system because they are the beachhead for the next generation of solutions, for example, life sciences is seen as an emerging area so it contains some developing relationships. Thus, business development is an essential community as a window to the future.

e. Finance. All the business units as well as corporate have a finance department—another set of communities.

f. Legal. This is generally at corporate headquarters but there may be occasions that external legal counsel will have to be brought in. Nevertheless, the opinion and insights of legal are important and could be critical, especially in the highly regulated industries.

g. Press. The public relations department as well as the communications departments will be in contact with the press. So they have to be in the loop in order to have the right message, to check that the message is not in conflict with other messages, and to be ready when and if the time is right to issue the appropriate press releases and notifications.

h. Development community who are building the product. This is an important community. They want to be at the table because it is their expertise that will be called upon to deliver the product in a timely and appropriate fashion. In addition, as happens all too often in many organizations, the development people don't speak with those in marketing or finance or even in sales, generating a distance between what is promised and what can economically or even technically be delivered. This community is a highly contributive member of the team.

l. Brand group. Anything that has the IBM name or association attached to it must go through a brand review and approval. The IBM brand is too important to risk any dilution or association with an inappropriate presentation or partnering. This group is the watchman of brand protection and preservation.

j. Global services group. This group takes the global view from a services perspective and makes sure that these interests are represented and protected as well.

In general, the team starts off extremely large. Then, it becomes smaller as it moves into the negotiation phase and even slims down even more as they enter the contract definition and finalization. Each person or interest group plays its role as the alliance moves from contract negotiation to the press release and approval stages; at that point in the process, the hourglass is narrowest.

The one IBM team involves every business unit at IBM and multiple stakeholders (communities). It is the ideal of the process which I describe in the alliance development metrics. It is a remarkable accomplishment to achieve such a symbiotic connection between diverse and complex interests as exist in a company as multifaceted and huge as IBM. The fact that the individuals and groups involved agree as a team on how to do this is, in itself, a marvel and then they do that which is so typical of IBM—they measure themselves as a team, too!

IBM has always had strong partnerships but has also had a concern and nagging issue about being co-operators as well as competitors with their partners. 1999 was the opportunity to make a significant change. The change has been implemented and is successful.

Communication

Whereas the first area IBM focused on was how to measure success, the second area they concentrate on is communication. Many companies suffer from fractures in their communications both internally and externally. Whether it's between lateral groups of executives at the same level but in different business units, or between those up and down the corporate hierarchy or across functions of the same group or business unit, communication is one of the key elements that can cause a company to be successful or fail in its goals. I call it the head and body of the dog. All too often the head of the dog is where the senior management resides and the rest of the organization is in the body of the dog. A few folks are in the tail of the dog, too. Now strategy tends to be developed in the head of the dog, and the hope is that at least there, the parts of the head are interrelating to each other. After all, if the parts of the head which have the benefit of proximity can't communicate, there isn't a lot of hope for the body.

So let me assume that there is acceptable communication between the head and its various parts. The next issue is whether the head of the dog is talking and communicating clearly to the body of the dog. That means going through the neck most often, which is rather narrow, and that is where a lot of the communication flow is cut off. The narrowness of the neck could be represented by gatekeepers who prevent information flow up to the head or down to the body. You will recognize these people as political organisms who try their hardest to interpret information and translate it rather than allowing it to flow of its own momentum. No matter where the blockage is, it could just be paucity of communication or flow, or actually being blocked by someone or someone's group. The body very often just doesn't get enough information and understanding of where the senior management head is going.

Of course, if there are multiple business units, each with its own heads and bodies, you have a compounded problem and the alliances which are created by various units may not only conflict and compete with each other, but there will also be little synergy or leverage between the units which could be highly detrimental to the organization's negotiating strategy and results.

So when Erdman said to me, "If it's key to your strategy, people get it," those few words told me a thousand more.

At IBM, in the software group, the head and the body of the dog are in sync regarding their alliances, the communication is superb, and the one IBM team process insures that messages are delivered about the program internally and externally. The one IBM team also ensures that the sales force is given and supported in what they need because that is where revenues will grow.

Any kinds of changes to this program are done in a similar manner. For example, in late 2000, IBM found out that they needed to update the strategic alliances program to include territorially specific alliances, for example, those in the financial industry for Japan needed to have applications providers that were Japan-specific because they were the best alliances for that purpose.

The team at IBM updated their program to allow for this because many of their global providers didn't have the best offering in Japan. That kind of flexibility will go a long way to make a huge company like IBM appear flexible and customer centered.

Often, IBM goes to their global suppliers, and says this is what our intelligence work shows us, feature by feature, regarding our customer's satisfaction, and in these arenas we have found that another supplier is the leader. Unless their global provider can deliver at the same level of quality, they adjust the arrangement so that the customer is well served. After all, that's what it's all about, isn't it?

IBM believes in doing their homework both internally across the organization and externally with their suppliers and customers. Their programs are updated constantly and communications about changes and updates are spread across the company about their alliances. They use a number of ways to communicate internally and externally. Inside IBM they have a newsletter which is published for thousands across IBM. Employees can customize the newsletter that they receive so that they can select areas of their particular interest as well as receiving flashes as each new alliance is signed. IBM generally announces new alliances internally before going public and they post the content on the sales force site. This way a salesperson can find out who the ISVs are in Detroit, who can sell a solution on CRM in a particular industry. They have multiple ways to search. One way to search is to ask who the key CRM suppliers are, how they are positioned against all competitors in this space, what their relationship is with IBM, and how IBM is partnering with them, as well as discover the status of all the partnering elements.

For example, if the salesperson sees a research and development partnership, he can ask to see the pharmaceutical process and learn to understand the necessary outlay at the front end. They can also ask what it takes to build such a product, and so on. Their sales representatives have to know on the day the alliance is signed that not everything is ready to sell so they can see in this process when the product will be available.

To meet the immediacy and information requirements of their sales force, IBM has plugged into their processes the entire concept-launch process for their partnering projects so that sales representatives can understand the project flow; the up-sell and cross-sell and forward-sell opportunities or limitations. The team updates that system every day—from the underlying measurement system as well as from the IBM system—and feeds this to the sales representatives daily.

IBM syndicates content across the company. They have one editorial team that works on everything in their alliances, so someone in editorial will have the responsibility to place the information across the company so other employees can select what they want to see.

Michael Azzi is the communications person who works with the alliances team in the software group at IBM. For example, Azzi's team is working with the life sciences team to be sure that their unique industry messages are included, while they retain governance over the overall theme of the alliance. This means streamlining all announcements to be sure that they are aligned and focused on the strategy developed for external communications.

Understanding Roles and Responsibilities

The third area that IBM focuses on is the understanding of roles and responsibilities. There are three subsets to this factor:

1. The accountability and responsibility for each process step.

   Under each process step there has to be a description of what has to be done, which group has to do it, and templates of how to do the job so that if that person leaves the job, the next person knows what to do. It is also very helpful that inside the IBM alliance team is a support infrastructure to maintain the tools and day-to-day support for people who use them.

   One example is the process chart that shows a pipeline all the way to execution. In the pipeline phase are lots of templates that the alliances team built which are integrated with the execution program. Since their alliances were three years in length, at year two they automatically included a step involving some refinement on the execution side. This takes into account that IBM was able to learn alongside their partners, and the processes are seen as living breathing things.

This flexibility is part of IBM's management success. Erdman manages those team members who are supporters of the process. They are project management experts from every discipline in IBM—sales, marketing, and development—and they show the knowledge and the awareness and concern for all of those interest groups. Erdman has cherry-picked the very best, experienced people within the company in each function to make up her team. Within her existing partner program, she already had a good start, but Erdman is a worldly and experienced long-timer with IBM. She has lived and worked for IBM in Japan and has learned from living in that group-oriented culture how important it is to create a group and team where people are not only strong in process development but are also good in people skills. Her long-term experience with IBM has also taught her to make sure that whatever she builds into a process must not be something that is separate from the existing system because it will ultimately be rejected as a foreign organism.

2. The management system.

Because Erdman and her group built the alliance management program based on the underpinnings of the IBM management system, these interlocking systems established:

➤ How she and her team were to measure themselves on how they executed the program in the marketplace as a team.

➤ How they decided what and with whom to market.

➤ How to deal with things when they went wrong when they needed to resolve conflict.

All of these issues had precedents within the IBM management system so there was no need for Erdman and her team to re-create that wheel.

They put in place a steering executive committee that made sure that what it came out with would stick. This provided the senior level sponsorship which enabled Erdman's group to then build communities of people with specialized skills, including development resources, press resources, legal resources, finance, contracts, and business development—people across every business division and unit. Every single business unit president had to allocate resources to this alliances project.

Also various operating plans were built with regard to revenue reporting, as well as the status of technology, including where the ISVs contribute. Templates were developed regarding the selection of technology or where it would be better for IBM to select a services provider. Then they tracked activities and outcomes in order to see if, when IBM products were selected, whether they needed development or fine-tuning or maybe even practice guides. The IBM team worked with the ISVs in order to ensure that their levels of competency increased and were customer focused and appropriate.

A key factor in all of this was that IBM did not change the reward systems to make the alliances program stick. The alliances program was fundamental to IBM strategy and had been stated as such by all levels of senior management. The strategy was why they had the program in place at all. The entire alliance program was strategic and was seen to start with the customer who wanted a solution, which could include IBM products along with non-IBM products and services. Because of these customer needs, the ISV activities were all seen to be critical to IBM's overall market strategy.

3. Management of senior executives upward as well as the executive sponsor role.

A difficult part of every alliance is to know how to manage *up* to senior management on the alliance. This means being able to understand the reporting process upward in the organization for the alliances and their results.

IBM has an advantage here because they have the entire approach upward to management within their management system—all the financial measures, the operational measures, how to build a community of partners, how to integrate alliance activity into the measurement system, all the way to and from Palmisano, the CEO, to the field representative in a small town.

There certainly are lots of different divisions inside IBM but every one of the businesses in the annual report is a part of the alliance process. This means that within their own line (unit) measurements, they have an understanding and tracking of who the key alliances are: Each senior vice president unit head inside IBM who has an alliance partner key to their business unit has metrics associated with that alliance. These corresponding metrics and information are all shared across business units, and they will all participate in the alliance process.

Mentioned earlier, a major alliance for IBM is Siebel Corporation. There are multiple activities within each business unit with Siebel Corporation so that each business unit has its corporate objectives, which relate to how they make their products work better together.

Each unit is responsible for their metrics, which must connect into the alliance group metrics. They have a total share for IBM's objectives as well. For example, the software group has gained lots of share in the DB2 (database 2) technology, and they have outpaced Oracle. This metric has become part of the alliance process and is a main line metric.

Part of the management system is a process that Erdman's group built that handles key issues within the alliance in such a way that every unit is communicating daily as to how things are going in the account with good tracking across the team. When there is a problem—they have weekly reviews—they use their own collaboration tools and databases, and their own technology to track the status on technology enablement as well as the sales activities. In this way, a person on the team can mine the data to see what is behind the status report and the problem or issue that has been highlighted. They can click on a status box and go deeper into the information and activities.

This system allows you to click on the relevant box on the screen related to the alliance. The system then shows the responsible executive and technology specialist, as well as the nature of why that particular box is showing a warning color (yellow) and the sub boxes where the technology specialist will have his or her comment. That set of tracking tools is right on the weekly case report. If it's green, then they don't have to look deeper. Red and yellow show a series of accelerating problems that can then be addressed.

Inside IBM, the management system gives Palmisano visibility into each of IBM's many alliances.

In addition, the executive sponsors report separately through the IBM management system not as a separate review but as a normal part of their agenda of things to review and notice.

This is another critical success factor and one many companies do not implement. Unless alliances become part of the normal executive review agenda, they will never be allocated the kinds of resources, expertise, and relevant metrics that make the best returns for alliance investments.

On a quarterly basis, IBM also has senior leadership reviews of their alliances, which are the result of a close working structure between the particular sponsoring senior executive and their alliance managers. The executive sponsor on each alliance has a day-to-day relationship with the part-ner executives.

An additional executive coverage inside IBM provides added support and communication. Often IBM does go-to-market activities together with their product and service development groups. Their senior executives reg-ularly visit and talk to partners together. The senior sales executive would also be involved with these customer-facing activities and various sector executives would get involved as necessary. This is the way that IBM makes the partner and customer-facing activities an across IBM effort.

Through all of this activity, in the software group and alliances, Azzi is a hub for all communications activity when there is a need for external media communications. He approves all announcements and communications for the software group.

One of the differentiating activities that IBM does that distinguishes them from other companies in the field, is their care and training of the executive sponsor. This role is seen as an important one, not just a titular appointment.

In many companies, I have seen the executive sponsorship taken lightly, and the performance of sponsors in those companies is less than accept-able, which does not please either the internal alliance managers or the partners.

At IBM, the executive sponsor is not left to create what his or her role and responsibilities are. Once the executive sponsor is identified, the alliances team spends lots of time with each of them, going through their expected roles and responsibilities. IBM has sponsored training calls in which the sponsor and their team members participate because a sponsor may designate some of his or her people to help with each relationship. The executive sponsor training call is not just on one occasion. They have many calls and refresher sessions, which could be teleconferences or in-person sessions, wherein all the rest of the team's roles are laid out.

For example, during the transition period when IBM has committed to entering into the alliance and the contract may or may not have been signed, there will be a detailed description and role-play for all team members, including the sponsor, for behavior that is acceptable or unacceptable. This is the part in the process where they have moved from strategy to selection of the alliance and are ready to announce the relationship. They are now moving into the field execution and have a new set of items to focus on. The alliances team will create a transition call to bring the executive sponsor and the field executives together. These are the people who sit alongside the brand and development executives and are now being trained to go through the next steps of field activities. These calls will last one or two hours. Those who work in these teams are prepared to be in a participative mode to make the transition and are highly collaborative and committed to bringing all the players together.

The enormity of the task of streamlining an organization as complex as IBM does pose some particular challenges. Here are a few that Erdman shared with me:

The Strategy

IBM sets the strategy. Because the alliance partners and IBM will grow together, staying in step with corporate changes is key. This is a difficult area, and it is not always perfect. It is tricky to expect that all alliance partners are going to be perfect forever, so IBM has a process to deal with issues that come up. They assume that some issues they will be less than successful at resolving.

As we discussed in Chapters One through Four, there are lots of strategy changes that can take place. There is strategy change in markets, financial challenges, portfolio changes, and management changes. There is constant evolution in the marketplace and that is part of the fun and the difficulty for all of these alliances.

Execution of the Alliance

Even with the best planning and the greatest team, the execution and implementation of the alliance is the most important set of elements. IBM has a specific focus here.

Don't just assign the alliance is the general feeling. There is a strong implementation focus at IBM. They have a fundamental premise in the way they set up their management systems with leads, opportunities, and customer business, so that senior management can see the contribution of the partner daily. This is not, however, what the partner sees. IBM has put in place field sales tools so they know what is going on with the alliance in the field. They have discovered that communication to their field people is just as important as to the senior vice president. They don't want the alliance partner's representative in Chicago to not know the essence of the alliance, nor do they want the IBM representative, for that matter, to be in the dark about daily alliance activities. IBM has learned that sales force tools are as important as upward management, and these must be effective, accurate, and provide daily information.

So what are the lessons learned by IBM that can be applied to you in your company? IBM has added their lessons learned to their process because the learning gave them an opportunity to fine-tune their approach.

The major learning came from those who were not adopting the process willingly. Instead of castigating them, they asked them why they were challenging the process. The answers enabled them to make changes that were relevant and important. Now continuous feedback loops and learning from the field is part of their process and the alliance team regularly encourages people to put in their comments and changes. For example, comments that say *this didn't work* and *do it this way* are enormously valuable and are shared with the teams and changes are made.

Other bells and whistles that IBM have for their partners come from using their own technology. They have collaboration sites for their partners to access for many purposes of the partnership. This leads to better collaboration (through their Lotus division's tools and more). IBM also contributes their marketing forces. This type of support varies by partner in terms of their ability or willingness to use Web-based technology.

Many of the metrics that we have outlined in earlier chapters are covered by the IBM approach. Here is a list of just a few:

➤ The alliance plan is aligned continually with the strategic plan by applying the mainline management systems and shared objectives within each management unit.

➤ Buy-in is fundamental to their strategy.

➤ Compensation for the alliances team includes both bonuses and rewards on the success of process as well as the success of alliance.

➤ They build and manage the process and facilitate the alliance and so share in that success.

Erdman feels strongly about this:

"You must have the balance, have to have people facilitating the building of the process so it is robust enough so you can run your business and also have them helping the rest of the team to play a role."

➤ Although it is an IBM policy to not talk about compensation, it is clear that the compensation issues are part of the corporate plan and alliances are incorporated in that compensation discussion.

➤ The interrelationship between the communications people and the alliance group and business units is so good that they work effectively together.

    a. IBM has created a repeatable process—each partnership deserves its own announcement.

    b. They have an internal process where they create talking points and background for questions and answers; they also construct the announcement with the partner and support it with media relations.

    c. They have the partner issue the announcement over the wire, but it is a joint announcement of the parties regarding the date and the goal of the alliance.

➤ There is a buy-in from many organizations because there are so many stakeholders within the company and each agreement has a hardware, software, services, and possibly even a financing part to it. The partner may commit to going to market with IBM brands. They need a minimum requirement of commitments with high percentages such as 40 percent to 50 percent of sales of each of the IBM products that are in the agreements. So for the announcement, they need all the IBM people in those divisions in the announcement, to sign off on the commitment. There is also a community of other partners, who may or may not compete with the new partner so they don't show the announcement to the other partners, but they do show it to the IBM account manager for that other partner. If there is a sense that the partner may feel that the new partnership may impede their relationship, then they will take that into account and may have a conversation with the other partner to reassure them that they are not moving other business away from them to the new partner. This would include assurances that they are not going to market with both their existing and new partners in the same space. The research and planning that goes into these activities generally prevents these potential conflicts from happening. But the communications groups in the software and alliances group that is led by Azzi help to feed internal communications among all business units. Rarely does IBM find that partners have the same capabilities that IBM has from a communications

FIGURE 7.2 IBM Strategic Alliance Process for Independent Software Vendor (ISV or Developer) Relations

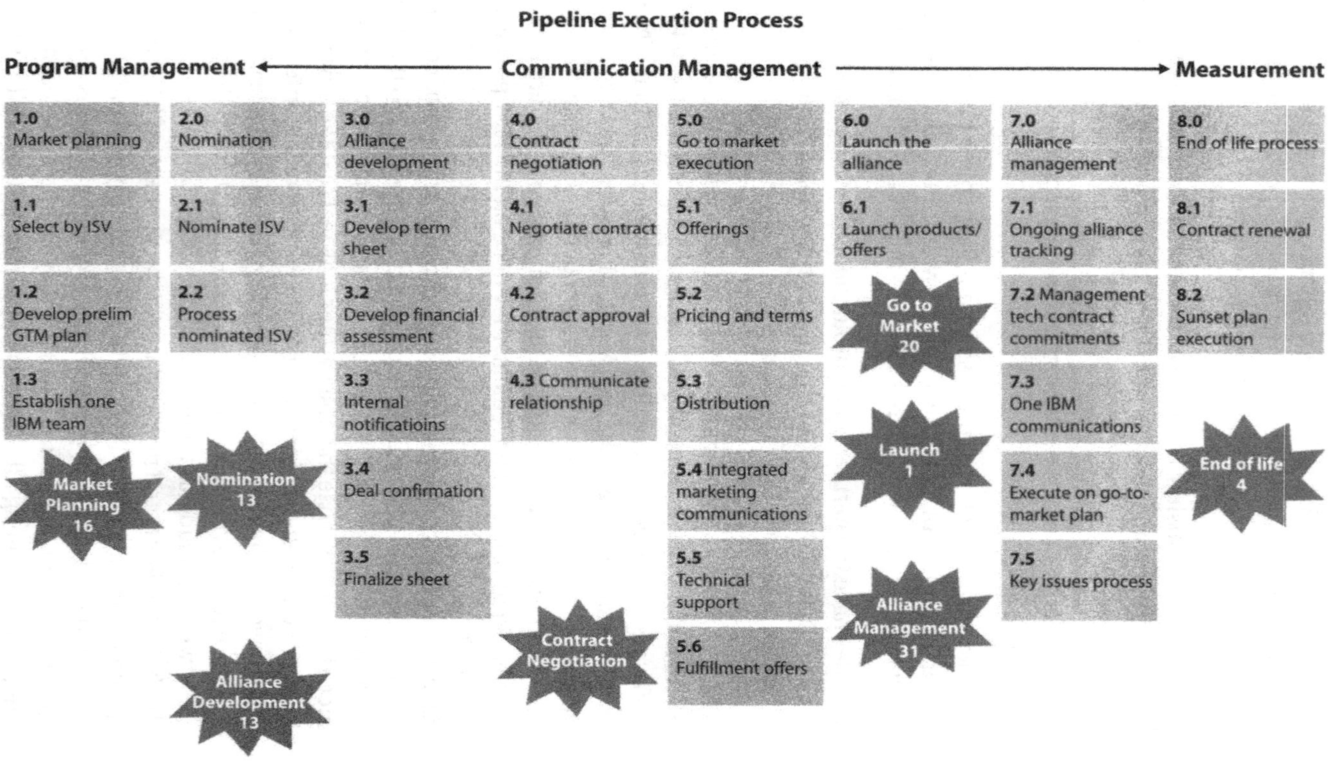

Pipeline Execution Process

Program Management	Communication Management	Measurement

1.0 Market planning	**2.0** Nomination	**3.0** Alliance development	**4.0** Contract negotiation	**5.0** Go to market execution	**6.0** Launch the alliance	**7.0** Alliance management	**8.0** End of life process
1.1 Select by ISV	**2.1** Nominate ISV	**3.1** Develop term sheet	**4.1** Negotiate contract	**5.1** Offerings	**6.1** Launch products/ offers	**7.1** Ongoing alliance tracking	**8.1** Contract renewal
1.2 Develop prelim GTM plan	**2.2** Process nominated ISV	**3.2** Develop financial assessment	**4.2** Contract approval	**5.2** Pricing and terms		**7.2** Management tech contract commitments	**8.2** Sunset plan execution
1.3 Establish one IBM team		**3.3** Internal notificatioins	**4.3** Communicate relationship	**5.3** Distribution		**7.3** One IBM communications	
		3.4 Deal confirmation		**5.4** Integrated marketing communications		**7.4** Execute on go-to- market plan	
		3.5 Finalize sheet		**5.5** Technical support		**7.5** Key issues process	
				5.6 Fulfillment offers			

Market Planning 16

Nomination 13

Alliance Development 13

Contract Negotiation

Go to Market 20

Launch 1

Alliance Management 31

End of life 4

standpoint. Some software providers are sophisticated but not all—so in most cases, IBM does the majority of the media relations work.

The ISV program at IBM is a stand alone and unique partnering program. The reason is that the ISV companies are the pure partners with whom IBM goes to market. In other areas of IBM, often units will announce a partnership with a customer because the customer is paying a great deal of money for that privilege and has just given IBM a huge contract. In the ISV program, that is not the case.

The alliance team in the software group can be justly proud. They have created a metrics system and process which has become part of the DNA of IBM, not an insignificant feat, and have incorporated into 147 steps just about everything that an alliance manager or senior executive could possibly want in a system that tells everything you need to know about a specific alliance or the alliance portfolio as a whole. Figure 7.2 outlines the multiple processes in broad categories that IBM has created for their alliances.

Figure 7.2 steps through the process description that I have outlined in this chapter and provides most of the details that we have covered. Do not be intimidated! It works for IBM. It may be too detailed for your company, but with the complexity and global nature of today's IBM, it makes sense for them. However, what is worthy of emulation is the discipline and commitment that IBM has made to the whole concept and activity surrounding alliances and the alignment they have achieved in multiple areas of a highly complex organization.

In Chapter Eight, we will look at another highly complex organization that will, I believe, become the gold standard of how to do an integration of an acquisition—the HP integration process of its acquisition of Compaq.

The Hewlett-Packard/Compaq Merger: An Integration Process Managed as an Alliance

It was the deal they said would never happen. But Hewlett Packard Company (HP) CEO Carly Fiorina should never have been underestimated. Nor should the critics have undervalued the power of the two organizations that are now one. Other important factors that positively influenced this acquisition were a consolidating market and the determination of those who believed that this was the right thing for both companies. What is the result? An integration story that I believe will go down in history as one of the finest. The reason is that it has been handled with *relationship focus* from the beginning. Clearly, this was an acquisition by HP. Yet, the integration process has been managed with every metric that a good alliance includes, not the least of which is mutuality and attention to compatibility challenges.

These are the metrics that will be addressed in this chapter:

1. Alliance development metrics. Conceptualization, strategic alignment and fit, collaborating with a potential competitor, cultural fit.

2. Alliance implementation metrics. Operationalization and implementation launch.

3. The alliance life cycle. Conceptualization, strategic development, planning, internal buy-in, creation of the operating plan, launch and startup moving into hockey stick (high growth of the actual integration process pre- and post-launch), and professionalizing of the alliance with the integration team moving into permanent positions a year post-merger.

4. The stakeholders. We will also look at the alliance/merger from the point of view of a number of the stakeholders—partners and their various teams, management of each partner, and external analysts.

In short, the story of the HP merger with Compaq is in microcosm a good example of many metrics that are shared by multiple alliances, not just acquisitions and mergers.

The integration story begins with Fiorina and Michael Capellas, CEO of Compaq. Both wanted two people to be involved from the beginning, one from each company. The people they chose were critical. They had to be individuals who had already built a following, that is, a level of respect and acceptability within their own companies. In many post-merger integrations, this is the first and often most critical mistake. A person who may be in a staff position and is seen to be targeted for a more senior opportunity uses the integration process as a way to elevate his or her respectability and leverage for future exposure by leading the integration team. Or, it may be the CEOs themselves who lead the team. In terms of authority, CEOs certainly do have it, and therefore, the team which will be doing the work has to have a different composition. The people in charge must already have internal political and experiential capital and respect. Those people were Jeff Clarke, former CFO of Compaq, and Harry W. (Webb) McKinney, formerly the senior leader of the global sales force of HP. (The metric here was to select the right team leader and measure him or her regarding the appropriate skills and talents.)

Clarke's restraint, ability, and negotiation skills are superb. It was clear that he would generate the right responses within Compaq. Clarke had lived acquisition integration issues firsthand, having been part of the Compaq acquisition of Digital Equipment. Less than wonderful, the Compaq/Digital Equipment acquisition encountered many of the normal problems of cultural mismatches and other residual concerns that linger on for years after acquisitions. He was therefore familiar with what could go wrong and how to do it differently so as to make things go right. Clarke's entrepreneurial spirit and energy was boundless and contributive to the commitment that would be necessary to make the integration effort succeed.

McKinney was the HP co-leader. His reputation was golden within HP because he had been head of the global HP sales force and was known as a *doer*—someone who delivered what he promised. He also had a tested and tried understanding, appreciation, and love for the HP culture and a true familiarity with the HP way. He could therefore anticipate and appreciate the issues that might be important to HP history. McKinney was a thirty-two-year veteran of HP and was recognized as someone who knew his way around, both pre-and post-Fiorina, and could bridge some of the internal gaps that would still exist in those groups that were not entirely on-board with the deal.

The integration process could *not* have been as effective without the internal networks that Clarke and McKinney had already built over decades with their companies.

It is helpful to look at the time line for the merger because it gives some idea of the pressure and enormity of the task. The integration team provided Figure 8.1 as follows:

On September 3, 2001, the first group of employees was selected to become the initial team for the integration process. Each of the co-leaders selected their best people, measured on the following selection metrics and criteria that they:

1. Would be able to run with this project and be innovative.

2. Could move quickly.

3. Had a good network of people and relationships that would be accessible for a task of this nature.

4. Exhibited leadership qualities.

5. Had good ideas, could complete things in a timely fashion, and were dedicated.

Among those chosen, there was a feeling of being special because of having been chosen and recognized as a valuable contributor—someone who was thought of as having an open mind and abilities that would be of value in the new organization. Did this mean that those who were not in the integration team were the *un-chosen?* It was important that those feelings and resentments didn't grow so that the organization was seen to be elitist rather

FIGURE 8.1 Key Points on the Time Line of the HP/Compaq acquisition

1.	**September 3, 2001**	Merger announced
2.	**September 11, 2001**	World Trade Center attack
3.	**October 1, 2001**	Compaq pre-announces revenue and earnings per share shortfall for September (3rd quarter 2001)
4.	**November 20, 2001**	HP reports 4th quarter 2001 results of 0.19 EPS (consensus of 0.08)
5.	**December 7, 2001**	Packard Foundation announces decision to vote against the merger
6.	**December 19, 2001**	Letter to HP shareholders titled "HP Position on Compaq Merger"
7.	**January 25, 2002**	Compaq financial analysts meeting in New York
8.	**January 29, 2002**	Compaq presentation to ISS
9.	**February 4, 2002**	Proxy statement/prospectus issued to HP and Compaq shareholders
10.	**February 27, 2002**	HP securities analysts meeting in New York—reaffirms $2.5B in merger synergies and 12% accretion to HP shareholders
11.	**March 5, 2002**	ISS recommends approval of merger
12.	**March 19, 2002**	Special meeting of HP shareholders on merger in Palo Alto, CA
13.	**March 20, 2002**	Investor approval of merger
14.	**April 23-24, 2002**	Trial at Chancery Court in Delaware (Hewlett vs. HP)
15.	**April 30, 2002**	Lawsuit dismissed by Chancery Court
16.	**May 3, 2002**	Merger completed
17.	**June 4, 2002**	HP security analysts meeting in New York—$2.5B in merger synergies will be achieved in 2003, one year ahead of plan
18.		Further increase overall merger synergies to $3.0B by 2004
19.	**August 27, 2002**	HP reports 3rd quarter 2002 results of 0.14 pro forma EPS
20.	**November 11, 2002**	Capellas resigns
21.	**November 20, 2002**	HP reports 4th quarter 2002 results of 0.24 pro forma EPS
22.	**December 3, 2002**	HP reports $3B of merger savings will be achieved in 2003

THE INTEGRATION PROCESS CONTINUES...

than inclusive, which was very much part of the HP culture. The message was sent out and, indeed, it carried the ring of truth: Everyone is a contributor.

Together, McKinney and Clarke began to build the team. This could be called the alliance development metrics for this merger. The metrics had to be carefully designed, including who would participate from each company and how would they be measured. The co-leaders knew that selection of the teams would report to the first group already chosen (how, who, and why) would be one of the issues on which the success or failure of the integration of the merger would be judged.

A tremendous amount was learned from the interplay between the two co-leaders of the pre-merger teams from the very first moments of activity. The first move was that the decision body had executives from both companies: four from HP and three from Compaq. These were the first people to decide who would be in the clean room. They asked each person to bring their best direct report executive onto the team, and he or she brought their top person, and so on, as the transition team was organized.

This meant some people had to relinquish their positions. One example was supply chain management which involved huge billion-dollar purchasing agreements and relationships. Ed Penzel who ran such an area for Compaq gave up his role to Gilles Bouchard who ran the HP supply chain. Was there pain? Certainly. It was clear that there were only going to be twenty-five leaders from each company who would build their teams; choices had to be made.

Entering into the clean room was done by a process whereby human resources approved each entry. Those persons who had to leave their existing jobs did so with no knowledge or guarantee that they could return to any job, least of all their current ones. So this was, for many, a great leap of faith. They didn't want to grow the teams too fast or get too big. The issues of team creation also had to do with the proprietary data to which each team member had access. The decision was made that data would not be valuable longer than about six months, so they decided that team members would take three months or six months off and then go back to work.

Sensitive data were an issue. After all, they could conceivably be competitors again if the proxy battle didn't go the way they wanted it to. For the most sensitive data, such as prices paid by Compaq to Intel Corporation and most strategic relationships, which comprised over $4 billion in activities, the two companies asked a consulting firm to have access to the data and blind them to it, sanitizing the information so that if they got information back, it would not be competitive or damaging should the merger not go through. This would have been the metric (transfer and security of data) for the disintegration process, if the deal were not approved.

The entire integration process had to be predicated on Plan A if the merger went through and Plan B if it didn't. This meant that parallel sets of metrics had to be developed to deal with either situation.

The integration team started at two hundred and fifty people and grew to five hundred people. At its peak fifteen hundred people were in the merger integration office. Since the first thing they did was to create an integration steering committee that was led by Fiorina and Capellas, both Clarke and McKinney worked directly for that group which met every Thursday afternoon. On that committee was also Bob Wayman, CFO; Bob Napier, chief information officer (CIO); and Sue Bowick, head of human resources. This was a small team that could make final decisions on all the processes that flowed into that meeting.

Fiorina dedicated half a day every week to resolve concerns in which issue escalations happened. At her disposal was the collective intelligence of that entire committee. The result was consistency, collaboration, clear metrics, and the right people who were empowered to make things happen fast.

Wednesday was the day every week on which the full integration meeting was held with McKinney and Clarke and their reports and team. The issues that evolved from that meeting were taken into the Thursday meeting with Fiorina, Capellas, and their top committee members.

The Wednesday meeting put the metrics of this alliance process to the test. There was a rigorous and detailed process, well mapped, using engineering scheduling techniques such as program evaluation review technique (PERT) and Gannt charts. There were a couple of major themes: One was the concept of *adopt and go*. This was a development metric but would soon become the important implementation metric. Using *adopt and go*, came from some of HP's former history. When HP had decided to spin off the division that ultimately was called Agilent, the test and measurement business, they created an approach called *clone and go* where it was necessary to actually clone the process, for example, the human resources process.

Now in the merger, they adapted that approach to apply to situations where there were duplicate overlapping processes from both companies, for example, in a finance department or in their go-to-market strategy where each company had its own process and the need arose to choose one. So they created *adopt and go*. The key of *adopt and go* was to drive speed in integration. Instead of taking the best players from both teams, they decided to leave the key group of each team together (e.g., in the football analogy, defense) in the belief that they were already a winning team together and would play better that way rather than breaking them up. As Clarke said:

> "We want the best who play best together, and we will adopt a process, and if it's 'good enough,' we will accept it rather than trying to blend it."

This became a critical success factor in the integration process. For example, the HP Unix business was more profitable, had better market share, and a larger customer base than Compaq's so the decision was made to go with HP's approach. On the other hand, the Compaq product sets that run Microsoft's Windows NT had a more profitable business model and also had number one market share, so the decision was made to close the products sets in this area that were from HP.

It is important to remember that one of the underlying issues behind this merger was that this was a merger of consolidation. When designing the metrics over which the merger success would be measured, this was critical. Years later as analysts will debate the success or failure of the merger, the consolidation issues and cost savings will be key success factors worthy of mention. This was an implementation metric of huge importance to external analysts and shareholders.

It was a given that the companies competed in many areas, which meant that the general idea was to take the best of each product line and convert customers over to it so that they would not be left with two brands or two departments.

The goal was always to pick the one that was best. Across many of these situations, the commercial decision was clear because of metrics that related to each company's external market share as well as their profitability metrics.

Another factor was the way that the integration teams were set up. There were twenty-five teams, one for each business group and one for each function such as finance, human resources, and so on.

There were four business groups for the new HP: enterprise, services, imaging and printing, and personal computing. The teams also included the legal, human resources, finance, and go-to-market teams.

They decided to color code the companies, making Compaq red and HP blue. The teams were asked to have a red Compaq and a blue HP leader on each team, but here is the key, as Clarke said to me laughingly:

"Webb and I wanted to have just one throat to choke, one person who would speak for the team, so the co-leaders had to come to agreement in order to speak with one mouth and both had to have good understanding of the issues to do that."

Choosing red and blue leaders was another key element to the success of the integration process. This meant having one from each company in place so that when there were detailed questions from one side of which the other side had no knowledge, they could flow information to each other and transfer knowledge this way. This method caused balance and accountability and worked very well. The alliance metric here falls into the area of operationalization of the relationship and would specifically be used to allocate accountability for results to the managers about their performance.

This core nucleus, comprising twenty-five teams, really became the responsible people for all functions, such as the supply chain team who chose the suppliers which would be the key ones for the combined company—a highly debated issue.

The time invested in the pre-merger integration has paid off royally. The rollout has been spectacular, but the proof is in the fact that the integrated company by the second quarter of 2003 had saved over $3.5 billion in costs —that's real money!

The communications program for this integration is another critical success factor. It was like a smoothly planned and executed military campaign.

The employees had to be educated on their new processes and, of course, most importantly, on the new customer information, although the integration team at the height of its numbers in the clean room was more than fifteen hundred people that nevertheless comprised only 1 percent of the total population of the new HP which was over 150,000 employees. This meant that 99 percent of the employee base would have to implement the integration teams' decisions and know what to do in their *new* jobs. The challenge was on May 3, 2002, when they planned to launch the new company: How could the teams translate over 1 million hours of effort into understandable information bits for the total employee population? Furthermore, because the representatives from each company were able to see only half the data because the other half which belonged to their partner (who was also potentially their competitor if the deal did not go through), was not permitted to be revealed to them—how would they know what to do? This was the dilemma of having two parallel sets of alliance implementation metrics regarding operationalizing the alliance in place at all times.

Clarke is certain that this merger integration process would not have been as successful as it has been if not for the companies' Intranets which served as the differentiator between success and failure. He knows about which he speaks! During the 1988 Compaq integration of Digital Equipment, Clarke was part of the integration team from the Digital Equipment side. Due to the state of the industry at that time, most people had personal computers (PCs). Each company had huge databases, but there was no electronic communal access point to data for all the parties. The Intranet allowed both HP and Compaq to have an enormous amount of data deployed instantly on May 3, 2002, to everyone in the joined company, employees as well as customers and partners. They put out their product road maps, including which ones they would phase out or sell, the go-to-market structure, and so on. Everyone learned about it instantly, everyone was watching the Intranet, and they had tens of thousands of downloads from organizational charts to how management would work together, to the economics of new business models including levels of costs to cut, launch plans, playbooks, and sales tactics, including gains against competitors, customer data, and more. New account managers could see all the data for all those years they had competed against each other and learn how they would move forward together. Just a few short years ago without the proliferation of intranets and the Internet, this could not have happened. It's no small irony that in the complicated merger of two leading technology companies, technology is what has made it a successful integration.

In other mergers, often there are huge fights between the pre-merger teams as executives jockey for political position and gains. This didn't happen because it was clear from the beginning that Fiorina would make the final call. So the Wednesday teams knew if they brought the right decision to those meetings on Wednesday, they would get a final decision on Thursday. Certainly, Capellas had his opinion, he said his piece, they would debate, they would use the data to inform themselves, they would let the data drive the decision, and then Fiorina had the last say.

This does not, however, minimize the critical role that Capellas had to play in this merger. He had to sell the deal externally, meet with Compaq employees and customers, and get them to move culturally, emotionally, and financially over to the merged company. His role was vital and brilliantly executed.

The cultural integration was one of the greatest concerns that both companies had. Rightfully so. In my research at Caltech, I have found that 60 percent of all alliances and over 80 percent of all acquisitions fail because of the lack of good cultural integration. This metric is one of the most important ones to measure, and that can be done only if there is first a recognition that there are differences, then that the differences are identified, and, finally, that a process is implemented to rationalize the differences so that they don't disfunctionalize the organization.

No doubt Compaq and HP had vastly different cultures. The cultural integration had to begin at the top. McKinney and Clarke had to integrate themselves as a working unit. They spent a lot of time together. They also gathered the top twenty people of the core teams and went through an exercise in order to develop a common language. One phrase that came up a lot was the idea of *a moose on the table*—it was heard many times a day. It meant identify the real issue and have debate on it.

Another metric was the important aspect of communication which was both a metric on its own as well as part of the cultural metric, seen in both the alliance development and alliance implementation metrics. The teams had to decide on common communication tools. HP is very voice-mail-oriented and Compaq is very e-mail-oriented. All the Compaq folks had Blackberry pagers and sent e-mail messages all day during meetings, and HP people would check cell phones for voice mail. For example, on one occasion, McKinney sent Clarke an urgent voice mail message and was frustrated when Clarke didn't return the call immediately, but when he logged on to his computer, he found that Clarke had responded by e-mail.

One of the ways that the organization continued to measure cultural integration post-merger was the rollout of the same series of workshops that were initiated in the clean room where teams of people participated and raised issues of concern including developing a common language. These workshops were mandatory throughout the organization; everyone had to participate.

On a blank chart, facilitators would ask HP employees to describe their culture, then describe the Compaq culture as they saw it. Then the Compaq people did the same regarding HP. Some of the characteristics for Compaq employees were that they were Texan, aggressive, shoot-first-aim-later kinds of people. HP people were seen as bureaucratic, although innovative and very process-oriented. Each company wrote the positives and negatives of the other company; for example, HP is a great brand with loyal employees, but they were slow to change with less proactive reactions to the market. Compaq was seen as more oriented to command and control with faster decisions (which Compaq saw as the *pros* and HP saw as the *cons!*).

The key was talking about culture and getting to know each other. The amazing outcome was that there were fewer red and blue culture issues than they expected because people began to bond by function. For example, the finance people spoke to each other and bonded, so did the HR people, information technology, marketing, sales, and so on. The personal computing group was more interested in competing against Dell Computer Corporation than in clashing against each other. There is nothing as powerful as a common enemy to resolve internal issues—it worked here. On one occasion, a comment was made that it was impossible to tell who was red or blue at a certain point in the integration process, unless you looked at their laptop computers.

The cultural integration challenges were taken very seriously. Not only was there a cultural due diligence done in the early stages where several thousand people from both companies were interviewed, but the teams also looked to model what the cultures were and then mapped the various company's strengths and weaknesses. The *adopt-and-go* approach was applied to culture, too, with the goal of building one new and stronger culture for one new strong company. They designed a new culture with some of the following elements:

➤ Core values of the company.

➤ Corporate objectives.

➤ Behavior.

The behavioral continuum was very black and white. First, they outlined what was acceptable behavior and contrasted it to what was not acceptable. Then they did the same for what is legal and not legal. Then they specified the standards of business conduct all the way to the characteristics of self-actualized leadership. This comparison of bad, good, better, and best enabled HP to set the stage for the present activities which are focused on embedding this new culture worldwide throughout the entire employee base, a significant undertaking that will take some time.

The 17,000 cultural workshops that were done in the first three months of the company's new life set the stage for this major cultural change. The workshops not only welcomed everyone to the new team, but also outlined what this new HP does, how the new HP behaves, and its values and new operating models with the roles, objectives, and responsibilities and how they work together. All of this material was pushed into the HP market before the launch, inviting a few thousand of the top HP managers to an orientation and education session on what to do, how to communicate, and the details of the new HP and their roles in it. When the metric of cultural integration is examined, it can be seen that the expectations for cultural analysis, change, and implementation were met.

The energy that went into a superb integration is now moving forward into new insights about governance bodies and how to plan and drive the company beyond the place it now is for future success.

Of all the observations of Fiorina I received in preparing this chapter, this is the one that stood out, and I heard it again and again: "She has better stamina than any executive I have ever seen." Clarke added to that:

> "She has more energy and is tireless. There were many times when we might have wanted to go into what would we do if this didn't work. She never did that once. Carly was forthright on all occasions, all through the ups and downs of losing support of the HP family foundations, then support of the HP families, then the stress of the proxy votes, and all the attacks by the press. It was never ending. But Carly had complete commitment. She was on the road all the time. If she had blinked or taken time to step back and not fight to the end, we would not have made it. The merger would not have happened. The reason it happened came from her feeling that she had to change the DNA of HP and that this was the best way to do it. This was not just a *feeling* she had. It was based on data. She *knew* that we were saving money with the consolidation; she knew it because she saw the data and she was right there, sitting in the meetings, as more and more data came in proving over and over again that this was the right thing to do. The data proved to her that this could and would work, and the more the data rolled in, the more confidence it gave her to speak so well publicly about the merger, its viability, and the reasons it must go through."

The metrics of this process arose from the data that both groups of teams were developing and gathering. All the data were recorded through the integration process which they called the integration plan of record (IPOR). This was a process for which each team leader was responsible, that is, every week they had to detail all the cost savings, implementation, and integration plans and map them out for Clarke and McKinney. They had to walk into the Wednesday meeting with a red or yellow status on items. The red status issues would be raised to the steering committee level. Green coding represented their commitment that they were completing their tasks.

Every Monday there was a sub-team who worked for McKinney and Clarke. They would talk through the ratings to be sure they were on track. Then all ratings would be summarized and taken to the committee.

For example, some of the metrics were to track the numbers of *adopt-and-go* decisions, how many of these decisions were made, those implemented, those that had implications to intellectual property issues, the support issues regarding new management teams, and how these issues related to cost savings.

When HP and Compaq announced the merger in 2001, they promised that they would save $2.5 billion in costs by 2004. In six months after the deal was implemented, they hit $2.4 billion, and one year after the merger, it was $3.5 billion. Who knows where the savings will be in another year or so. There is no way that this merger can be called anything but successful.

The value capture process was highly complex, one of the most difficult areas for alliance implementation metrics. The metrics that HP used to make this happen are important. Following are some of the areas for value capture and a variety of differing financial savings that were and are being tracked:

1. Procurement.

2. Program cancellations of overlapping marketing programs.

3. Facility closures.

Then the teams tracked each action that would lead to the execution of the financial savings. The IPOR included the description of the action, for example, the *adopt-and-go* decision in one instance was to go to the Compaq industry standard server product as the surviving product rather than HP's option.

The actions that followed that decision took the tactical coordination of road maps to lead to that result:

➤ Close out engineering.

➤ Communication to customers.

➤ Transition plan for customers.

➤ Lay off engineers on net server side.

➤ Reset of sales strategy.

Every decision had hundreds of implications, so having the nuclear group who were empowered with a clear vision of *adopt and go* gave great clarity.

One of the key process people in the integration team was Barbara Braun. Her title has remained as vice president of integration. Braun explained how the integration expertise was developed:

> "We first did benchmarking around the best practices in the merger field. We looked across a number of industries to see why mergers fail and started to collect best practices and get a road map around what good integration looks like. We didn't just stop at a single benchmarking point in time. We have continued to do it once a quarter for as long as we have been on this project."

Braun agreed with the key success factors that others in the integration team had told me:

➤ That the right leadership and decision authority were in place with huge planning and the ability to drive their plan in a rigorous, consistent, and measurable way..

➤ That the purpose for the acquisition was clear, for consolidation purposes, that the approach taken was to holistically integrate two companies into one. The idea was not to:

  ➤ *Milk* one company for certain assets and liquidate or sell off other parts of it.

  ➤ Acquire for portfolio purposes.

  ➤ Acquire to build a group of companies by acquisition (see Chapter Five on Avnet's strategy for consolidation and growth)

One important factor that Braun added is that HP had come up with the rule that they would not disband their integration effort until 80 percent of their IPOR was reached. Her research had shown that many of the companies that fail in mergers do so because they disband their integration efforts too soon. Her experience showed her that mergers failed when the team had to redo their entire integration plan once two years passed and they found that they were in chaos.

There is no question that it could have been much simpler if the approach to integration would have been what Cisco Systems commonly did in their acquisitions, that is, announce: HP has acquired Compaq. So here is the way HP does things. Welcome to HP. End of discussion. HP did not do that. The reason is that their goal was integration, taking the best of all the remaining assets of both companies and using the *adopt-and-go* approach to accept the best of one of the companies and go forward. So the issue arises of who is best? And who knows who is best? Of course, the customers had to be the arbiter of this. So the team engaged those who faced the customers (often the sales representatives) when there was an account where there was a Compaq/HP overlap, to ask the customer what they thought of the merger, what they would like to see as an outcome, and which product or service was superior.

Metrics in any integration are never simple. We have looked at the structural cost savings which are significant as one metric. But the company also measured their success by constituency. The constituencies were customers, employees, shareholders, and partners. Throughout the pre- and post-merger integration process to this day, HP is still focusing their metrics on these stakeholder constituencies.

Another important metric is the issue of compensation. HP has aligned compensation with strategy and has institutionalized integrated planning and reporting methodology with strategic planning and financial planning and performance. This includes variable pay which is generally bonus-related. This shows that the company is putting its money where its mouth is, always the acid test in any change movement.

McKinney and Clarke stayed involved in the integration team until the end of February 2003 when Clarke was appointed executive vice president of supply chain and customer relations and McKinney was appointed executive vice president of merger integration and organizational effectiveness. This consistency and continuity had the effect of adding another important alliance implementation metric—socialization (acceptance within the organization) of the integration process seen in Chapter Four. In other words, it wasn't a deal-making orientation, that is, do the deal, do the integration, cap it with a time schedule of six months and consider it done. Rather the metrics of integration had to be met, and once they were, the process continued so that the integration was seen as an integral part of the entire life cycle of the alliance and relationship between these two entities as they came together.

Although everyone in the clean room was reassigned, the integration office continues to exist with the milestones of the IPOR still being followed by all the former integration team leaders in their various jobs because they were focused on multiple years, not just until the merger was complete. The road map has not changed. Everyone has been very rigorous in executing the plan evident in the HP results which have exceeded expectations regardless of the horrendous technology markets of 2002 and 2003.

In Clarke's new role, he is involved in the company's businesses processes and supply chain management. McKinney is still in the integration role. Because his skills are big program management (as a former executive vice president of the HP sales force he was used to running large programs), his role will expand beyond integration into driving the company to achieve the leadership it wants in a variety of areas for the future. HP is already a leader but they have long-term strategic objectives. McKinney and his team, including Braun, will be looking at what the next steps are for HP strategically, operationally, and culturally.

I was fortunate to trace the path of one executive from Compaq, vice president Leigh Morrison, as she moved into the clean room and then into her new HP assignment. Her story pulls together all the insights that I have touched on above in this remarkable event but tells it from an angle which is deep inside the activities of the company as well as the clean room operations. It's a viewpoint that tells the human side of this corporate integration which is one of the metrics that through my research at Caltech, I have found to be a key factor in the failure of alliances and merger integrations.

The challenge was:

How to take a longtime employee of one of the partners and integrate his or her knowledge and competency with another longtime employee of the other partner in a team that could be both collaborators and competitors at the same time?

This is a common challenge of many alliance partners. HP found a way to do it that is a lesson in the integration of dissimilar cultures, personalities, and goals.

Morrison is one of those unique executives who is understated yet full of knowledge, integrity, and skill. She was one of the earliest employees at Compaq and lived the startup and emerging phase of the company, seeing it go through many stages of its life cycle including its acquisition by HP. Her perspective as a longtimer both in the industry and in the company is valuable because the changes affected her personally as well as professionally and involved some substantial risks and leaps of faith.

When Morrison actually went into the clean room, she was asked to lead the go-to-market team for the Americas for Compaq. Because there was always a team of two, one from each company, she had a counterpart, a colleague from HP, Mike Heal. Their job was to build a field, customer-facing organization. Everyone they selected left their old jobs behind with no guarantee that they could return there if the merger didn't go through and stepped into this never-never land of risk and excitement.

Jim Milton was leading North America for Compaq. He called Morrison in October 2001 and said:

"Leigh, would you be willing to come into the clean room to lead the go-to-market project?" Morrison had said that she would think about it and then called him and said, "Yes I want to do this." But then the proxy battles started, and the integration team stopped bringing new people in so Morrison's entry was delayed.

Morrison joined the clean room 1 February 2002. The teams had kept the key go-to-market people out until they really needed them because they were facing the customer and were too valuable to potentially lose if the merger didn't go through.

Finally the time came when the need was intense to have the expertise in the clean room on how to organize and build the field organization and so in January, Morrison received another call which said she needed to start in February. Morrison had been with Compaq for 19 years. The risk she would take was huge. She and her husband talked about it a lot. She tells me that she will never forget the moment that the call came to her. She was visiting an alliance partner of Compaq, Oracle, when the call arrived.

"We need you to go into the clean room now." Milton said.

"Jim, I must have a guarantee that I will have some sort of job if this thing does or doesn't go through."

"Leigh, no one has a guarantee. You need to have some element of trust here." Morrison had worked for Milton for 4 years, since the Digital Equipment integration which she was also involved in. "You have to trust me," he repeated. Morrison took a huge breath and said, "OK, I'll do it."

The dynamics of the clean room, according to Morrison, were challenging. They were most of the time in a building in Palo Alto, with the large proportion of their time spent on conference calls between Houston, and Palo Alto. Only on two occasions did the whole team for go-to-market from all over the world come together in Palo Alto. One of the meetings was very tense because at that time it looked as if the merger wouldn't go through. They had to keep telling their teams that they have to go forward as if it was going to happen and remind the teams that they had to keep each other from having side conversations about the rumors and the merger being on or off because that was a waste of time. The closer the merger was, the more stressful and exciting it was. They had a couple of false starts based on launch days minus 90 or 60 or 30 to the date of the actual launch. Finally, when the date was pushed forward, it gave them more time to do what they needed to do. But there were only so many decisions that could take place before people actually took on their new roles.

The time came for some of the permanent appointments to be made in confidence. Because only a few people would know these appointments, certain code names were created. Milton was named NABU, named but not announced. When he was announced, Milton had responsibility for all the Americas including the enterprise systems group, sales, and storage, services, and software. He had a peer for the personal systems group called NABU PSG, another peer for the IPG (imaging printing group) called NABU IPG, and a final person for the services group called NABU for HP services.

Milton is the senior vice president and general manager for the Americas and the other NABUs report through their general manager as well as to Milton for the Americas, so their code names were *The Four Tenors*.

One fundamental theme that Capellas and Fiorina gave them was that they must present one face to the customer. So they knew that any go-to-market plan would have to have a model that did not confuse the customer. If there was a debate of a certain decision and Morrison and her colleague could not agree, then Milton was the tiebreaker.

This kind of conflict resolution mechanism is an important one in every alliance. Seen in the alliance implementation metrics, conflict resolution is a skill and process that is necessary for all alliance managers. Another element of good alliance management is the character of the alliance manager and whether he or she can be trusted. The alliance group and senior management are interested stakeholders in measuring this quality in their reports. Morrison passed that test with flying colors.

Certainly, many debates took place about what would be right for the new HP and what was the best way to do something. There was also enormous emotional commitment, doubt, pain, and worry. Morrison shared with me some of the agonizing that went on when critical decisions had to be made, with trust as an important element.

When they started the project, Morrison and her counterpart, Heal, had three different organizational charts so there was lots of debate on how to do everything. They decided to go with one organization structure with a vertical structure after much argument and discussion. They presented that with a recommendation to Milton. He listened, debated, and thought a lot about it. Finally, Milton decided why he liked one particular structure and then asked the teams to debate why the other structure would be better. Then he said, "Let me sleep on it." This discussion went on for two weeks. Finally, on a Friday, Milton decided. Morrison was in Houston and Milton called her. Her phone had not stopped because everyone was calling her, asking her what the new organization will look like?

> "That was the hardest thing to do" Morrison confided to me. "All of these people are my friends and colleagues, and I knew how worried they were for their own futures. And, in the meantime, they were trying to stay focused on the business and on the customers. It was very trying."

That night Morrison got on the plane at Houston. Milton had made his decision on the organizational structure, which meant that jobs would be decided, roles defined, and many people's lives would change. Morrison flew home relieved that at last, finally, she and her colleagues and friends knew what the organization would look like. But as she landed and turned on her cell phone, it rang. It was Milton.

> "Leigh, I have changed my mind. I believe that the organization that we must build is one that saves the most jobs and people. That must be our major focus, and it will serve HP well. Frankly, the people issues are more important to me than the issues of cost savings, and I truly believe in my heart that the cost savings will come if we make sure the people issues are taken care of."

The irony of this difficult decision by Milton is that he made the decision the HP way, with consideration of people and community as fundamental principles. However, Milton was from Compaq. He passed the trust test, as did Morrison, and another former Compaq senior executive, Peter Black-more who, when he had his first staff meeting, went through each and every résumé of the people he had selected. He spoke in detail about why they had been selected and their accomplishments—something that has stood them all in good stead since then. Decisions had been made for value, not favoritism. These are the elements that develop trust in a partnership.

The go-to-market metrics were a challenge. There was a need for specifics of the roles, customer interfaces, every aspect of the planning. So they came up with the concept of playbooks. This concept is not new for Compaq.

Every person in the customer facing organization was given a guide so that on the launch day, they would know how to get information for a customer, and how to work an issue in the field. Every person in the field organization was assigned a buddy from the other company so they knew where to go for information.

Following is an example of one of the playbooks (Figure 8.2) which gives a clear indication of what was to be learned, measured, and executed. This one is the North America Enterprise Systems Country Managers Playbook for goals and actions.

FIGURE 8.2 GOALS & ACTIONS FOR ESG COUNTRY MANAGERS

North America Enterprise Systems Group
Document Number: 3.1.2
Document Name: ESG Country manager playbook
Version: v.1.8
Date of Revision: 4/11/02
Valid from: 4/1/02 to 7/1/02

Document Owner: XXXXXXX

North America ESG country manager playbook
This document is a suggested action plan for all ESG country managers in the new HP. It is a starting point to determine the critical actions that must be taken to help operationalize the HP and Compaq merger. The focus is to help ensure that we are aggressively in front of customers and partners to drive revenue and customer satisfaction as well as to ensure that we engage with our HP and Compaq counterparts to quickly integrate our organizations and our plans.

"**Important Note:** Until C+1 HP and Compaq are required by law to continue to act as two separate competing companies. Any activities discussed in this document which require sharing of non-public or confidential information are not permitted prior to C+1 unless the activities are conducted through the HP/Compaq clean room/clean team process."

(continued)

The one-page integration goals.

Please see the following key integration goals. How you achieve these goals is up to you, but action-item detail follows should you need it. It is vital we focus on these priorities:

Pri	Category	Goal
H	Basics	**Learn the messages** of the new HP by participating in the merger launch events and reading material found in the "Selling in the new HP" Toolkit (URL on cover of this document). Start with the "Getting started with the Toolkit" link.
H	Business	**Leverage current processes.** Execute in "Business as usual" mode for the HP and Compaq sides of your business. Execute with HP tools/process in the HP realm, and Compaq tools/process in the Compaq realm.
H	Business	**Hone the launch communication plan** for your country and ensure we are sending the right messages via the right media to your customers, partners, employees, shareholders and PR/AR community.
H	Customer	**Achieve your two separate P&Ls until you receive an integrated one.** Continue to drive aggressively all revenue opportunities. Look for methods to cross-sell the broader array of products, solutions and services available to you in all your accounts.
H	Customer	**Talk with your customers and partners immediately.** Ensure your sales teams immediately share details of the merger with customers and partners at all levels. Include your HP/Compaq counterpart. Schedule executive sponsors as appropriate.
H	Customer	**Determine and address revenue/customers at risk.** In your accounts, determine what relationships and big deals are at risk and identify where HP/Compaq are competing. Quickly escalate issues to your management for assistance in resolution as appropriate.
H	Employee	**Aggressively and prudently select your organization.** Work with HR to roll out your organization quickly ensuring equal consideration for both HP and Compaq employees. Implement a quick, fair, and sound process.
H	Employee	**Immediately create unified teams.** Drive interaction at the lowest level between HP and Compaq individuals on the same accounts. Get people talking and working together quickly.
H	People	**Stay close to your team.** Be open, supportive, and optimistic. Develop strategies to retain key employees.

(continued)

Pri	Category	Goal
M	Business	**Learn the new side of your business** from those who know it.
M	Business	**Drive cross-group and cross-company leverage.** Although we have strong group P&Ls, understand how you can work collaboratively with your other country managers to drive a consistent customer experience.

To find the material referenced below as residing in the "selling in the new HP" Web site, use the link included on the cover page of this document.

Actions for ESG Country Managers.

Country group managers should execute the following actions. ('L' refers to the official Launch day for the new company; thus 'L-6' means six days prior to Launch.)

Date	Category	Action/Resource
L-7	Internal	**Attend Leadership Summit**
L-7	Internal	Dialog with Your Region General Manager. Talk with your Region general manager and review key near term actions to drive integration.
L-7	Internal	**Dialog with Region Integration Lead.** Meet with your ESG region integration leader for a debrief on all merger-related activity including a review of the "ramp plan." Your ESG region integration lead has been active since January planning how your group's integration will occur in your region.
L-7	People	**Review Client Business Manager Selection.** Review the work to-date on the selection process for Client Business Managers (the lead on our most important global accounts) in your country. Escalate if you see issues. Insure that the levels of the customer organization in which the CBM operates are reviewed.
L-6	Legal	**Conduct Legal Review.** Meet with your region lawyers to understand the full ramifications of combining legal entities, work council rules, etc., especially understanding restrictions on sharing information about accounts and merging your organization. Instruct your country legal to review this playbook (and the other playbooks for your organization) and comment on and address any legal implications.
L-6	Marketing	**Review Marketing Communications Plan.** Review the marketing communications plan with your marketing team understanding the ramp down of pre-merger messages and ramp-up of post-merger messages.

(continued)

Date	Category	Action/Resource
L-6	Launch	**Review Launch Communication Plan.** You have 3 launch communication leads for your region (one for business customers & partners, consumer customers & partners, and employees), with one as the overall leader. Speak with your region launch leader about the launch communication process and ensure it is well planned and effective. Additionally, map out a plan to ensure that appropriate PR/AR communication occurs in your country coordinated with your country manager counterparts.
L-5	Internal	**Learn the New Side of Your Business.** Seek out individuals from the company not of your heritage to understand how that business runs in your country. Learn the nuances and issues by speaking with your manager, the incumbent person who did not get your job and others as appropriate. Understand their terms and acronyms. Learn the financial metrics, reporting systems, etc. Review the documents available to you in the confidential "e-Room" Web site.
L-4	Personal	**Create an Aggressive 60-Day Personal Communication Plan.** Create an aggressive personal schedule that puts you in front of customers, partners, and employees. Block out time that can be filled in by your sales management team. Show coverage across your business. Determine if other executives are required in your accounts and schedule as appropriate.
L-4	Employee	**Customize Playbooks.** Speak with your group integration lead and obtain copies of all relevant playbooks (1st line sales manager, end-user sales playbook and partner playbooks) that defined specifically what various roles in your organization should do on Launch and beyond to achieve integration. Have your team: 1) Customize the *actions and dates* (being aware of local holidays) as appropriate for all playbooks for your country. 2) Customize content for any known country legal restrictions (e.g., sharing of customer information). Ensure that legal signs off on final playbooks prior to delivery to employees. 3) Adjust goal priorities as appropriate. 4) Ensure that the playbooks are delivered to your organization for Launch either through e-mail or by posting them in the toolkit under the regional customization section prior to Launch.

(continued)

Date	Category	Action/Resource
L-4	Finance	**Drive Your Two P&Ls.** You have two P&Ls to manage, one from the HP side and one from Compaq. Review your revenue targets, expense targets and margin targets provided. Assess challenges and opportunities.
L-4	HR	**Identify Top-Tier Performers.** Work with HR to obtain lists from both the HP and the Compaq sides of the top performers in the country. Work with HR on approaches to retain key employees. Begin development of retention plans.
L-4	Internal	**Create Country Distribution Lists.** Create one for all employees and one for all sales managers across both HP and Compaq. Include all CBMs in the sales manager distribution list.
L-3	Training	**Review the 'Selling in the New HP" Toolkit.** Briefly scan the Web-based toolkit (URL found on the first page of this document) so that you understand it exists and the types of information available. This is the primary source for sales and selling support related information.
L-3	Training	**Learn Key New HP Messages and Merger Detail.** Learn merger detail by reviewing the "Selling in the new HP Toolkit." Refer to the URL on the first page of this document. Follow the "Getting started with the Toolkit" link to start. This gives you information on the merger, acronyms, product road maps, etc. Rehearse this message—you will be giving it many times.
L-3	Employee	**Learn the Quota and Compensation Plan.** Review with HR the plan for quota and compensation migration. Be sure you understand the plan to encourage HP and Compaq interaction on accounts.
L-3	Multiple	**Learn about Merger Information and Issue Management.** From the toolkit, learn about the Merger Information and Issue Center (MIIC) in your region. This is an approach to ensure that we respond quickly to issues that arise at Launch and beyond that are not already planned for in other integration approaches. Ensure that your region integration team is effectively implementing and staffing the MIIC in your country.
L-3	Internal	**Prepare for Launch Kick-off Conference Call.** Plan with your other group country managers, region GM, and group region integration leader a kick-off conference call on Launch with your new organization. Determine if there will be a separate call per group or a single call with all group general managers and whether there will be country level calls. Develop ideas on how you can personalize this. Be

(continued)

Date	Category	Action/Resource
		sure to develop thoughts around reaching out to the employees from the company not of your heritage.
L-1	Comm	**Create Your Launch Welcome Message for Managers.** Write a brief message to your new organization for *all managers* welcoming them to the new HP and setting the tone for the future. In this message indicate: 1) Your personal welcome and excitement concerning the merger. 2) Outline details for the launch communication for your country. 3) The importance of their role in driving the cultural and process changes needed to achieve effective integration. Emphasize the importance of staying close to employees and the need to escalate employee issues as appropriate. 4) The need for continued leadership from all managers, whether or not they were chosen for the position of their choice. 5) The importance to stay very close to customers and your expectations that they will drive aggressive call plans with customers. 6) Indicate importance of executing against playbooks, both their individual playbook and the one for their sales teams. They should review the end-user sales playbook to understand/support the action items given to their sales teams. 7) Ask managers to review the "Selling in the new HP" toolkit (give the URL as found on the cover of this document), starting with the "Getting started with the Toolkit" link on the Toolkit homepage. 8) Indicate they should drive immediately toward unifying account strategies and teams *where legally permissible.* Ask them to share the account/employee spreadsheet as appropriate to facilitate that unification. Indicate that we will operate with dual account managers for many accounts until the organization decisions can be cascaded to arrive at a single account manager. 9) Attach the sales manager playbook. 10) Attach the end-user sales playbook. 11) Attach partner playbooks (volume, enterprise, retail) as appropriate. 12) Attach the post-merger country organization document. 13) Attach the "*named account spreadsheet.*" 14) Attach the "*partner spreadsheet.*"

(continued)

Date	Category	Action/Resource
L-1	Comm	**Create Your Launch Welcome Message for All Employees.** Write a brief message to your new organization for *all employees in your organization* welcoming them to the new HP and setting the tone for the future. In this message indicate: 1) Your personal welcome and excitement concerning the merger. 2) Outline details for the launch communication for your country. 3) Given legal approval, emphasize the need to immediately start acting as one integrated account team. In those accounts/partners where both HP and Compaq are present, this means we have two teams with two leaders working together. 4) Ask employees to review the "Selling in the new HP" toolkit (give the URL as found on the cover of this document), starting with the "Getting started with the Toolkit" link on the Toolkit homepage. 5) Emphasize the importance of executing role-specific playbooks that will help with integration—indicate they are attached. 6) Attach the end-user sales playbook and partner play-books (value, volume and consumer) as appropriate.
L	Internal	**Conduct Your First Meeting with Direct Reports.** Hold a meeting either face-to-face or over the phone with your direct report team. In this meeting you should: 1) Optimistically rally your team around the important integration effort ahead. Emphasize their role in driving the change processes to ensure a smooth integration. 2) Review the process for selecting sales managers and the rest of your organization. Indicate that one of the goals of the integration was to significantly increase the number of direct selling professionals. Indicate that a fair and speedy process will be used. Consider involving HR in the discussion. 3) Review any legal restrictions that may be in place (e.g., inability to share account data in some countries). 4) Review the playbook and toolkit strategy. Distribute the sales manager playbook, walk through it, and indicate that you expect it to be executed. Emphasize that your selling teams will use playbooks and the toolkit. 5) Ask your team to quickly learn the key new HP messages, compensation plan, and other important items in the toolkit.

(continued)

Date	Category	Action/Resource
		6) Share account and partner assignments spreadsheet with your sales managers so they can communicate within their organizations to drive joint Compaq/HP interaction.
		7) Explain that until we have all account assignments set, we will be keeping all account teams in place. Emphasize the need for all account managers and sales managers to share account information immediately with their counterparts and create one face to the customer through the two sales teams.
		8) Indicate that each account manager, where legally permissible, must immediately coordinate communication of the new HP message to their assigned accounts with their counterpart from HP or Compaq.
		9) Send the message that we will use existing mechanisms, approaches, tools, etc., until integration is operationalized.
		10) Dialog with your team on holding "mixer" meetings with the sales teams to begin Compaq/HP interaction.
		11) Communicate your personal 60-day communication schedule and ask your direct reports to immediately prepare a similar aggressive schedule for themselves and their teams. Ensure coordination. Ask your team to fill in blocks of your schedule as appropriate.
		12) Review key-employee retention plan.
		13) Encourage your team to aggressively attack and exploit synergies between the two companies. Look for places where you can "adopt and go" rather than invent a new process or system.
L	Internal	**Participate in Group Launch Calls.** Participate in the conference call with your group region general manager and their direct reports to get grounded on near term actions.
L	Comm	**Send Your Launch All-Employee Welcome E-mail.** Send your welcome message just created to your distribution list of country employees.
L	Comm	**Send Your Launch Managers Welcome E-mail.** Send your welcome message just created to your distribution list of sales managers.
L+1	Customer	**Determine deals and customers at risk.** Look at all major deals in flight and identify deals and customers at risk. Review any work already done at the region level on this. Develop strategy on how to minimize risk in these areas. Maintain a list and aggressive mechanism to address these risk situations.

(continued)

Date	Category	Action/Resource
L+3	Employee	**Build Your Organization.** Work with your local integration team and HR to understand the full organization rollout process including time frames when various levels will be named and announced. Create an aggressive schedule. Understand the list of candidates that you will interview for your direct reports. Create an interview schedule and work with HR on the timing of interviewing viable candidates. Realize that speed to integration is one of the key success factors for the merger. Aggressively push to define your new organization quickly.
L+7	Customer/ Partner	**Learn about Customer Data Transfer Notification.** Read about customer data transfer notification requirements and the actions being taken by HP to comply. Information on the Customer Data Transfer Notification Process can be found in the Selling in the New HP Toolkit.
April/ May/ June	Internal	**Focus on Revenue and Customers.** Drive both the HP and Compaq sides of your organization to maximize sales activity, revenue, margin, and customer satisfaction. It is vital that we do not slow down our efforts and offer our competitors an opening. Ensure that all managers understand the sequencing of the different HP and Compaq fiscal quarters during the initial period so they don't ask people to do atypical things when trying to drive the most revenue.
April/ May	Personal	**Aggressively Execute Your 60-Day Communication Plan.** Develop and execute a personal 60-day communications plan, driving a fast-paced schedule so that you can carry the new message.
April/ May/ June	Internal	**Stay Close to Your Organization.** Review with your direct report team the key-employee retention strategies, understand issues and address as appropriate. Conduct weekly staff meetings with your entire group (potentially with your HP/Compaq counterpart) to address any confusions, missed expectations, etc., targeting care of the employee. Stay very close to your employees during this time of change.

(continued)

Date	Category	Action/Resource
L+5	Customer	**Define an Offensive Attack Strategy.** In addition to your plans to protect your installed base, consider selecting a small number of competitive opportunities where the new HP provides a competitive advantage not previously available from HP or Compaq individually. Define attack plans for these accounts. Keep the competition busy protecting their turf while we integrate. Highlight this effort to your organization to drive confidence and enthusiasm in the "added value" of the new HP.
L+5	HR	**Implement Key Employee Retention Plan.** Identify any top performers at risk and escalate as appropriate.
L+5	Internal	**Rationalize Your Forecast.** For product forecasting, continue with current forecasting methods for both the HP and Compaq sides of your business, ensuring that we are not double counting revenue opportunity on the same deal.
L+7	Employee	**Drive Clarity with Your Direct Reports.** Schedule 1-on-1 sessions with all of your direct reports, spending extra time with those of the different company heritage. Communicate your strategy and their role in more detail.
L+10	Personal	**Learn about Your Benefits.** For ongoing updates about your compensation and benefits refer to the Total Rewards Interim Guide at wwwwwwww
L+30	Employee	**Select Direct Reports.** Work with HR to interview, select, and announce your direct reports.
L+30	Internal	**Complete Effective Transition from Plan to Action.** Work with your regional Integration Manager to ensure integration plan is complete and being implemented, with clear milestones and scheduled progress checkpoint reviews.
April/ May/ June	Comm	**Communicate Integration Success Often.** Publish an internal "integration update" message to your organization citing successes to-date, areas of focus and near, term goals. Assign ownership to create this message for your review. Use this as an opportunity to send any new messages to your team.

As you can see from the playbook, every detail was considered. Importantly, all benefits were rationalized, a hugely critical issue for all employees. On launch day, every single one of the 150,000 employees were on one e-mail system, and new signage was placed in every major site—not just a banner but actual new signage. All product lines were complete. They had protection plans for customers moving to new products from those that were being phased out. All product road maps out three years were done on day one. Everyone knew how to get access to all sites, and all sites were rationalized as HP. Their first paychecks were identified as HP. When someone called any office, the phone was answered "Welcome to the new HP" for two months after the launch day.

Morrison laughed when she remembered her days at Tandem Computers and then Digital Equipment:

> "This was light years ahead as an integration process. At Tandem in Cupertino the signage didn't change for six months until the CEO decided he wanted a board meeting there. That was when they changed the sign."

They learned the date the new company was going to be launched in the clean room. All level three managers were identified, but it was not announced by 12 April. The launch date kept moving and was finally announced on 7 May 2002. By 24 April 2002, all the level three managers were invited to a secret meeting in San Francisco, at the Hilton. The instructions were clear:

> "You are not to wear any logo'd item. You are not to register in the name of the company. You cannot talk to anyone about anything. The name of the conference will be Lessons in Leadership and will not have the names of either company anywhere."

Fiorina was concerned about the press and any leaks, but she felt it was essential to get the leaders of the new company together. This was the first time many of the employees in the top three levels had met her. Fiorina spoke without notes, as is her habit. Fiorina spoke about how it was all coming together one idea at a time. She used the metaphor of the Golden Gate Bridge and how no one thought it could be done, but it was and that every one of these leaders needed to keep their focus on the end game. She took difficult questions and was so impressive that everyone from the pre-merger companies were completely won over. Additionally, lots of HP people hadn't met Capellas. All of the people who reported directly to him did breakout sessions so that they had time to interact with each other. Then Peter Blackmore (former senior executive at Compaq who had been given a leadership role at HP) had another meeting at the Airport Hyatt with his team to further get to know each other.

All of the three hundred people who attended this meeting had to sign nondisclosure agreements. They were all given instructions not to refer to HP at all. Every meeting room had lots of security. During the executive presentations, no hotel employees or outsiders were permitted to enter.

It was the best kept secret. No one guessed, no one leaked to the press, and no one knew that this was going on.

When thinking about implementation metrics, the implementation launch was a critical factor in this alliance, whereas for many companies, launching the implementation of the alliance is a time for great public fanfare. In this case, the byword was confidentiality and trust until the word was given to go forward. Keeping a *secret* of such huge proportions was an expected outcome of being part of the implementation launch—and they did it.

Meantime Milton was planning the launch days for the Americas. He wanted the launch done in sixteen cities across the country and every employee in the region to be there, with every senior executive so that the message would be consistent sent, and received . They had to find a venue that could take three thousand people in New York and fifteen hundred in San Jose, California. Morrison arranged the San Jose Convention Center for the first launch event. She was to set the pace. The first day was HP employees only. The afternoon was devoted to all of their combined alliance partners, independent software vendors, and channel partners. The following day Milton and his peers talked about the product line and that day was customers only and a representative of various product groups. There were breakout sessions, product road maps, and, of course, again, everyone had to sign nondisclosure agreements.

The major theme was: This is going to be hard work. We are going to prove to the nay-sayers that we can do it. But we need to remind each other to have fun, too. It was commented that Fiorina said that a lot. One day Morrison and her team took it to heart.

Can fun be a metric? One example that Morrison shared with me showed that for them it was.

It was six o'clock Pacific time on a Monday morning. Everyone was exhausted, they had been working around the clock, and they didn't seem to be getting anywhere. They certainly were not having much fun. Heal, Morrison's counterpart at HP said, "We aren't making progress." They agreed. "Also, we aren't having fun." They decided they needed to get around this issue, made some jokes, and set another time for the discussion. Fiorina's admonition that fun was an important part of the integration process was taken seriously and became a measurement for the teams in many difficult discussions.

What Made This Alliance Work

If I were to differentiate this merger/alliance integration from all others, there were specific characteristics that made it work. All of them relate to the fact that the merger and its metrics were managed before and after deal closure, as if the situation were an alliance. This approach took a lot of the factors out of the integration process that cause other mergers to fail. It was also a merger that took place for various structural reasons that are different from other types of mergers that are for growth and new markets such as the stated goals for the AOL Time Warner deal. Here are a few of the differences in the HP/Compaq merger:

ALLIANCE DEVELOPMENT: STRATEGIC AND STRUCTURAL ELEMENTS

1. It is a merger of consolidation in an industry that needs it badly (it wasn't a merger for growth; one in which one company was buying the other to enter a market where they had aspirations, for example, AOL/Time Warner).

2. There were substantial cost savings available—$3.5 billion worth of overlaps due to the consolidation by the second quarter of 2003 with more to come. To put this in perspective, remember that the entire movie industry had record box office receipts of just $9 billion in 2002.

ALLIANCE IMPLEMENTATION: THE OPERATIONALIZATION OF THE INTEGRATION PROCESS

1. They put two senior executives who were used to making company-level decisions in charge of the merger planning and execution (prior to the merger McKinney led the HP sales force and Clarke was the Compaq CFO). Too often, a key staff person or up-and-coming executive will be

asked to lead a merger. Fiorina decided to put two executives in charge who already led critical company-level decision processes.

2. The CEO—Fiorina—stayed directly and intimately involved in all the decision processes. She held a weekly half-day merger integration meeting where escalations, clarifications and core decisions were made. McKinney and Clarke had one-stop access to her on the many key strategies and tactics they needed to debate, decide, and deploy.

3. They created a framework for speed of decision making which they called *adopt and go*. Simply put, they looked at how HP and Compaq alternatively ran a function or process, picked (adopted) one or the other and transitioned the alternative company's process (go) to it ASAP. For example, they adopted the HP treasury processes and immediately shifted the Compaq processes to the HP ones. In turn, they adopted the Compaq information technology planning process and quickly shifted the HP data and planning efforts to the Compaq modules.

4. They executed with hard discipline. This is the critical *blocking and tackling* where many mergers (notably Digital Equipment/Compaq) go awry. This included establishing over twenty teams (each with both HP and Compaq leaders) but then assigning one of the two leaders to be the one *throat to choke* per se for McKinney and Clarke to hold accountable. This included rigorous red/yellow/green charts highlighting implementation timetables, and so on. It also required over 1 million people-hours of investment in planning before the merger was approved—they didn't underestimate the challenge.

ALLIANCE IMPLEMENTATION: THE IMPLEMENTATION LAUNCH

1. Debate about which team was best (or good enough) happened at the lower levels of the integration team, was negotiated, argued, debated, and agreed. No attempt was made to create the animal of consensus that ends up being a fourteen-humped camel with two legs that can neither stand, run, nor function.

2. Clarity existed about the approach—no duplication. Once the decision was made, no second guessing. *Adopt and go!*

3. The hierarchy of decision structures was clear: We debate, we can't agree, it goes up, they can't agree, it goes up. The Fiorina/Capellas/

Clarke/McKinney committee has the last word. *Adopt and go* and make it good enough—not perfect.

4. They had two leaders who were highly empowered to lead rather than staff people.

5. There were open door and regular weekly meeting processes with the CEO and an empowered steering committee to make decisions weekly.

6. They resourced the transition team well enough and more thoroughly than most planned mergers in history. There were over 1 million hours invested in the transition process. This intense effort allowed the merger to succeed as well as aligning many of the cost savings.

7. Communications were a focused commitment of the entire integration process.

8. Team members preserved the confidentiality necessary in this delicate set of circumstances until the time was right to go public with the new HP.

The HP integration process is a benchmark standard to which few companies will rise. However, the structural, human, and process excellence which we have covered in this chapter has laid out how managing an acquisition as if it were a valued alliance and relationship can lead to huge returns and ultimate success. If success is measured as the return to shareholders, employees, and customers, then most acquisitions will fill the annals of failures because approximately 85 percent of all acquisitions fail on these metrics. The HP acquisition is proving to return the cost savings, the customer satisfaction, and the sustainability of building one consolidated organization in an industry cycle that is one of the worst in recent history. Not an insignificant achievement.

Chapter Nine will examine two companies that couldn't be more different: One is private, the other is public, one is family owned, and the other still has its entrepreneur as chairman but is far from the family driven company that it once was. Both companies serve their customers with great interest and care and have used alliances to grow their businesses.

The Large Companies That Act Small

S taples was created out of one person's frustration and need for immediate service. Late one evening, Thomas G. Stemberg, the founder of Staples, needed a printer ribbon to replace the one he was using, which had broken. He could not find one anywhere. From that need came an idea. From that idea came the office supplies superstore industry with the opening of its first store in Brighton (Boston) in May 1986. Stemberg is Chairman of Staples and was CEO from January 1986 when he founded the company until February 2002. Now the CEO is Ronald Sargent, also a longtimer with the company since 1989. Sargent shared with me the goal of the company: to provide small business owners the same low prices on office supplies previously enjoyed only by large corporations. Staples is now an $11-billion retailer of office supplies, business services, furniture, and technology to consumers and businesses from home-based businesses to Fortune 500 companies in North America and throughout Europe. Customers can shop at Staples in whatever way they choose, either by walking in, calling in, or logging on.

No matter how large Staples has become, their primary customer remains the individual and small business owner. In that respect, they are a large company that must consistently think small. They are similar to ValleyCrest Companies, which has become the biggest in their industry of landscape services and still owned by one family. They, too, maintain their competitive advantage by serving one customer at a time, whether it is a landscape architect, a developer, a corporation, city, county, state, the US Olympics Committee, a home owners association, or, in select cases, an individual.

This chapter will look at the metrics that these two companies use to make sure that the alliances that they have in place stay at the high level of commitment and service on which both companies pride themselves.

For Staples, it's all about making sure that the alliances they have, can deliver the results they want. That sounds trite because every company wants to get the best results. But Staples gets so many requests every month for alliances that they have had to become very analytical about the partners they select and what they actually call an alliance and treat as such, rather than a commodity-type relationship. The metrics become critical to enable them to differentiate between those relationships that they want to accelerate into more integrated relationships, and those they do not. This also gives them their definition of success and, consequently, the metrics to know the alliances that they want to terminate.

Jeff Scheman, who is in charge of alliances for Staples, spelled out some of the metrics that they use at Staples. First, how they define their customer is the *small business in the power user segment.*

Every discussion regarding potential alliances has to first meet this test:

1. All the alliances start with the question: How does partnering with this company serve unmet or difficult needs for the small business or power user? The power user consumes lots of office supplies in his or her home office, especially ink, toner, paper, and computer accessories. These office supply users are Staples' key customers, their pride and joy, indeed, their bread and butter. They are always thinking about the unmet needs for that group and how to bring them something of value that they may not be able to get by themselves. The acid test is: Will this product or service from Staples make the power user customer's life easier? Some of these ideas trickle up from inside the organization, others come from outside the company.

2. Every alliance opportunity is only evaluated once Staples has considered whether they want to offer the product or services themselves. If they can't do it themselves, only then do they question how they can work with others to meet the customer needs. These make-or-buy decisions are fundamental and not atypical of a company that is relatively early in its growth life cycle where partnering is just beginning to become more important.

3. The third metric that is important to Staples is finding other organizations that serve that same constituency and with the same understand-

ing of how important the customer is—the commitment level of the partner to the same quality of services and products will be a key factor in the early partner evaluation process. It is a critical criterion for partner qualification in the early part of the alliance development metrics as well (Chapter Three).

4. The next metric is the senior executive sponsorship of the alliance in both companies. Staples feels that unless that level of commitment exists in both partners, the alliance cannot succeed.

5. Articulation of goals and strategic alignment are two more metrics that Scheman emphasized, in that the alliances that Staples creates have to be squarely in the *sweet spot* of each company's strategic goals. The partners have to be able to articulate what they are.

6. The above metrics will ensure that during implementation, when the partnership runs into difficulties (Scheman called them speed bumps), both parties can dip into the goodwill, executive support, and strategic alignment that will ensure success.

7. The implementation metrics are all about communication, managing expectations, and reminding each team of the broader vision and mission of the alliance when things get tough. Staples' culture is to share and debate. For some of their partners, this is not culturally acceptable. Staples' culture prefers to exchange ideas and push each other to think through the issues, bringing into the open the rough points in order to work them through.

8. The revenues metrics will look at whether the alliance has proven to be a profitable way to acquire the right kind of customer or to service the customer they already have, making customer retention another metric.

9. Leveraging of an existing relationship is important to Staples. One of the concerns they have is trying to do too much too fast. To prevent this, there is a focus on prioritization in the numbers of alliances, what is done in each alliance, and the outcomes that are expected in the short- and long-term relationship.

10. Another interesting metric and mode of alliance management is that there is no hand-off process when it comes to the implementation of alliances. Scheman described the alliances that he helped to negotiate and create. Now he manages them. He generally will work with no more than five or six relationships at a time, not fifty.

11. The next goal is to be sure that the teams within all partners view the alliance the same way, as doing the right thing for the customer in the right way. Although looking at stakeholder analysis is important to Staples, it chooses very few metrics to examine, so that people will not spend a lot of time filling out charts but serving the customers.

12. Learning is captured by trying to keep the team together, so that they are all there for the pilot and then for the rollout. This way, learning can be done experientially and captured by observation. They document what they can, but most of it is anecdotal and verbal. Staples does evolve best practices, but unlike an engineering and sales driven organization such as Avnet, they prefer to have discussions rather than quantified processes and metrics.

13. Executive communication. A very small group communicates often with each other. Scheman talks with his boss, with Ron Sargent, the CEO, and Stemberg, the chairman, weekly to monthly. They have a formal meeting where the alliance managers talk about the alliance with the chairman and CEO monthly or every other month. Those meetings create the documentation around their activities. They present to each other what is working, or not, and why, and share the learning among each other. It is important to get the right feedback from partners. The goal is that the team work toward a common ground.

Communication processes involve weekly phone calls with every partner, although the alliance managers are in touch more frequently. They set up a scheduled call at a regular time. If it doesn't happen, it becomes known and communicated that that should not be repeated behavior. Commitment to the partnership is key.

Much of this approach is the historical legacy of Staples. It was clear that one person's need became the need of many for whom convenience, accessibility, availability of products and services, and cost are the imperatives. When Stemberg founded the business in 1986, he couldn't afford to do any advertising. For many years, it was the habit of Staples to conduct database marketing and direct mail. The heritage of the company is that it serves small business, which has led to enormous success as Staples has moved into that market. They are different from other retailers in that regard, too, because fully two thirds of their sales are to small businesses. So it's logical to realize that the company believed that to spend a great deal of their marketing budget on television advertising and broad-based promotion would be a mistake. Most of their focused resources and marketing go in a targeted fashion to small businesses. They are constantly on the lookout for opportunities and partnerships that can help them to continue to serve that market.

Staples has over 4 million customers who come through their stores every single week and relationships with more than 8 million customers. They could sell them many other things that they need and want. However, in order to keep their customers happy, they are careful to test the products and services first and then to have clear evaluation metrics in place in order to glean the information they need from the pilot. They analyze the results, and only roll out the product when and where it will be appropriate. Huge value is placed on customer loyalty and brand value coming from the trust their customers place in them. They cannot afford to offer a service or product that does not meet their stringent quality standards. After all, it is their brand that is at stake. Out of this has come the most interesting of the Staples alliances, which are what they call *virtual alliances*. These are alliances for services that take many forms.

Virtual alliances always have customer satisfaction and brand issues in mind. Staples tested legal services and medical services. The most successful test which has become a valuable alliance for them is their payroll services alliance with Automatic Data Processing Inc. (ADP).

The on-line and off-line stores are a perfect referral vehicle for numbers of leads for payroll services. Staples then forwards the leads to ADP, and when ADP provides payroll, it has a revenue-sharing arrangement that lasts only for a period of time. There is great trust that has built up regarding the ADP relationship, but it was based on the original evaluation of brand value matching to brand value, which is the metric that we discussed in alliance development. Then the alliance is measured again in implementation with metrics that refer to numbers of referrals, satisfaction of customers, and an increase or decrease of activity related to the ADP services.

Other services have also been successful alliances. One is in the area of printing services, which Staples refers to as Taylor Printing. This is perfect for the customer who doesn't have the ability or desire to do printing themselves.

Another alliance is for their Internet services where they created a relationship with Microsoft Corporation, and yet another, with a company that provides warranty services. Because of the volume of the Staples business, each of these alliances represents a large block of business for the companies with whom they partner, especially the ones that are smaller. However, even with larger companies Staples' referrals provide a significant amount of business.

Staples has developed an alliance with United Parcel Service (UPS) to do their shipping. They negotiated a rate with UPS that is the same contract rate that UPS offers to individuals directly. The purpose of this alliance was to help the customer consider Staples as his or her shipping point.

In addition to product-related services and virtual alliances, they also have some unusual services such as those from a company called Upromise. This company has a relationship with certain vendors so that each time a customer buys from them, the company (in this case, Staples) will credit the customer's account and that money is set aside for a college education for the customer's child. This way Staples can include in its database of alliances, the relationship with such a company that will assist them to create more value than the service or product itself has on its own. It's a savings-type plan that is considered by all parties to have added value and makes Staples a retailer and preferred service provider.

Staples has at least another fifty of these value-sharing arrangements which may not be called alliances but, in fact, are measured like them in that they fit with my definition of alliances which is:

Business relationships for mutual benefit between two or more parties who have compatible and complementary business interests and goals.

Staples and their alliances share information, products, and services, and the customers and vendors all thrive on the relationships.

Staples is developing an alliance with Starbucks. Because Starbucks and Staples have a cultural and belief system that is similar in terms of their joint commitments to social responsibility, their commonality of purpose has been a major factor in helping their business interests come together.

This is also entirely consistent with the research[1] which I have done on why so many alliances fail. My research found that the business reasons for entering into an alliance were inversely proportional to the compatibility issues over time, which means that the business reasons were given a lot of

---

[1]Research by Larraine Segil into 235 companies at Caltech on compatibility challenges in alliances and how to make failing alliances succeed. Go to www.vantagepartners.com and click on Larraine Segil.

attention by the executives negotiating the relationship early on in relationship development, but the compatibility issues were paid much less attention. However, an interesting thing happened over time. The compatibility issues became more important and the business issues became less important; they intersected at about halfway through the term of the alliance which was exactly when 60 percent of alliances failed.

Vice President Scheman manages the alliances group at Staples quantitatively and qualitatively by using specific metrics, and by taking into account the company strategies, brands, and more. The company would not enter into any alliance without the appropriate metrics to make it valuable. These metrics are consistent with the alliance development metrics in Chapter Three. For example:

Strategic alignment. This metric would involve the measuring of the baseline of strategic importance of the opportunity to each partner. Then both partners would track that level throughout the alliance, making sure that if the strategic importance of the relationship were to change, each team would be aware of that change and be able to decide whether or not to take action to support or challenge it.

Brand evaluation. This is a critical metric for a company with a brand as valuable as Staples. Additionally, their partners, companies with high value brands, such as American Express Company, with whom they have a points program in which customers can gain points for using their AmEx card, are equally concerned that their brands are presented at the right level of importance. Important for both partners is that the brand values of both organizations are protected.

Planning. Creating the strategic and operational plan for the alliance is another set of metrics in which both teams (Staples and their partner) are expected to participate. The good relationships between their alliance managers will contribute to this.

Team Selection. Staples and their partners heavily emphasized the selection of the right people to manage their partnerships. Those people are measured on their performance and ability to work as a member of a team, too.

Staples had some interesting experiences during the dotcom bubble when everyone wanted to partner with them. The company managed to keep their strategic focus during the dotcom era. Even though the percentage of revenues from alliances was not huge, the potential was. Alliances are seen as a critical brand differentiator for Staples by their CEO and board. As they go forward and certainly over the next five years, alliances will become more important, particularly as they move into Europe establishing a differentiated offering enabling them to become the Wal-Mart of office supplies superstores.

Cross-border alliances are going to be more important in Staples' future. They have grown the business in Europe so far through acquisition and organic growth, expanding into the delivery and catalog business in that region. Staples is aware that there is much to learn about the different cultures and customer needs in Europe. They are constantly looking for additions to their domestic and international teams.

The real difference between Staples and many other retailers—this is one of the similarities between them and the other company I will be featuring in Chapter Nine—is that, in general, retailers talk partnership but what they really mean is:

The more I get, the less you get.

That kind of approach assumes that a finite pot of information is available, which is, in Sargent's opinion, a short-sighted view of the world. His perspective and his strategy for the company moving forward, is "the more we both get, the more there is for everyone to have." As Staples' sophistication grows, so does their view of the world and the mutuality and collaborative aspects of their partnerships.

Staples now negotiates differently with some of their vendors in supplier relationships. Their approach now is "Don't just give me a good price, rather, let's share data so that we could split some of the costs, too."

For example, Staples provides IBM with office supplies and has discussed with them that if IBM could reduce small orders, the reduction could save Staples money and they would be willing to share the savings with the customer.

Now seventeen years old, Staples continues to grow aggressively and will be starting between seventy-five and ninety stores in 2003. It's difficult to think about the niceties of partnering while the company is still in this high growth (hockey stick) stage. Only when their alliances start to generate significant revenues or profit will the partnering competency become an internal mandate. In the meantime, Staples is proud of the alliances they have.

I spoke with David Fingerman from Fleet Bank Financial Services (Fleet Bank), who manages the alliance with Staples from Fleet Bank's side, who had the following to say:

"We knew Staples well, since they had been a customer of ours for some time. We had provided them financial services for some of their banking needs, so when we received the call, it was as if from an old friend. Of course, Staples and Fleet Bank are geographically located close to each other, so in addition to our relationship of banking services, this was a natural outgrowth. But we were still delighted and pleased, as well as interested in the opportunity. Staples has an amazing brand, and the idea of co-branding our Fleet Bank brand, which is known in the Northeastern part of the United States, with theirs, was an exciting possibility."

Fingerman's style is charming and low key, so it's understandable that he and Scheman of Staples created a good relationship which has only become better and stronger over time. Fingerman explained the rationale for the alliance:

"Staples is refocusing their energies on the small business customer, and they have been excited by that for some years. At Fleet Bank, we have a small business group, where we focus on businesses that are $10 million and below in sales. Our objective is to increase market share by providing exceptional value at prices profitable for Fleet Bank so the Staples concept was appealing to us. They wanted to expand the offerings in their stores by providing related products and services for small businesses. Staples asked if Fleet Bank would be willing to have a physical presence in their stores and reach out to shoppers and offer them small business financial services. One of their key requirements was to customize the offerings from the small business owner's perspective so they would get a service from Fleet Bank and Staples combined that would be unique. Fleet Bank felt there would be great leverage for their brand since Staples has such a strong presence in the community."

The financial services idea was one that Staples had had for some time and tested the idea in Canada, where they launched an Internet-based banking service. It was quite successful, and Fleet Bank examined it closely.

Their conclusion was that the Internet approach was not the way to go in the launching of this service in the United States, but that they would rather do a series of physical locations in the United States as a pilot and see how they succeeded. As Fingerman said:

> "We were pleased that at least there was some empirical evidence that this offering would work, and so we were encouraged to look at the opportunity for some locations in the Northeast where we are strongly represented. Personal service is a phenomenon of the United States small business owner. We felt that they would not be ready to take the leap to all-Internet-based banking but would continue to value highly the banker's personal relationship with them."

The program is now in pilot in three locations in Massachusetts, New Jersey, and Pennsylvania. If it meets both partners' objectives, they will roll it out to all the Northeast locations where Fleet Bank does business (Fleet Bank operates from New Jersey to Maine).

Staples certainly has a national interest in doing the program, but because Fleet Bank does not have a national presence in all the states, it agreed that Staples could take this program to other locations with leading banks only with the understanding that if it were successful, that Staples would not assign the program to a Fleet Bank competitor within the Northeastern region.

Some of the metrics used are traditional sales volume per employee, translating that data into revenues per customer, and then rolling that up to look at return on investment (ROI) and payback on their mutual investments.

Fleet Bank made a physical investment. They decided to develop a customized kiosk that was 150 sq. ft. At the time, they thought it would be important to stand out. The kiosk is visible and highly merchandised. Staples shared in some of the setup expenses. Fleet Bank decided *not* to do external marketing because they didn't want to compete with their branch offices. Staples was very helpful in that they gave Fleet Bank access to their Business Rewards–Frequent Shopper list and collaborated with Fleet Bank so that the bank could call these customers and introduce them to the concept. When Fleet Bank and Staples each presented a grand opening, they invited each Business Rewards customer to participate and had a very good response. The focus remained to pursue the Staples customer base.

This program has turned out to be good in that Fleet Bank is achieving higher business checking account sales (which is their core product) in the Staples' locations, higher than they achieved in the average branch. But it still wasn't high enough to justify the overall investment in the program. Fingerman mentioned how they had changed the program once they started implementation, based on the results thus far:

"We discovered that there were a good portion of shoppers in Staples who are consumers (not small business owners) and that about 50 percent was small business. We found that our salespeople were spending lots of time and energy engaging consumers in conversation who were not small businesses but were interested in personal accounts. So we modified our offerings. In the early part of 2003, we re-opened the program with a more balanced approach to businesses and consumers so that we are targeting every shopper now. If they have business accounts, we go that route, and if they are personal, we open personal accounts for them. So it's going well, but it's much too early to tell."

One of the key issues for both Fleet Bank and Staples is the whole area of sustainability. If the objective is to target Staples shoppers, the question remains: Are there enough *new* shoppers coming into Staples to sustain sales volume? Only time will tell. Both Fingerman and Scheman are committed to partnering in some way and have the staying power and patience to wait as the program evolves.

When it came to metrics, the stated goal for Staples was to make Fleet Bank successful so that they would roll out the program in different locations and act as the prototype for Staples to take the program to other institutions nationwide. Staples is a financially driven company and because they are giving up space in their stores, there has to be a financially acceptable payoff.

Besides increased revenues and other financial benefits derived from placing the kiosks in the stores, Staples also gets brand stickiness (the willingness of people to visit the stores more often for banking business and possibly increase their Staples purchases while there) and brand building by having the Fleet Bank program in-house. It also becomes even more attractive as the one-stop shop for small businesses.

Culturally, there certainly are differences between the two companies. Fleet Bank's culture is not typical in the conservative sense of most banks.

They are very profit-driven and doing this program at a time when the economy is not doing well is not without risk. Fingerman commented:

> "I was very pleased to see that our senior management was willing to look at innovative opportunities. But we still are financially driven and have to meet our financial goals. From the Staples side, their chairman, Tom Stemberg was directly involved in the program whereas Fleet Bank's CEO who became chairman in 2003, Chad Gifford, was certainly aware of the program but backed off completely and moved on to other projects. So we were delighted that Tom was engaged, and even though clearly having someone of such seniority and importance involved had its challenges. Nevertheless, this helped us all to cut through questions quickly and made a big statement to Staples store employees that this was important. So there was no real resistance at the store level—which was an important element for success."

Fingerman and Scheman work very hard to have their associates team and communicate well. At times, because of the cultural differences when people get miffed or misinterpreted, they have encouraged close working and renewed relationships. The goal is to look for other opportunities to partner. It must also be remembered that Fleet Bank has a banking business with Staples, so their overriding concern is not to lose their customer, regardless of the success or failure of the alliance.

Some of the cultural differences between the two companies are that Staples is a discounter, so lowest price and free is the mantra which made them so successful. In financial services, the focus of Fleet Bank is value. It's a different approach. Giving things away for free or discounting them greatly is not considered by Fleet Bank to be the long term way to develop banking relationships. As Fingerman said, "This approach might get the relationship short term but won't keep it long term." These are philosophical differences that continue to be negotiated and worked through.

The pilot continues—the metrics are in place and at the end of the pilot, they will depend on those to decide whether to do the rollout (which due to economic times might happen a little slower than anticipated), cancel the project, or do it differently. Good implementation leads to good reviews and re-launch, and a good pilot will lead to a careful and well-planned implementation. The Fleet Bank/Staples approach works for their corporate cultures. Although neither company has fully institutionalized installed alliance management programs, they do have informal but repeatable processes.

Staples looks at their alliances from a portfolio approach. They perform a gap analysis to see the gaps in services or products or geographic regions which they want to fill; those then become part of their strategic planning process.

ValleyCrest Company

ValleyCrest Companies (ValleyCrest) is certainly not the size of Staples, but they are another company that depends on the goodwill and satisfaction of the individual customer. They, too, were started from an idea of one man, one family, and one need. The idea grew as has the company and now boasts over 7500 employees. It is the largest landscape services company in the United States. It is privately held by the same family that started it. The alliances of ValleyCrest are with their customers as compared to many of the other companies in this book who are partnering with others to serve their customers better.

ValleyCrest is one of the best-kept corporate secrets. You see their work everywhere. For example, it is the landscape company responsible for the amazing gardens at The Getty Center in Los Angeles, it will implement the immense renovation and redesign of the Baltimore Zoo, and it serviced the landscape needs for the United States Olympic Committee in both Los Angeles and Atlanta. You see their handiwork at the Bellagio in Las Vegas as well as Caesars Palace, Aviara Golf Club in Carlsbad, California, Cisco Systems's campus, Lawrence J. Ellison's residence (if you happened to drop in for tea), Best Buy's headquarters in Eden Prairie, Minnesota, and, of course, The Walt Disney Company and Universal Studio theme parks in Florida and Harvard University in Boston.

This company has grown internally 15 percent to 20 percent per annum for the past fifty years. How many companies can boast that metric! That means that they are growing at a rate of $80 million in annual revenues some years—not an insignificant amount for a family held company.

Burton Sperber and his brother Stuart, Burton's son Richard (who now runs the company), and their employee family of 7500 are all committed to the same values. Burton Sperber, a gruff, down-to-earth man with no frills or need for obfuscation, says it like he sees it. He writes his goals on three pages which then are communicated to the entire organization in typed form but still in his words. He doesn't call them metrics, but that's exactly what they are. He applies them to the internal alliances that exist between his people and the external alliances that they have with customers. In Burton Sperber's mind, these are the only two kinds of partnerships that matter. He has created a series of alliance development and implementation metrics that center around the belief system of the company and how that belief system must be communicated both internally to internal partners and externally to the customer who is their main and central alliance or partner. Burton Sperber says:

> "Our ethics: Respect, Responsibility, Results—we train our people to do what is right. If we know what is right, we will do the right thing."

This means that the metrics of quality and performance for the customer are specified, and people are held accountable for their delivery by Valley-Crest.

Burton Sperber includes words to live by. These words are also the baseline metrics by which people are evaluated in their internal and external performance with internal customers (helping each other) and external customers (those who buy their services and products):

> "Stay true. Never be ashamed of doing the right thing. Decide what you think is right and stick to it."
>
> "If you don't stand up for something, you will fall for anything."
>
> "To know what is right and not to do it is the worst cowardice."
>
> "Honesty is the cornerstone of our success without which confidence and ability to perform do not exist; our customer must find this out themselves."
>
> "Savor each of our jobs as if they are the last order or job we will get."
>
> "Work each job hard to satisfy each customer and look at each dollar we earn and spend as the one dollar we need to survive. We will be a better company in our customers' eyes."

These homilies are not just words to Burton Sperber, his team, and employees. In fact, when I recently gave a keynote address to his managers from all over the country and from all divisions, the comment I heard the most was this:

> "I have never worked for a company which was like this. This is like my family, my own business. I am so happy here I can't wait to get to work every day."

The average tenure of their managers is eleven years; hundreds of employees have been there for twenty or thirty years. They have second and third generations of employee families working for them. Every year they give away five new Ford F150s to encourage employees to work more safely. Every year in January, Burton offers a substantial amount of money to employees who stop smoking. He makes a point of ridiculing those who smoke in the hopes that they will stop and save their and others' lives.

Burton Sperber admonishes his people to do the following:

"This is a strange time in our country. Bad economy, employment, stock market, corporate corruption, and we are on the brink of war with most of the world not liking the United States. This is if you read the paper. You will get real depressed, so don't read the paper. We're really doing OK. Our employment is up. This year we will contribute $1 million to our 401k plan. We have good backlogs in development of $350 million. Be a solution to our customers and keep our employees working each job as if it was our only job, not just another job or order."

Good advice from a nuts and bolts businessman. The employees and customers love it. It works. Burton will "aw shucks" a lot, but he is one smart *head gardener* as he calls himself in the little internal booklet ValleyCrest has created.

They have made some acquisitions, all of which came to them. They are the leader in their industry now.

Roger Zino, who runs the maintenance division, is a fairly recent addition to the ValleyCrest family. He is different from the rest of the division presidents who were brought up in the company business. He did his undergraduate work at Georgetown University in accounting, was a chartered accountant with Arthur Andersen LLP, has an MBA degree from Harvard University and worked at Ford Motor Company on the line in an assembly plant. He joined McKinsey & Company in 1991 in their Los Angeles office where he spent ten years. ValleyCrest was his client. The reason he joined the company is that the industry, which was unknown to him beforehand, intrigued him. He loved their ethics, he loved the fact that in a privately held company one could do things for the long term, and most of all, he loved the company's devotion to its people. The pull of ValleyCrest for him was that it was not about numbers, it was and is about people. This fact was proven for him in many ways, one of which is the trip that Burt and Stuart Sperber arrange every year with the 65 or more senior managers and their spouses and children to Hawaii for a four-day vacation—a remarkable event. The company is not only a family company, it's a family.

Zino admits that the maintenance area is disaggregated from a structural standpoint. He believes that there are many ways to take the company into the next level of market penetration. The industry is regionalized with lots of local competitors, so the way is clear for a national competitor with high-end local services in place.

The main metrics that Zino has focused on for the maintenance division regarding the internal and external alliances that the company has with their customers and employees are:

1. Customer retention. They measure in detail their customer satisfaction and retention. Pamela Stark, a twenty-eight-year veteran and vice president of customer satisfaction, is an energetic person with creative skills who has generated state-of-the-art metrics in this area, especially about what drives customer retention. They look at retention as a lagging indicator—if you see a problem, you have a system-wide problem that must be addressed.

2. Profitability. This area is driven by their income statement because return on capital invested is controlled by capital expenditures and equipment ratios which are not difficult to watch.

3. Direct costs and overheads. Direct costs are the labor and materials that are needed in the landscape maintenance business to get the job done, and all those ratios have to be carefully watched. For example, in Atlanta the winter grass becomes dormant during the year. As a result, the service ratios will vary from season to season. Their labor cost is critical and is measured weekly as well as daily on a labor report. For example, they will estimate how long it takes to cut a hedge, and those projections are figured into a total labor projection which is then correlated with actual time spent. These data enable increases in efficiency and decreases in excess labor costs as well as better productivity. Of course, as in the business of Avnet and other companies, there is always a dynamic tension between investing ahead of the curve for growth and taking on excess equipment, management, and labor costs.

4. Revenue growth. This is measured in two ways—contract revenues and extras. It is always important to make sure that the contract revenues are showing growth and market penetration. The extras enable them to

bring the full value of the landscape services to the customers by making added suggestions along the way to make the property more attractive and upgrade materials, and so on.

5. People development issues. This is the training of foremen and others in order to ensure organic growth in skills but also the hiring and development of people to deal with industry and company growth and changes. Their 15 percent to 20 percent growth rate has to be planned for. Although the best branches can handle 20 percent growth, the best practices require planning and implementation of resources with good timing to ensure that a delicate balance of being resourced but not overloaded with unneeded overhead, is kept.

One of the key skills of the company is to take an industry with a low-wage workforce, primarily minority and female, and give them an opportunity in the company that most companies do not give. One of Burton Sperber's sayings is that they are "an equal opportunity employer by choice"—something that they did long before any government mandate called for it. The concept of equal opportunity by choice is a metric that Sperber uses to measure the progress and performance of his own company, as he puts it, "not because someone from the government told me to, but because it's the right thing to do."

The majority of their labor force is Hispanic in California and Florida and elsewhere in the nation; however, in Boston they have primarily a Portuguese workforce. Often they will go into a minority community and encourage the people who have talent and ambition to rise to the top, not because they are female or minority but because they are talented. Most of their higher paid foremen are minority employees. They have developers, builders, and property managers who have been with them for twenty-five years. As they grow older, often their sons and daughters join the company and even some of their customers have their second generation doing business with them over time.

Every year they have a management meeting for the officers and the children. The community feeling is such that the children all feel like cousins, and they take pictures of each child each year and share in their successes, sort of like a corporate kibbutz.

"You have to be pretty bad to get fired around here," Burt Sperber told me.

In their fifty-third year (Burton Sperber is seventy-three years old), they will have $611 million in annual revenues. They went public once, but after a short period of time, Burton, his brother Stuart, and officers of the company took the company private again. Their goal now is to keep the company in the family in perpetuity.

Burton Sperber told me about an event that concerned him greatly even though Valley Crest benefited from it:

A large competitor in the industry decided to do a rollup of multiple companies in a variety of different regions of the country. They bought over one hundred companies in less than a three-year period. However, they decided to sell the landscape construction portion of the business, writing off $300 million. ValleyCrest acquired that business and all their employees. Within one week they made sure those employees all got their paychecks and didn't miss a beat. By doing so, they acquired some of the deepest, embedded, and local knowledge of the industry as well as some very grateful, devoted, and loyal employees for the future. In one day, they hired eight hundred of their competitor's downsized employees, many of them business owners who were grateful and thrilled to be back in a family business that was well managed with a great home and comfort for them. They did it at a cost lower than the acquisition cost that the competitor had made and accelerated their own business growth dramatically.

"Look, I started the company when I was 19 years old, with no advanced degree in business, but I know this. Even though we have gone through tough times in the past, our ethics have always stayed the same. We strive to maintain full employment whenever we can. In hard times, and only if necessary, we have closed a few branches and attempted to transfer employees to other branches so that they are offered jobs somewhere else in the company. And we learned early that there is a lot of trust in this business. Most of the people who buy services and products from us are not technically knowledgeable about horticulture, and other competitors may try to shortchange the specifications, such as substituting less expensive plants or materials and still charge the same. We must run our company on our ethics. This sets us apart and makes us more valuable to the customer."

The metrics of not taking the customer for granted but constantly trying to think in the mind of the customer in order to provide what they want—

measuring customer satisfaction, customer loyalty, customer expectations, and actual delivery on those expectations—these are what ValleyCrest focuses on rather than how much money they can make from each customer deal.

Burton Sperber and his team know a fundamental truth: good customers instead of saying "How much can you save me?" say "How can I make this better?" Customers don't give money away, but they not only trust Valley-Crest to do the right thing for them, they work with them on making their projects better, not cheaper, creating landscapes that make their projects great. This idea of changing the conversation from *how much* to *how good* is part of the negotiation element of alliance development and alliance implementation metrics.

Burton Sperber named a number of customers with whom they work who have this special attitude. It is no surprise that they are the same customers that win the awards for the most outstanding landscapes. Customers like Steve Wynn of The Bellagio Hotel cares greatly about how the project looks. Rick Caruso of Caruso Affiliates who built the The Grove in Los Angeles and the Calabasas Commons, as well as shopping centers, goes personally to buy the trees for his projects to make sure that it is not "how much" but "how good". Donald Bren of the Irvine Company does the same as does The Walt Disney Company as seen in The Animal Kingdom where they selected the plants themselves.

ValleyCrest has also built many sports stadiums across the nation including the Angels stadium. The maintenance of every project is equally important in order to retain and sustain value.

Value is a word with great meaning to Burton Sperber. He tells the story that during the divestiture purchase of the eight hundred employees from their competitor, there were heavy negotiations in place. One item was for $30,000, and the company on the other side kept saying "What's the big deal? Write it off!" Burton Sperber's CFO said to them: "To you, a big company, that's nothing. But to Burt it's a lot—$30,000 is a lot because it's his own money."

Besides the money, Burt Sperber puts more credence in people than in anything else. He says he and his brother now mentor and oversee because he doesn't want his heirs to make the same mistakes he made.

I have no doubt that the metrics that Burt Sperber has put into the DNA of his company mean that his and his brother's presence is more than just mentoring. They are a walking embodiment of the things that count daily in ValleyCrest Companies.

Stuart Sperber agrees:

"We don't keep our thumbs on our people, we want people with entrepreneurial spirit to help build the company and bring things along. It's not the money that builds the company, it's the people."

In many family businesses, it's the family that ultimately breaks things up with internal issues—not at ValleyCrest.

Stuart Sperber is an unusual man who does not let sibling rivalry get in the way of his relationship with his brother and their company: "I love my brother dearly. We are each other's best friends, and I respect him greatly. He is brilliant. I am willing to work for him and with him."

The issue of sibling rivalry is one of the less obvious metrics that applies to companies that are family driven or controlled. It infiltrates the issues of succession between family members (parents, children, and siblings) and ego. These are difficult things to measure or even to talk about, but those who see them at their worst will tell you that many successful and lucrative businesses have been destroyed by these problems. In their internal alliances with their employees as well as their external alliances with their customers, family-controlled companies must create a process for handling the concerns of sibling or family rivalries and emotions.

ValleyCrest has succeeded in this arena. I give great credit to Stuart Sperber for his determination to make this family relationship and business work well and his willingness to work with and for his brother. Ego and sibling rivalry have not destroyed this family business, and that is why their partnership is so effective. They disagree often and work it out. Although in public companies, the metrics may be all about the quantitative elements as well as the culture, in family-held companies, the family relationship is an important metric in itself because conflict will destroy the business faster than any return on invested capital or other metric.

Stuart Sperber pays particular attention to Valley Crest Tree Company, which he and Burton founded, and now is headed by Robert Crudup, a twenty-five-year veteran. Valley Crest Tree has the best reputation of any tree grower and mover in California. They have built a company that is known as the standard of the industry. Landscape architects and agencies call for Valley Crest Tree specifications or equal.

To round out the offering of horticultural services, ValleyCrest Golf Course Maintenance is a division which maintains over forty courses throughout the United States. Their U.S. Lawns is a franchise business with over one hundred franchises which provide landscape maintenance business opportunity to the small owner.

Now Richard Sperber, son of Burton Sperber and the president of the company, has extended their employee benefits to include ValleyCrest University where they train people to increase their job responsibility and conduct project management on important initiatives. As Tom Donnelly, a twenty-two-year veteran and president of ValleyCrest Landscape Development says:

> "This is one of the great benefits of our company. We train the trainers, and we look for high-potential people. We look at all our laborers to be future foremen. We will need twelve hundred additional foremen in the next few years, and so it is critical for us to train the supervisors at our university to train the foremen locally. We are an operations-oriented company, so the senior managers train the trainers. Burt does his thing, giving people the ethics and vision, and we use our senior operations people who can teach those skills. Carrie James is a former school teacher, and she develops the curriculum. We take the supervisors into the field and set up job scenarios and show them what is done right and teach them how to interpret plans properly and how to develop a schedule. We do cross training and show them how other people are contributing to their success, and why team involvement is so critical. We show them how to estimate a job and why certain decisions are made and how they could impact them, so that they can understand the dynamics behind all of these processes and they become part of the team."

In order to increase the customer loyalty metrics, they have created a preconstruction services department. This is an expertise that they deploy through talented people who know how to create cost estimates from ideas as sketchy as those drawn on a paper napkin in a discussion over breakfast. After spending time with the customer and understanding their goals and dreams, they help them put together a budget they have customized from off-the-shelf software. This helps them with their ability to think and act like owners instead of thinking and acting as a contractor. They become closer and more valuable to their customers—a definite competitive advantage.

So, to summarize the metrics that come out of the ValleyCrest story, here are those that are most valued and implemented by the company:

1. Alliance development metrics.

   a. The alliance is with the customer (both internal and external)—customer development and specification creation—getting into the customer's head early in the decision cycle.

   b. Negotiation—changing the conversation from how much to how good.

   c. Ethics—create the standard, measure the customers by it, measure yourself by it, and the dollars will come.

   d. Make each customer the only one—measure each job as the critical one—place priority on each customer so that the partnership is clear from the beginning in terms of quality and performance expectations.

   e. Define success for the customer—that now becomes your measurement.

   f. Do what is right, not what is expedient.

2. Alliance implementation metrics.

   a. Define expectations and success continually.

   b. Change the conversation from how much to how much more can we serve you?

   c. Educate the customer about ValleyCrest value—show them how to trust you.

   d. Don't take the customer for granted—measure service and relationship building.

   e. Being part of the ValleyCrest family means we will take care of you if you take care of the customer—we will measure you on that and you can measure us on our promise.

Staples and ValleyCrest Companies—two very different companies with a very similar focus on the individual customer: Each customer is as valuable as the ones before and after, the ethics and the care of the relationship are critical success factors, and the main metrics are those that will deliver all the financial returns desired.

CHAPTER TEN

Hotels and Hyundai

In this chapter, I have gathered together a number of case illustrations of companies and individuals who have achieved excellence in the entire process of developing and implementing alliances with the kind of metrics that are relevant to their businesses and who are worthy of notice. They are diverse: Peninsula Hotel Beverly Hills, California; The BALSAMS Grand Resort Hotel in the farthest Northeastern part of the United States; and The Hyundai Motor Company (Hyundai), the Korean conglomerate, and experiences in some of their early cross-border alliances. The basis of the programs at The BALSAMS and Peninsula Beverly Hills and the connection to the Hyundai way of partnering is the commitment to a community and tapping into the basic human need to be part of one. Another key factor is recognizing and living with integrity. A common factor in all the examples in this chapter is also the informality of process (it's not written but rather learned by observation and experience) and the certainty of metrics—defined expectations, behaviors, and outcomes—which are part of the informal evaluation systems of these organizations.

My goal in presenting these various examples of informal approaches to you in this chapter is to demonstrate that even if your company is not partial to the development of templates, formal processes, and management tools, you can still be successful with informal metrics as long as they are observed in action, consistent, and valued by the organization and its leaders. The stories and experiences of the companies in this chapter will cover different situations, but the common theme is that metrics can be created and customized to fit any kind of organization in any diverse industry. My hope is that these illustrations will inspire you to look differently at your alliances and think of them in creative ways, considering aspects that are in the informal arena, which could serve as observable examples-in-action in order to improve those relationships.

Hyundai

Hoon Chung is an unassuming man, that is, until he begins to speak. Then it becomes clear that he is a person of great substance and depth. Born in South Korea and schooled there, he came to the United States in 1962 as a graduate student and finished his Ph.D. at the University of Pennsylvania in 1970. His first job was assistant professor at Illinois State University where he taught for eight years. After three years in Japan as an exchange professor, he joined the presidential staff as economic advisor for the president of Korea until the president was assassinated. Chung became deputy minister of finance before moving to the Economic Development Bank and finally going to Hyundai as executive vice president, responsible for international finance for the whole group. A couple of years later, he became CEO of the Engineering Construction Company, which, as a peculiarity of the Korean Chaebol corporate structure, acts as the holding company for the entire group. The owner of the largest portion, Chung Ju Yong, was CEO of the holding company until 1990. When he decided to run for the presidency of the country, Chung succeeded him as chairman of the holding company. He ran it until the end of 1992. In the Chaebol (Korean consortium), the chairman is overall group chairman and is no longer responsible for the business of engineering construction but looks after the whole business group of fifty subsidiaries and decides on any business investments and the making of strategic alliances—deciding both on the viability and kinds of strategic investments as well as finding partners for the investment and monitoring the alliance implementation.

It's ironic that alliance management in Western cultures is yet to be given the highest of all priorities among senior managers. Yet at Hyundai, the responsibility for these relationships is so enormous and important, that only the chairman, the most powerful and respected of all the Chaebol executives, is charged with alliance decisions and strategy. This is a highly significant position; partnering with the Hyundai business group was not undertaken lightly—they earned $90 billion in revenues and comprised 20 percent of Korea's gross domestic product. The responsibilities associated with the chairmanship are huge because not only is this the largest business group in Korea with employees of 170,000, but with its alliances, their employees total over 1 million people. There are 16 million people in the entire Korean work force which gives some indication of the power and scope of Hyundai as a partner for any company, anywhere in the world, small or large.

Chung eventually moved on to become part of The World Bank Group, when they set up a department to advise member countries on private sector development and asked Chung to advise them on Asia's participation in this activity.

Chung has said, "I like to make trouble," by which statement he means he is not afraid of new ideas, innovative approaches, and entrepreneurial leaps of faith. But after traveling with him in China and watching him on a number of occasions as he negotiated for terms, kept pushing gently, then not so gently, as he probed generalized statements for more specifics, more numbers, more data, and proof of statements, he makes a formidable partner of great strength, knowledge, and substance.

The metrics that Chung has applied to alliance development and implementation are practices that were devoted to deriving value over long periods of time. Of the approximately five hundred agreements with which he was involved primarily, many have lasted for decades. Thus, the development metrics had to be focused on the long-term relationship benefit for all parties.

The interesting dichotomy that arises out of the proclivity of Hyundai to partner is that they had no formal requirement or process but partnered using a case-by-case approach. This approach may appear as if there were no metrics, but, in fact, there were a number of clear mandates that were used to partner well:

1. Is the partner willing to develop a long-term, intimate relationship with the Chaebol?

2. Are the needs of the Chaebol being served by the partnership? Issues such as these were not recognized by various automobile companies from the United States when Hyundai wanted to learn how to become a fully fledged automobile manufacturing company.

3. Is the partner willing to transfer knowledge to the Chaebol which will enable them to become more competitive or to fulfill a need that is particular to the Chaebol?

4. Are the long-term strategic interests of both partners being met? This means that a partner from outside Korea would not be welcome if all they wanted was a low-cost manufacturer and had in mind to dismiss the relationship if the cost structure looked better in another part of the world without working collaboratively to create the optimum situation in Korea first.

5. The Chaebol is a community. This is probably the driving factor of its creation and continuation. Any partner with a member of the Chaebol is joining the community, albeit indirectly. The metrics of suitability, commonality of purpose and longevity of commitment all feed into that value. Although not written, these are key factors to the suitability of a partner for the opportunity.

Chung explained how an alliance with a United States automobile manufacturer had some challenges due to expectations which were incompatible with the above metrics:

"For example, Hyundai Auto or Motors is a passenger-car maker and is the only original car maker outside the five developed countries. There was an alliance with Ford Motors in the 1980s when I got to Hyundai, but I could see that it was doomed to failure. The reason it didn't survive had to do with the definition of success and the expectations of each partner. The alliance didn't survive since expectations weren't aligned. Ford wanted a partner to produce in Korea at less cost—they wanted an original equipment manufacturer's relationship. Hyundai might not at that time have had the technology, but we definitely had the ambition to become an original automobile manufacturer."

The processes that were followed in the development of the alliance were perfectly acceptable. However, the analysis of the relationship by each partner was very different. When applying our pyramid analysis (Figure 3.2 from Chapter Three; see below), it can be seen that Ford saw Hyundai as an outsourcing manufacturer partner, who would do what they were asked to do and no more.

The level on which the United States automobile manufacturer saw Hyundai was at the lowest or lower levels of the pyramid of alliances. However, Hyundai saw themselves as integrated partners, higher up on the pyramid. One of the key opportunities and benefits from their point of view in the partnership was the embedded knowledge that could transfer between Ford and themselves. They imagined that there would be two-way exchanges of knowledge, that is, not just Ford giving them an order with specifications, but rather, their communications would give rise to the creative opportunity to design and launch a car manufacturing operation for the Korean market as well as abroad, developing Hyundai into a substantial

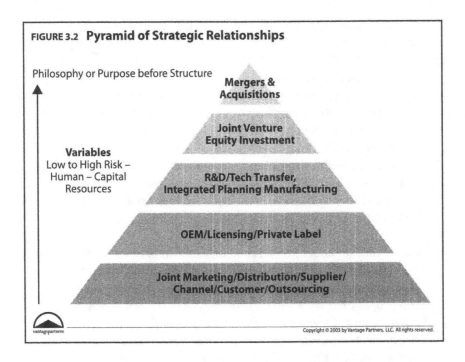

FIGURE 3.2 **Pyramid of Strategic Relationships**

force in the automobile market. At least that was the dream. However, Ford Motor Company (Ford) never heard the dream nor did they understand it. They saw the relationship as a contractual manufacturing one, an outsourcing deal, not an alliance at all. Recently, I spoke at an outsourcing summit[1] on when managing an outsourcing relationship as an alliance can be a competitive advantage. This would have been one of those strategic opportunities for both companies, but it didn't happen.

So after three years, Hyundai, under the chairmanship of Chung, dissolved its relationship with Ford and approached Mitsubishi Motors Corporation (Mitsubishi) in Japan.

Chung recalls how the relationship with the Japanese company evolved:

"We gave them a 5 percent share and created a co-production system—parts like engines were made only in Hyundai and electronic controls were produced by Mitsubishi."

---

[1]The World Outsourcing Summit 2003 in Rancho Mirage, California.

Using our pyramid analytical tool again is helpful here to see how Chung changed the conversation with this partner. First, he looked at the relationship from a holistic point of view. As we caution in our consultations with companies, look at purpose and philosophy first before deciding on the legal structure you will choose. The reason is that you may well change the legal structure, depending on what comes out of the purpose and philosophy discussions. The outcome of his philosophical analysis was that the overall strategic goals of both Mitsubishi and Hyundai could only be served if there were sufficient potential in the alliance for the long term, if the learning was two-way, and if each party treated the other as a worthy partner, with value and contributions to be made in multiple areas, not just in a narrowly defined manufacturing capability. Chung commented:

"I knew that we could not succeed unless whatever we, as the leaders, decided upon was flexible and rewarding enough so that it would last decades and survive the test of time. You see, when we told the Ford people what we wanted for the next decade in our relationship with them, and the extent of our dream, they really didn't believe us. They made certain assumptions and these were not discussed. They assumed that the Koreans would never reach there and would give it up. But we did do it nevertheless. Within the next five years, Hyundai had its own design produced by people we hired from Italy. Ford overestimated the power of their capital and technology and underestimated the potential of the Korean spirit and drive. Ford was not unique and many other Western companies did the same thing. That is why we partnered better with the Japanese. They understood the Korean potential. So with Mitsubishi, we wanted to integrate more with them in partnering."

The pyramid analytical tool (Figure 3.2 in Chapter Three and in this chapter) shows that Hyundai used multiple levels of the pyramid which is exactly how to integrate the relationship in many ways by creating an equity investment and share, a license, a co-production agreement for the design and manufacturing technology, and a long-term commitment which was culturally preferable to both companies from a country culture and relationship based point of view.

Another reason for the failure of the Ford/Hyundai relationship was the influence on Ford by General Motors Company (GMC) positioning in Korea. The GMC local subsidiary had sold part of their equity to Daewoo which was the largest automobile company in Korea. Ford felt pressured to create a Korean-based alliance because their major competitor GMC had one and wanted to capture what they understood to be a growing market.

Hyundai and its family of companies entertained mainly four kinds of alliances: joint ventures, licensing of technology, exclusive distribution agreements, and a variety of consortia, mainly in the construction industry. The Chaebol is a mix of wholly and minority-owned companies. When the Chaebol and its companies are small, they want to keep all activities in the family, literally for relatives. This is an incestuous kind of relationship which is called the *inbreeding* Chaebol and can be quite corrupt with lots of self dealing and internal activities that are not revealed. But if a Chaebol wants to go to the world market and is considering bringing in new capital from outside investors, they have to be much more transparent. When foreign investors come into the family and technology is imported, which means that the Chaebol will develop a variety of commercial relationships giving them access to foreign markets, the intrafamily business approach doesn't work. This has led to the improvement in corporate governance by the Chaebols. Partnering with companies such as Ford or GMC means that the excellent due diligence that foreign companies do has forced change upon Korean companies in their wish to grow faster.

Chung explains,

"Open economies are better. Lots of Chaebols were opened up to foreign scrutiny in the past decade. It has been better for partnering."

The other interesting outcome has been that the strategic alliances that were structured as joint ventures with the Chaebol were much more profitable than many of their wholly owned activities mainly because they had separate accounting systems which meant that they had no need to support the lagging subsidiaries of the holding company and were often created to answer a need in a particular area of growth. The growth areas were mainly international.

Knowledge transfer has been a solid metric of every alliance in which Chung has participated. While he was with the World Bank Group, he used knowledge as a metric in many activities.

"Knowledge is not exclusively a patented technology," Chung commented, "It's much broader. The most important knowledge that needs to be transferred is corporate culture. In general, Korean firms are hierarchically organized and so have many layers of purported decision makers. Actually, there is only one man who decides. All the layers below that top manager are not free to express themselves and are expected to defer successively to the top. Although there may be ten people puttering around in senior management, none of them count, only the one at the top. So, if you bring a foreign shareholder who places an executive in the company who represents their interests, and if that executive is subordinate to a Korean manager and if he speaks out, the culture will be shocked. But this is exactly what must happen. Although it is shocking to see the countercultural activity, it's critical to bring about change."

Chung has lived in many cultures. His concept of cross-border alliances includes the blending of cultures as a good outcome of knowledge transfer:

"My experience tells me that you will have a good joint venture when you have less micromanagement and business becomes more structured in that you know who does what job and that people are exchanging horizontal communication rather than everything going upwards. Free debate and communication are valuable. Sometimes, it is important in cross-cultural alliances, especially in Korean ones, that you have a separate joint venture not run the same way as the other subsidiaries of the Chaebol. Another intangible benefit is if you mix traditional hierarchical Korean organizational cultures with a Western mentality of a free-flowing organizational structure, you will create a lot of tension in the beginning, and in the first and second year, nothing seems to be going right, but when you get over that stage, the tension produces a much better dynamic and result."

The perspective that Chung brings is the long term—creating alliances that last and are expected to only reach real results after years together. How few Western companies have that staying power!

"It's important to be there for the long haul," Chung continues, "There is so much to be learned. The knowledge about marketing is brought by foreign partners, but they gain a lot, too. That partner establishes a beachhead in a foreign country, and once he lands there and establishes a local presence, he can go much further in that country. GMC came in and established a joint venture to produce a car. Then they created an auto financing company. Before GMC, the purchaser could only pay cash or go to a consumer finance bank. When auto financing became part of the new organization, it was eventually more profitable for GMC than the manufacturing side."

Chung is something of an expert in China. Nowadays he spends a lot of time negotiating huge construction deals in China for Western companies and has strong feelings about the areas for new opportunity:

"This is what China is today. There are many absentee businesses. As an economy develops, incomes go up and people need new enterprises. For example, nowadays in China, 80 percent of food produced there is consumed without profit within a week or so after the harvest. So the food produced in China is catering to a very fragmented market. With transportation and processing, this market is now becoming less fragmented and the likes of Del Monte Foods or a competitor will be everywhere. Then there will be competition. Logistical development will reduce production costs and give higher utility for consumers. These are the areas for investment. In the past, we have seen foreigners set up factories in China with cheap labor from which they shipped products to other parts of the world. Now, other people can do the same thing at lower wages, for example, in Sri Lanka, so now China has to look for ways to increase and upgrade value, and this means increasing their activities in the service sector. The next opportunity in China will be to look for partners in the service sector such as hospitals, schools, and education. Thereafter, telecommunications, then transportation, harbors, ports, airports, and, finally, research and development and scientific research."

Chung had some advice for companies partnering with those in smaller countries with less developed markets:

"We wanted to partner with many different companies when I was at Hyundai. However, many of those companies didn't want to partner with us. The other guys had many options—why come to Korea, which is such a tiny market, with a dictatorship not far away, where it was Chaebol family-dominated? This is the difficult part of alliance building when you are based in a developing economy. It's really parallel to being a small company. In Korea, our limiting factors are our own government, which acts as a heavy regulating agency with miles of red tape and regulations, and if you are Korean, you have no choice but to live under this. But if the partner learns of this, he expects you to remove it and you can't. So you agree with your partner that this is bad for the country and the business, but there is an industry that lives on this bureaucracy. This is when you earn your keep for the foreign partners by trying to run interference, help facilitate, and improve the situation. But you can't change it and that remains a limiting factor for Korean/Western alliances."

Chung admitted that the most wonderful part of alliances for him was the building of social relationships:

"Sometimes, even if you are at the top of the organization, you cannot effectively persuade your own people that certain things have to be done differently. It's difficult to tell a boss that you disagree with him, since in Korea, that behavior could mean that you could lose your job. But you can use the foreign partner as the reason for change sometimes with his knowledge and sometimes with implied consent. He is not only the agent of change, he is also the ammunition for you to make change. Through him, your horizons become broadened."

Many of the metrics that we use in the West are not applicable in the Korean environment. The whole concept of an alliances group with a series of rewards and compensatory structures particularly for that group is not a familiar one. USAA (an insurance company for veterans and their families in the United States), for example, in a benchmark study in which I was the subject matter expert for sales and marketing alliances, rewarded their alliance managers for the success of the process, not the success of the alliance. This was because they found that alliance managers were willing to take on difficult alliances that might not be as successful as the easier ones, where these were good for the company and its subscribers (who are also shareowners).

In Korea, the concept of performance bonuses and rewards that were tied to the alliance in any way, were unknown.

Chung explained, "Your performance record will improve, but we didn't have specific compensation for building alliances." This has a lot to do with the cultural aspect of a country where the good of the Chaebol or group is paramount, so that individual rewards are seen to come from group, not individual, success.

Another issue that in many Asian cultures is different from Western cultures, particularly with regard to alliance managers, is the role of women in alliance management positions. I have found in the past twenty years that whereas there were no more than 5 percent of the executive participants in my classes at Caltech who were women, now there are normally 15 percent. When it comes to different cultures, because I present programs and give talks worldwide, as a Western woman, I know that I am permitted many opportunities and much more authority in many Asian cultures than their own women are availed. It is rare to find women there in positions of authority or with the responsibility for a strategically important alliance.

Chung agreed.

"Women have a very difficult time and the higher you go up in the organization, the more prejudiced they are. This is changing very fast in smaller companies but in the big companies, there is a lot of discrimination. These are some of the bad things about Korean business. But there is some strength. Korean companies can take a lot of beating, and when times are bad, the Korean employee will more willingly accept pay cuts rather than laying off people and are willing to put up with long hours throughout the organization, from the top guy to the new employee. This has nothing to do with the family—rather, it's the cultural aspect of the Korean workforce. Our rewards are not just compensation. The company commits to take care of employees' families for the rest of their lives. While I was chairman, there was a flood, and we lost many people. However, it was my commitment to the surviving families that their members will be taken care of for the rest of their lives and their children until they have graduated from college. This is an informal system, not a social security system, but we carry a lasting sense of responsibility on behalf of the managers and people who devote their time to the company."

For this reason, as you could well imagine, the situation is very competitive for positions in companies: It's a lifetime guarantee. Because alliances involve some measure of risk, the irony is that *not* being compensated on either process or success, and having a lifetime guarantee, means that alliance managers in Korea see the opportunity as equivalent to any other opportunity in the organization. When we look at the stakeholder analysis for those in the alliances groups in Western organizations, we see that the alliance group has to work hard to make sure that a position in the alliance organization has a career path and a future series of opportunities for those who choose this challenging kind of project. Measuring performance of alliance managers in Korea is the same as measuring performance of any manager.

Chung understands well these differences in the value of employment, the need for performance metrics in alliance managers, and the path to a good career in the Japanese and Korean cultures:

> "Unfortunately, many Westerners don't understand the subtleties of the cultural differences. The Japanese are different since they are actually less hierarchical. Culturally, they do not encourage anyone sticking out above the rest. The old Japanese saying is that the nail that sticks out will be knocked down. However, the Korean culture is different in that one man comes out and takes responsibility. He makes decisions whereas in Japan one person will not come out and would rather take the consensus from chief advisors. This is why the Japanese do well when it comes to high technology products but are not that flexible when they have to move into new markets. The Koreans take their jobs more seriously than many Americans do—since it means lifetime support and also the culture respects people who are devoted to their jobs. For this reason, there is also very strong camaraderie and esprit de corps among the workers. Another difference from Japan is that face is much more important there. If your company doesn't do well, you have to hide since you cannot file bankruptcy as an individual. So you will see a business man who is bankrupt who cannot rise to success again. In Korea there are many bankrupt companies which come back again and succeed, so we are similar to the United States in that regard."

These kinds of insights can make the difference between success and failure of cross-border alliances with Asian companies for Western companies. Those companies who understand the differences will increase their potential for success.

There are now lots of examples of successful Korean alliances, especially the large engineering companies such as Parsons Corporation in California, information technology companies that have partnered with Korea

Telecom Corporation, and in banking where there are now over eight hundred banks in Korea that are from the United States. The Carlyle Group, an investment house, owns 35 percent of the KorAm Bank. The banking sector before the crisis was only for Koreans and in Chung's opinion that is why they had a financial crisis. "Bringing in different credit and culture is good," he concluded.

Chung's experiences at the World Bank Group also involved alliance skills:

> "World Bank is not a bank—it's an advisor armed with cash which they lend to governments with no interest for 40 years for poorer countries. The bank carries a big stick, metaphorically, and depending on the ideology of top management (they are appointed by the United States president for a five-year term), so the policies will be set. President Bush didn't touch the person appointed by President Clinton, James Wolfensohn. The governance consists of a governing board, and the G7 (global leading countries that are major economic powers) finance ministers really set the policy tone and the allocation of their contributions, which comprise 90 percent of resources. The World Bank sells bonds into the market, and the bond is guaranteed by the governments and is much better than treasury bonds and is lower than the London Interbank Lending Rate (LIBOR)."

There are certain areas in which commercial capital will not invest, for example, a rural clinic, primary schools, hospitals, and drinking water supplies. The World Bank Group fills that investment gap. They apply very detailed scrutiny of all contractors with well-disciplined and highly educated staff. When the people from the World Bank Group speak, the governments that they invest in listen.

Chung was very specific:

> "There are pretty good metrics imposed by the World Bank, but some of the governments are so bad that no one can fix them. For example, Nigeria is an example of enormous corruption. It is almost impossible to partner when you know your partner is corrupt. And that applies to business as well as government."

This is a golden truth of all alliance metrics: The process may be terrific and the metrics may be detailed and comprehensive, but if the will is not there and the ethics don't support the use of valid measurements and accountability (as in many emerging economies but also in companies that are unethical and lack integrity), it will be impossible to partner with these countries, governments, or companies.

The example and experience of Chung give some insight into the challenges of doing cross-border alliances. It is clear that even a wonderful relationship may still lead to failure due to government restrictions and the difficulties of cultural beliefs that lead to different attitudes to decision making and change.

The BALSAMS

So let's move from the enormity of Hyundai and The World Bank Group to a small hotel called The BALSAMS and their customer recognition program.

The idea of partnering with the customer was the key factor illustrated with the ValleyCrest example in Chapter Nine. The BALSAMS and The Peninsula Hotels have similar value systems to ValleyCrest and their results in customer partnerships have also been successful. Learning about how these organizations partner with their customers includes learning by informal observation and reinforcement rather than a formal set of processes. However, there are metrics:

➤ Whether the behavior was done.

➤ Customer response was good.

➤ Standards were met.

➤ Partner expectations were exceeded.

The BALSAMS is a remote resort in the northern White Mountains near the Canadian border. The guests have to go through the Laurentian Mountains to reach the hotel, or if they are from New York, they have to go through Vermont. So this has to be a place that they are coming to on purpose. When The BALSAMS recognized this fact, they began to hold as their highest successes, their returning guests. They began to reward their returning guests in a multitude of ways. Out of this reward system grew their industry best practice customer recognition program.

The BALSAMS has multiple guests who have many homes. At home, they often don't know their neighbors. This hotel becomes more their home than other places because everyone greets, knows, and wants them to be happy there. Steve Barba, the general manager, and The BALSAMS have tapped into fundamental human needs for community in an impersonal world.

Barba told me the day we spoke that he had just returned from a small celebration which happens almost every day in the season—the giving of a gift to a 25-, 20-, or 10-year returning guest.

The customer recognition program is founded on a number of beliefs:

➤ The best partner that the hotel has is their customer.

➤ Customer metrics are all that matter.

➤ Returning customers are proof of value that is far more important than any number that they could measure.

The guest recognition program starts in a small way. Guests get a bottle of maple syrup and a handwritten card with a *welcome back* message. The BALSAMS has 100,000 names on their list for the guest newsletter. The only reason they make a change on the list is if someone moves or dies. They continue to mail the newsletter twice a year. They have found that the returning guest takes on the referral process and sends it to their friends.

The hotel offers the American plan of three meals a day with a full choice of all menus and no charge for anything extra such as skiing, golf, or tennis. The goal is to give the guest the feeling that the hotel is their home away from home, and if they bring their friends, they can invite them to dinner, to golf, or attend the nightclubs or any of the restaurants and bars, at no additional cost. The menus change every day and if you stay there for a week, you will never see the same food twice. The nightclub cabaret shows change every night. All activities are spontaneous and created to be more than you could possibly do. The idea that is so powerful and is translatable to many other kinds of alliances is this:

You get it all when you stay here. You are entitled to it all, but we know that there is no way that you can take and use it all. So that is the powerful tool we use to encourage you to come back. It is a combination of familiarity, belonging, customization, and abundance.

Barba has been there forty-five years, his lifetime, and was a thirteen-year-old caddie when he started. Barba affirmed the compelling business and value proposition for his customers:

"We have seen it repeatedly. It's the aspect of being entitled to it all but not being able to get it all which is our competitive advantage. There is always something to come back for."

The BALSAMS has a coding system that enables them to say *welcome back* triggered by the system when the front desk hands the keys to the bellman to take the guest to the room. They attempt to place people in the same room they had the year before if they liked it. If the code says they are returnees, then the bellman doesn't talk about where things are at the hotel but rather tells the guest about what's new and what's going on that night so they might know there is a special speaker or chamber music. This way the bellman looks as if he is being spontaneous, but its all part of the training. On the other hand, if the guest is new, then he will go through the orientation, for example, when the guest enters the dining room, he or she will be assigned a table that will be his or her table. The new guest will remain in that captain's section and will be served according to a team effort called *the chef du range system* in the industry—an approach in which a bit of Russian and French service has been combined. The service approach is a team effort with a captain and four-waiter staff, one of whom buses tables. The waiters work together: One takes the order, and another goes to the kitchen and delivers the order to the table in the same order it was taken. The idea is that you never have to look for the waiter who went off to the kitchen and then forgot about you! The waitstaff get to know how you like your toast; or that your coffee is always caffeinated for the first cup then decaffeinated for the second and further cups. They become expert on the customary way you like to be served and make a record of it so all wait staff will know it. The result is that guests ask for the same wait staff and the same table; they are even willing to move their tables to get *their* waiter if the waiter is moved. People like to be at the same table year after year and to get to know those at the table next to them, too. Guests like things to stay the same. It seems to give security in a world that appears otherwise insecure.

Many hotels have customer recognition programs. The Ritz-Carlton Hotel was one of the first hotels to create one. Unfortunately, too many times the system does not seem to work accurately. At The BALSAMS, it is a small enough hotel to do this so that their reservations officers can have a guest on the phone, or even a guest's referral, and within seconds have the entire file available. They can talk with a full understanding of the family or individual and their preferences or needs. Barba tracks a *notable* guest list, so that every day he knows who is checking in and out and if there are any special individuals or families that should be especially recognized. Many families choose to spend their holidays there in groups of 12 or more for a week or so in the Christmas or Thanksgiving season or in the summer.

The BALSAMS has an 86 percent return rate. A doorman can note as the party of guests are checking in with New York license plates by looking on the list. If he is sharp, he could actually greet them by name. People are delighted to be remembered. This kind of activity connects to the integrated nature of the customer and supplier partnership—the community feeling that everyone naturally enjoys, the continuity of partnership over many years, the safety of returning to a place of comfort and good memories—all of these factors set the environment for the tacit negotiation which takes place without any conflict. This is what it costs for this feeling, here is where you get it, this is what you can expect from us (your metrics for our performance) and your perception of value (and willingness to pay our rates) is tied with our delivery of these expectations. These are the same metrics that I referred to in the alliance development and implementation metrics— strategic fit and alignment of partner interests and negotiation in both development and implementation. Also, the team selection (The BALSAMS chooses as employees those who thrive when measured by these expectations) and the operationalization of these beliefs are clearly understood metrics, although they are transferred by observation and experience, not by being written down.

The hotel provides the employees with the tools so that they are enabled, if they are greeting guests in the first ten minutes of their arrival, to do a special job. In the guest's room, a card introduces the housekeeper and has pictures of the housekeeper on the card. She also tells them how long she has been there and what she likes about her work as well as a request to tell her what the guest might need, humanizing what is normally an invisible service.

Many contact the hotel. In all, they track about 250,000 inquiries that can be recognized so that if people call again, they will be in the file. For a 203 room hotel, this is a remarkable level of systemization and measurement. The BALSAMS has taken the traditional hospitality of an innkeeper playing a personal role and systematized it so that it is easier to implement. It shows that the implementation side of this customer alliance has been well designed, but most of all, it is bought into by every person who is part of the BALSAMS family.

Peninsula Beverly Hills

Another hotel in the tradition of excellence has a very different experience but is still based on similar metrics and the notion that community is exceptionally important, especially to those who travel extensively on business and who are faced with the impersonal accommodations that most hotels offer. I was fortunate to spend time with Ali Kasikci, the charismatic general manager of the Peninsula Beverly Hills.

Customer relationship management in the very personal sense of the word is the hallmark of Kasikci and his style and approach to Peninsula Beverly Hills. Kasikci installed a process that looked at value from the point of view of the customer rather than the hotelier. Expediency and profitability are two words that do not conflict with each other in his vocabulary:

> "We cannot do something that might be helpful to ourselves if it does not add value to our customer whom we see as the reason for our existence and very important partners. In that respect, we have to listen to the customers all the time and anticipate what they would want, as if it were our greatest wish for ourselves. For example, nothing is more irritating than to find that when you arrive in the early morning and have a meeting that you have to rush off to, that you cannot check into your room without paying for the night before. That makes no sense at all if the room is ready. That happened to me as a business traveller all the time. So, I decided at the Peninsula we would do it differently. Now you can check in any time of the day that you arrive— day or night in fact—it's twenty-four hours a day. If the day is twenty-four hours long, guests should be able to check in and check out at any time they like. Hotels should not force guests to adapt to the hotel's time frame. Instead, operations should accommodate guests according to guests' wishes."

Kasikci's statement is a good example of how the alliance development process involved a large amount of feedback and buy-in that is not something that Kasikci would unilaterally begin without finding out what the customer and partner thought about it. Nor could he unilaterally demand that his people do this without expecting some pushback from them. Hotel management is more about influencing rather than forcing people to perform well. So he began by discussing the idea with his marketing director, sales managers, and front office manager. These managers discussed it among themselves, and then they started to canvass customers, asking them for their feedback informally. They also talked about the concept to other managers in the hotel, basically co-opting involvement and buy-in from every stakeholder in the hotel family. This is a classical stakeholder analysis and the development of a buy-in process which we find in alliance development: conceptualization, internal negotiation, strategic fit of the concept with both the customer and the provider of the service, and most important, crossing the 'invisible wall' from corporate (Kasikci and his good idea) to operationalization (the managers and housekeepers who would have to implement the behavior).

Customers were delighted by the idea, especially those from Australia and New Zealand who had traveled for fourteen to seventeen hours and were longing to get immediate access to their rooms. Likewise for those who took the red-eye flights from other locations or were coming from the East Coast on the last flight and ended up at the hotel late in the evening, which was East Coast time in the early hours of the morning. Many of those guests were only in Los Angeles for the day and would not even spend an entire day in the hotel but would check in and leave on the same day such as on the red-eye flight back to New York, Boston, and Washington, D.C.

Once Kasikci had some internal support from his managerial group, he spoke with his executive housekeeper and her staff to determine whether this was operationally feasible. Could rooms be ready for arrival at any time of the day or night? The housekeeping staff collected data for two months about how many guests checked in and out at what time periods, and how many requested late departures and for what times. They could then examine patterns of guest behavior to see how many rooms would actually be required. They found that by 8:00 A.M. that at least ten rooms had been vacated by early departures so that the suggestion was feasible.

Kasikci is a smart businessman. His collaborative ways reach deep into the community. He passed the idea by a number of his competitors. This is a good example of another area of alliance metrics, the external stakeholder analysis. He knew that doing something like this might create some reactions in his competitors, so he took into account this important stakeholder, the external competitor, and factored it into his decision making. This was politic of him because the Beverly Hills hotel community is rather small. Everyone knows everyone else, and it would take about three seconds for other hotels to find out what The Peninsula was doing. As you could imagine, his competitors all said it would not work and that the Peninsula Beverly Hills would have to quickly give up the practice. The housekeeping staff was also hesitant, but their attitudes changed after in-depth discussions with the entire team, as well as focused conversation on how this could become a differentiating competitive advantage for the hotel in that small but prestigious and highly competitive market. The informal discussions met another metric—the strategic alignment of the decision to do this with the overall competitive positioning of the hotel in the marketplace, as well as the customer's goals and strategies of having the least amount of stress and wasted time in their ongoing commitment to stay continually at the Peninsula Beverly Hills.

Some of the operational concerns had to do with the issues of cleaning the rooms early in the day when guests might be sleeping. So the house staff was asked to be rather quiet, not converse in the hallways, and close and open doors quietly.

After six months of research, discussions, and buy-in (all part of the metrics approach I recommend in Chapter Three on alliance development), the hotel launched the practice using two of their most experienced and independent housekeepers. Housekeeping inspections were eliminated for the rooms done in the early morning. The predawn cleaning involved the use of much dimmer lighting rather than sunshine so the housekeepers had to adjust to this as well as to the need for proficiency in English because the housekeepers were charged with calling the front desk once the rooms were ready.

The system worked. Now housekeepers who take this shift are paid more than the regular shift pays. The option is offered to those for whom this work pattern is appealing. Those who choose this are generally housekeepers who want to leave earlier in the afternoons to spend time with family or take educational courses.

The costs involved were minimal, for example, new hand-held vacuum cleaners that were quieter were bought, which, if the experiment had failed, could have been used in other applications in the bar and restaurant, and there are some lost charges from late checkout and early arrival. However, Kasikci sees the loss of those charges as his long-term investment in customer loyalty. I agree with him; Peninsula Beverly Hills stands tall in the community for highly customized, specific, and thoughtful service to a discerning and well-heeled customer group.

As Kasikci explained, over a superb lunch in the restaurant of the hotel, where my husband and I are regular diners,

"This practice astonishes our customers. And it's relatively easy for us to do. It's all about thinking outside the box. Most hoteliers do things the same old way. I have worked and played all over the world, and many of our guests are international, worldly, and sophisticated. To astonish them with such a small gesture is rare—and it really came from trying to put myself into their shoes. Their eyes sparkle when we tell them that this option is available. And traveling as much as I have in the past, this was one of the major irritants, so it made all sorts of sense to me. We like to think out of the box here. For example, early on when people came from different countries and didn't have cell phones that worked well in the USA, we would make portable phones available to them in the hotel, and in this way they could leave their rooms and could receive calls anywhere on the hotel property. So there are many ways that we can astonish our customers, if we don't make excuses for operational reasons why things can't be done. This is something we should have done long ago."

Summary of Activities and Informal Processes

The process steps that we see in these alliances were followed carefully and are generic in the way that they can be applied to all alliances. Here is a summary of the activities and informal processes that were referred to in this chapter and were used by all three organizations:

1. Alliance development metrics.

   a. Careful conceptualization—idea development and long-term commitment.

   b. Strategic alignment with the overall message of the organization.

   c. Research into the feasibility and into competitive implications.

   d. Structuring.

   e. Cultural awareness and management.

   f. Creating buy-in.

   g. Internal negotiation with operating groups.

    h. Scenario planning.

    i. Team selection.

2. Alliance implementation metrics.

    a. Launch.

    b. Operationalization.

    c. Revision and re-evaluation.

Also, regarding the Peninsula Beverly Hills, the life cycle of the alliance with the customer has been noted and managed. Over the past five years, the practice has been transferred to more house staff, more customers are familiar with the practice, and some see it as the major reason why they choose the Peninsula Beverly Hills over other hotels in the area. The alliance with the customer is now in hockey stick mode and growing nicely while being carefully managed along with the entire customer relationship cycle which is, of course, what the Peninsula Beverly Hills is all about.

From the diverse experiences of Chung in an organization of 170,000 employees whose every move affects the political, social, and economic changes in their country to the 203-room The BALSAMS and the splendid jewel of all Peninsula hotels, the Peninsula Beverly Hills, the informal use of the alliance process which includes metrics large and small lends to more competency and repeatable and measurable alliances that can compete for excellence with the best in alliance management worldwide.

For most people, when the word *coffee* is mentioned, there is no other company that comes to mind but Starbucks. This remarkable feat in a matter of a short number of years has established a brand and market penetration that harkens back to the early days of the first fast food chains that created and defined the category. Starbucks has certainly defined the category of upscale, everyday, must-have coffee. Chapter Eleven delves into their brilliant alliance strategies and metrics.

Starbucks

The Mahatma Gandhi's Seven Deadly Sins

Wealth without Work
Pleasure without Conscience
Knowledge without Character
Business without Morality
Science without Humanity
Religion without Sacrifice
Politics without Principle

G andhi probably would not have drunk coffee if he were alive, but he would surely have appreciated a business like Starbucks. They live many of the tenets of the Gandhi belief system. In that way, the company is a phenomenon. That Howard Schultz pulled it off is a miracle. That the team that now runs it has grown Starbucks to its present size and will no doubt continue to increase its success worldwide is another miracle. Or perhaps not—perhaps partnering is the reason that Starbucks has been able to create a niche in an industry where there was none before. Starbucks' partners with their customers, with vendors, with distributors, and with each other. Their partnering philosophy therefore cuts across all parts of the company. It is clear that Starbucks' metrics are quite different from the normal metrics you might see in an alliance. The customer is seen as internal as well as external. The communities they touch are seen as alliances and are diligently, innovatively and consistently worked, managed, and measured as such. The consumer is seen as a partner, and their experience is constantly evaluated, cup by cup.

Orin Smith, CEO of Starbucks, who brought his knowledge of business and finance to the company in 1990, believes that partnering is part of the very core of the Starbucks belief system:

"We have done so much partnering, in one form or another; it is hard to find anything we do that we do not consider a partnership."

Howard Behar, who joined Starbucks about six months before Smith, with twenty-five years of retail background in the furniture business, also contributed to its huge success. He made up the second part of the company triumvirate of H2O (Howard Schultz, Howard Behar, and Orin Smith). Although he recently retired, Behar remains on the board and is still present in the company:

"The success of Starbucks is about one, plus one, plus one, equals ten. We had to keep doing things in many areas with many partners and customers until we reached the critical mass that established our premium brand in the market."

The company was doomed many times as Schultz snatched it away from its demise, begging, pleading, and convincing early investors that he wasn't crazy, that the concept would work, and then finally achieving his victory of building a brand that is beginning to rival McDonald's Corporation, Coca Cola Company, and The Walt Disney Company in the depth of its recognition worldwide.

But let's start at the beginning. To understand Starbucks' alliances, you must understand Starbucks' culture. Which means understanding Starbucks' history. It's a great story, the stuff of which dreams and ulcers are made.

Starbucks' History

Schultz was not the guy most destined to succeed.[1] In truth, his beginnings were so modest that he could just as well have turned to crime as to profit. The neighborhood in which he grew up was Brooklyn. His entire universe was narrow, and his ambitions were small. However, the seminal event in his life was the painful lack of fulfillment that he saw in his father, which led to his inability to be the mythical all-powerful dad about whom Schultz dreamed. Tragically, his father didn't live to see the great success of Starbucks; a fact that to this day has caused Schultz significant regret and pain.

---

[1]Some of the insights about Schultz were gained from his book, *Pour Your Heart into It— How Starbucks Built a Company One Cup at a Time*, authored with Dori Jones Yang (New York: Hyperion, 1997).

Nevertheless, the most powerful gift that his father did leave him was a drive to succeed and not to give up on his dream even though the odds were against him. What continued to bolster him through the early struggles to grow the company was the value of his supportive wife and family. What made him different from other CEOs then and today is the commitment he brought to community that differentiates Starbucks from many specialty retailers and certainly any other coffee and lifestyle experience purveyor.

This cultural set of values is what Howard Schultz is all about. Starbucks strongly reflects those beliefs, and those beliefs permeate every aspect of their alliances including the most important metrics that drive their relationship selection and management processes.

The H2O team was a group of opposites. Behar disarms you almost immediately because he is transparent in his meaning, without guile and totally straightforward:

> "I was always willing to experiment on new things. I don't believe in holding everything close to the vest, it's not productive. It is far better to try something new, and fail if necessary. Howard Schultz has always been adamant about the quality of the coffee and was willing to listen to different placement of the product. I was the advocate for the customer, willing to experiment on real estate. We all brought different things to the business."

The competitive advantage that Starbucks created from its early years was to take a supplier contract, change it into something much more, and finally, develop it into a truly integrated alliance. This core competency led to the alliance competency that exists today in the company. It started quietly, as the early supply relationships were developed. A very early relationship was with Costco Wholesale Corporation (Costco). Involving Costco caused a great debate among H2O. Costco is a discounter, and Starbucks is a premium coffee purveyor and provider of outstanding coffee experiences for their customers. The argument was: Could this alliance diminish their then-evolving brand? Surely the customers at Costco would not be of the same demographic characteristics as the customers in the retail stores? The irony of the outcome of this debate was that, indeed, Starbucks did supply coffee beans to Costco, but they avoided any brand issues by saying that the beans were roasted by Starbucks, rather than supplied by them. The supply relationship became a huge cash-flow factor for the company, enabling it to increase its rate of retail store growth. So the Costco relationship contributed to the fueling of the growth of Starbucks, the brand of the whole company became further known, and, of course, the rest is history. Nowadays, the Costco debate is muted because the company has grown the relationship so that it is much more integrated. Additionally, the Costco customers have changed to the demographic and sociographic characteristics that are more typical of Starbucks' retail store customers. In many ways, the discounter-aversion discussion is moot.

Another issue in most superstore discounter discussions is the huge leverage that the purchaser has in negotiating price with their suppliers. However, in the Costco relationship, Starbucks felt that they got fair pricing for it, and Costco saw their benefit in providing this upscale product as an element that enhanced their brand. The relationship has taken on the metrics of an alliance—brand equity, customer satisfaction, partner integration, needs analysis, careful team selection, relationship nurturing, service, and many of the implementation metrics recommended in Chapter Four. The result was that Starbucks managed to change the conversation that it had with Costco. It has done this with every major customer since then, so that it became much more about what would satisfy their mutual customers, rather than *how low can we get you to go in price*. As seen in my comments about Staples and ValleyCrest, when a supplier can change the customer's focus to *how great can we both do on quality* from *how much can I get you to lower the price*, the relationship has just begun to change into an alliance.

This kind of conversion is one of the methods that Starbucks uses so effectively wherever it does business. Take its international expansion as another example.

Starbucks' International Expansion

The European expansion is under way and continuing. It has, like the Asian expansion, been a careful learning and culturally sensitive experience for Starbucks. Peter Maslen, who used to run Starbucks International (until he retired very recently), is a highly talented executive who has lived in many cultures and has multilingual abilities. Maslen explained:

> "I have been with the company about four years and when I arrived, there were one hundred seventy to one hundred eighty stores nearly all in Asia. Starbucks had just acquired the UK-based Seattle Coffee Company which added about another fifty-eight stores. Howard

Behar was running the international business and had started it in 1996 when Starbucks went offshore in Japan."

The push into the non-United States jurisdictions started with the use of joint ventures and licensing agreements. The idea was that Starbucks wanted to have a control factor in all their relationships and was not interested in franchising.

"We are control freaks," said Behar, "We are not about to yield control of our brand to anyone. We want equity in our international activities, and we spend a whole lot of time making sure that the people we partner with are as close to us ethically, morally, culturally as possible."

Gandhi would have been proud.

Smith, Starbucks' CEO, has a macro and micro point of view about the importance of alliances for Starbucks, "If I define the concept of an alliance broadly, it has enormous impact and is integrated into every aspect of our business. If I define it more narrowly, still I would say the same thing."

When it comes to cultural fit, however, he is adamant about this point. "When we have partnered with those we didn't check out carefully enough, we have made mistakes. Obviously nothing is foolproof, but we spend an inordinate amount of time with our potential partners, we get to know their families, their communities, their business associates, and do a very careful due diligence on all that they have done, before we take the step of agreeing to partner. And we get multiple partnering requests every day so this is not a simple process."

For example, the Starbucks expansion into Japan started off rather slowly.

Behar explained.

"We were trying to do things the US way when we first went to Japan. We felt that speed was essential and so we knew that we had to partner. And we just could not understand all the Japanese requirements, and we kept pushing back against them. So, things got harder, not easier. Finally, we sat back and reevaluated the whole situation. We told ourselves—this is their country, their regulations, their concerns. We have to see it from their perspective and through their eyes. Let's go with the flow." They did, and immediately things started to improve.

In Japan, Starbucks wanted a partner as well as capital and experience so they created a 50/50 joint venture. Now it owns 40/40/20 because it has taken their Japanese operations public. In other markets, Starbucks' ownership varies from 5 percent to 20 percent. It also has many situations with licensing arrangements. However, as Behar explained, "When we evaluated the idea of franchising, the idea didn't have much appeal since our research told us that many franchise organizations have separate agendas, and we felt that this would be inconsistent with our culture. We like having control, so we didn't create a franchise organization."

Maslen clarified some of the limitations that Starbucks faces with the main metrics that count—people power.

"No matter how great the opportunity for Starbucks, the huge limiting factor is always people. We run out of people very quickly and can only go as fast in our expansion as the people we can develop. We are incredibly people-oriented. This is not like building another factory—it's all about people and relationships. For example, we know that the most profitable stores and highest frequency of visits and customer satisfaction is where the managers have been there one to two years, that is, where they have relationships with customers. Howard Behar always says that '*Starbucks is in the people business serving coffee*' and the whole organization believes that to be true."

When it comes to international expansion, initially, the company didn't have the depth or numbers of talent to go into many markets. That drove Starbucks to the idea of partnering. Then that became its first and preferred choice for international expansion strategy. Maslen continues:

"We understood as we went into various countries that we could attract higher calibers of companies who wanted to do business with us. Additionally, because of successes of the brand, we have lots of companies knocking on our doors. However, when it comes to the partner selection process, we turn over every stone. For example, let's say that we are thinking of entering a new country. Since we probably get over thirty legitimate inquiries every day from each country we are not in, when we go there, we have a pretty good idea of who is interested as well as candidates we could be interested in. That evaluation process could take eighteen to twenty-four months, and by the time we reduce the number to twenty companies, those candidates will be the ones who have strong balance sheets and brands. We then narrow the selection and cull the list down to three or four companies. These three or four companies come to Seattle and present to us, and we present to them. However, what we are really looking at is the cultural fit. If the company got into the final group, they are normally fine financially. So now the remaining open items are all about cultural fit and people values. The key question that is in our minds is: Are their values aligned with the vision of Starbucks? These are very personal, up-close decisions. We do it over a one-week period, but it has actually been two to three years of knowing these potential partners. They meet with the most senior people at Starbucks, and then they find a little time with a secretary or two, and possibly someone from the Starbucks' plant. What we are looking at, is every little interaction so that we can answer the question; Do they walk the talk and act the values of that which they espouse?"

Maslen, Smith, and Behar as well as Hank Suerth, who runs the business alliances group for the domestic activities of Starbucks, speak with one voice, as indeed all senior executives we met at the company do: "If you say it, you must live it."

For example, each one of them in his own way told me the same story which is illustrative of the meaning of the alliance development and implementation criteria which I emphasize so much in Chapters One through Four, called *cultural fit*. Here is Maslen's version:

"After a number of glasses of wine, one evening, when the week of evaluation ended, which was the culmination of the two years of due diligence, one of our potential partners, now relaxed and confident of the partnership deal, made a racist comment. At that moment, even though he didn't know it, the deal was over with that company. We were unanimous: If the leader can't walk the talk, it was an easy decision for us that we could not live with that company as part of the Starbucks' family."

Although you might think that this is too simplistic, remember that everything Starbucks does is aligned with how they see themselves. They are in a relatively simple business. With no barriers to entry, no technology, not costly-to-build stores, no patents, they have only their people, and so their vulnerability is their people. Globally, Starbucks is trying to build intimate moments with the masses. This sounds paradoxical, and it is, but if they can do it well, they will continue to grow strong worldwide.

Recently, Starbucks was named in *FORTUNE Magazine*'s top ten most admired companies,[2] and the Interbrand Consultancy in New York, who list the one hundred most valuable brands, included Starbucks. Maslen stressed the important point to keep in mind about these accolades:

> "If you look at all the brands featured in *FORTUNE Magazine* and Interbrand's list, Starbucks is probably the only one that got there without advertising. Now that sounds impossible until you think about the business we are in. Coffee is the most widely consumed beverage except water. China's coffee consumption is growing at double digits, and coffee has now passed the tea consumption of the United Kingdom. So people can enjoy coffee twice or more a day, and if we do it right, the world can drink coffee in our stores."

It is a fact that customers visit a Starbucks store over 18 times a month and some users come back twice a day. Maslen recalled when he was being trained as a barista (the people who make and serve the coffee in the retail stores) in a Starbucks store; he met a neighbor who has remained a good friend of his since that time. The relationships that are developed between baristas and their customers can be lasting and important to each party. For this reason, advertising is not necessary because people are coming into the store every day and being satisfied.

Although customer satisfaction is an important metric at every level of alliance development for Starbucks whether in creation or implementation , there are three metrics which are an integral part of what they do and measure in every area and region of the world. It is the three-part relationship that they have with what Starbucks defines as communities.

Starbucks and Its Communities

Smith clarified this well, "We need to play a role in three communities so we will earn our right to be there." The three communities are:

---

[2]Stein, Nicholas. 2003. America's most admired companies. *FORTUNE Magazine*, March, 81.

➤ Community around the store.

➤ Community at the country level and global level.

➤ Community of the coffee origin countries.

Smith expanded on the theme of community:

"The days are gone when a corporation and brand can march into a community and not give something back. Our mission is to go into a community and contribute to them. At the store level, we do lots of things in different countries in different times of the year. Recently in Seattle, there was a program around kids, literacy, and conservation. We collected children's books in stores, and the baristas read to disadvantaged kids in the community. Sometimes a customer will ask, 'What happened to my book that I donated?' So the barista will invite the customer to go with them to read to the children, and this ends up being an incredibly important experience for all concerned."

Maslen had lots of examples of the global and country level type of community involvement of the company. "In New Zealand, we had a program called 'lend a hand' where the customer and barista take a local cause and do it together. In the Philippines, the Starbucks Foundation and a local foundation took on a project to build a school in a particular area. In Korea, we collected money and donated the proceeds to an orphanage in North Korea."

This second kind of community, the community at large, is a major benefactor of Starbucks' generosity. Starbucks is a major contributor of cash to Care and many other charities.

Starbucks touches the third kind of community through a number of methods, one of which is its sponsorship of Conservation International. Starbucks' senior management is particularly proud of the company's involvement in the community of protecting the environment which includes the coffee-growing countries.

Behar explained:

"Coffee comes from the earth, and so we must stay close to that origin—so this goes hand in hand with our corporate social responsibility which should just really be seen as social responsibility. This cannot be only a program for Starbucks; it has to be how we live. It is a filter through which we pass your decision making. Like being a parent. Once you are a parent, you pass every decision affecting your child through the parent filter. You are forever changed once you are a parent. Then there are the human rights issues which have to start at home. We want to treat our workers around the world as we treat them here in the USA. We were the first company in our business to offer full health benefits to part-time workers, and we are trying to move our commitments forward an inch at a time as we are learning constantly how to do things better. If we treat each other well, then you should expect that we will treat our customers well. We do it because of our values, and the economic benefits flow from that. We would never treat our people badly in order to make more money. The first line of our mission statement is to treat each other with respect and dignity."

Smith has strong views on this community:

"We are in an industry that has, at origin, had a history of negative environmental impacts. This wasn't true so much when coffee was grown traditionally, but in recent decades, farmers have found it more profitable to cut down as many trees as they could in order to grow sun-grown coffee, not shade-grown. Now various environmental groups are concerned about bird sanctuaries, as well as other species. Additionally, when you go to sun-grown coffee, you are forced to use chemicals since the natural protection from shade is not there. So we work with Conservation International—an important alliance— which gives us thousands of people in the field along with our other alliances with NGOs (nongovernmental organizations) so that we can all combine our strength to save and regenerate endangered environments. We have done this in Mexico. There was an endangered area in Chiapas. So with Starbucks working with Conservation International, we were able to educate the farmers on shade-grown organic coffee and provided them the market for the product and doubled their income from the loans that were made and the higher prices the farmers got. The conditions that we set up are that they add trees and do not cut them down in the coffee lands. This has made a huge difference in parts that are covered and other parts where the land is not developed."

The environmental community is of huge importance to Starbucks, but it's not just an external issue. It is also all about the people it employs and serves. Smith continues:

"What we did in Chiapas is an example of something that became a win–win for the farmer and Conservation International and Starbucks. We get great coffee and also the sourcing of good quality coffee, which, with our growth, is always a challenge and the reinforcement of our culture. But this also adds a dimension that provides people with a noble purpose. One of the outcomes is not only creating great experiences for the customer but also for the people who work in the stores who are more aware of environmental issues than their parents were. It's important that they are proud of the company they work for. It is also important that they work with a product that is environmentally solid. Also we are able to take our good work and bring it alive in the stores so when we sell that shade-grown coffee, this gives our baristas a chance to talk about what we are doing."

Behar said it simply, "You have to keep your soul—doing what is right, not just what is profitable."

Maslen elaborated on the experiential nature of the business:

"You don't often hear of a cricket coach who learned his trade in the library. We know that in the international market, in order to be a good licensor, we need to play the game. It is for this, among other reasons, that we want to own a piece of each region. So, for example, in the Association of Southeast Asian Nations (ASEAN) markets, we own the stores in Thailand and Australia, and in the United Kingdom, we own the stores in that market and are busy negotiating to own one or more markets in the former Eastern Europe. We want to both own and license, so we can be a player and part of every market we are into."

Starbucks' Implementation Metrics for International: Related to Structure

Many of the implementation metrics in alliances are related to the legal structure that is chosen. Starbucks considers the joint venture to be their first choice for international markets because it is part of their philosophy that partners teach them as much as the partner learns from the knowledge that is transferred from Starbucks to them. As the licensor, their job is to provide the right to use the brand, the knowledge of the system, and how to run it as a business. Because most of its joint venture partners are bigger companies, Starbucks doesn't need to teach them how to run a business in general. They are there to provide the knowledge that is particular to Starbucks' business and which overlays general business knowledge.

Maslen explained the international metrics that Starbucks uses:

> "We use two sets of metrics: first, the balanced scorecard for a market business unit like The Philippines, Hong Kong, or Germany. Then, we look at the following:

1. Brand strategy: How does the consumer use the brand and also a strength, weakness, opportunity, and threat analysis (SWOT) which gives us our all-important evaluation of brand health?

2. We look at our profit and loss statement for the business even though we may not own any of it and may only be a licensor. This is the financial metric.

3. We look at metrics that enable us to track how the stores are performing in our customers' eyes and whether we deliver on our promise. This is what we call the *snapshot*."

Starbucks considers metrics number 1 and number 3 to be the early warnings and number 2 to be the rear view mirror. They also look at the equity value of the investment if they hold equity.

What is now becoming a key internal asset of the company is the knowledge capture initiative that is developing. It is about 70 percent complete. It is the gathering of all the combined experiences which they have had around the world into the harvesting of key learnings gained and the incorporation of those learnings into their future market activities. When Maslen first started with the company some four years ago, they had manuals in the stores but none about how to run a Starbucks business unit. At that time, the company imparted knowledge of the business tribally (storytelling by one person to another, one team to another), but it realized it had to capture it in a more formal way. Now the knowledge captured is becoming one of the most important assets of the company.

This system of knowledge transfer is designed to harvest what the company doesn't know and was designed to allow people to contribute bright ideas. At the moment, it is international only but eventually the United States will use it, too. As it is being developed, everything is being done from the perspective of being useful and applicable for the domestic market.

Maslen added some details to the partner selection process for the international market:

"On the day we decide that a particular company is the one, we sign the letter of intent. This is the simplest document that is descriptive of what the final agreement will look like, but it is nonbinding. That is a very important point. Then we go into an intense period of planning and create a strategic plan for the market. This could take six months. After that, we create an operating plan, and only when that is done, is the final agreement signed. Any partner could walk away until that moment. However, every partner we have worked with has respected the confidential transfer of knowledge that happens during this time, and no partner has walked away thus far. Once we get through this time and sign the final agreement, next, most of the management of the new business unit will come to Seattle. For example, with the launch in Mexico, the first six store managers came to Seattle for twelve weeks of training. This is very expensive, time consuming, and difficult. Although it doesn't take twelve weeks to learn the technicalities of opening and closing stores, it does take twelve weeks to understand the culture and brand of Starbucks. The store managers graduate and do a fun presentation to everyone in Seattle, and they go back to start the new stores. They are considered to be founders of that company, and they are the DNA of that country's organization. Starbucks sends people back with them, and at least one person to live in their business for six months."

Wonderful stories circulate in Starbucks about how people have changed their lives and reached dreams they could never have imagined. Maslen told me one such story:

"When we open a new country unit, we also send someone from within our Starbucks system who wants to live there permanently and joins that country group. For example, in Greece—there was a young guy who came to the US to study. To make money while he was here, he worked at Starbucks. He ended up working for us for ten years. Then he heard about the launch of Starbucks in Greece. So he interviewed for the general manager's position and went back to Greece to manage it. Never in his wildest dreams, when he came here as a student, could he have imagined that happening. It's a wonderful story and makes us really happy to see that happen."

Starbucks has also created what they call the *Star team*. These are the Starbucks and coffee experts who go to the new store launched in a different country and make sure that the customers' experience on day one is the same as worldwide. This assistance takes the pressure off the team there for the start-up phase.

Learning about Starbucks was originally transferred from the domestic operations, where the company started, to the international group. Now the tide is turning. The international group continues to take much of their good learning from the United States business but now they are also giving back to the United States by contributing some of their international creations and innovations. One of those is the *coffee master* program, which has also contributed some of its graduates into the Star team.

The coffee master is like the wine sommelier. These are employees who have taken extra classes and have become expert in different coffees. They learn how to brew all different kinds of coffee, they read and study about the origins of coffee, and then they become coffee masters. These experts compete within their stores to become the coffee master for the region.

Starbucks has even designed computer games for their coffee master contestants to play, and quizzes so that becoming an expert is fun. This spreads to all stores in the region and zone. Eventually, someone graduates as the coffee ambassador for the region—such as the coffee master for a country like Japan or a major coffee city such as Seattle. These coffee masters also get to be candidates for membership on the Star team and travel around the world to promote the brand.

Maslen was responsible for the idea. It came about when he and Behar were in Kuwait City, and a young man from India, highly educated, gave an amazing coffee tasting lecture. It was forty-six degrees Celsius as they sat in a pool of sweat but they were inspired. Maslen wrote about it on the plane home, he presented it in Seattle, and then they rolled it out in Japan. Now they have a coffee master conference in local markets and the coffee masters participate in the Starbucks leadership conference. It is expected that the United States stores will do this within the near future. As Maslen said,

"This is one example of being able to bring things back to the mother ship. Another example is cream-based Frappucino—which all came from the Asian stores. We believe, in the international business unit, that the best ideas will come from outside the company, and our job is to recognize and roll them out to the whole company."

Everyone at Starbucks agrees that when things go wrong in their partnerships, and where they have struggled, it was because they ignored their own principles in partner selection. For example, the Swiss-Austrian Business Group was selected three years ago. It was a public company that overextended itself and stretched its management too thin. The parent company could not support Starbucks in either a managerial or capital way. So Starbucks bought the company back. Now business is doing well again in that region.

A whole world of opportunity exists for Starbucks, as well as many markets that have yet to be penetrated. The consumer wants various types of products, and Starbucks is making their impact on some of them: the tea market as well as the ready-to-drink tea market with their very own brand, Tazo Tea; and the coffee market and the ready-to-drink coffee market, as well as ice cream. A $101-billion market is available, and Starbucks can continue to build a strong business which complements their core business in those markets.

As Hank Suerth, head of business alliances which are the domestic relationships at Starbucks, said, "It is really about relationship management, selection of the right alliance, and marrying the strength of two organizations in a market rather than doing it alone. We believe totally in these values:

1. Importance of sharing common vision and goals.

2. Mutuality of benefits.

3. Together we can do a better job than apart."

Maslen adds, "And we learn so much from our partners, the same way as the partners learn from us. And that is where the value of partnering makes Starbucks a much stronger brand and presence in the market."

Suerth has taken the domestic alliances of Starbucks and made them blossom and grow. In his energetic way (as a former Big Ten basketball and baseball player of considerable skill and a continuing athlete), he strides with long legs across the colorful floors of Starbucks headquarters, starting his day early and ending it late. His enthusiasm for the brand, culture, products, partners, and the concepts around which partnering takes place at Starbucks is enormously appealing. His skills at relationship building make both internal and external alliances part of his DNA. His experience in the North American Coffee Partnership, the hugely successful joint venture with PepsiCo that gave rise to the cannot-stop-drinking-it Frappucino®, is invaluable to the company. His committed management of relationships with partners in good times and bad facilitate even the toughest collaborations.

Suerth's group is responsible for all the business in the United States that is not in the retail stores—and it is considerable. This business includes the PepsiCo, alliance mentioned above, with Doubleshot (a yummy pick-me-up bottled drink), Frappucino, Dreyers Grand Ice Cream, the alliance with Kraft regarding distribution for Starbucks in the supermarkets, and supply arrangements for companies like United Airlines and Barnes & Noble. In addition, Suerth is responsible for alliances with colleges, universities, travel and leisure, hospitality, and more. Suerth is a busy guy.

This means he has to be organized. Our consulting firm, The Lared Group (now Vantage Partners), has been working with Starbucks on a number of strategic alliance-related projects over the past years and has watched Suerth multiprocess many alliance issues, while mentoring younger employees (a role he enjoys) and driving the business forward. Because he was president of a consumer electronics company before joining Starbucks, he has excellent management skills, which are a prerequisite to being a good alliance manager, or what he calls a *mutuality advocate*.

> "Over 25 percent of Starbucks' customers first became involved with our brand through an experience in a place other than the Starbucks retail store. So it is essential that this experience is a good one, or it will affect our brand negatively. The consumer does not differentiate the source of the coffee experience they received but rather the quality of the experience."

The metrics that are of great importance to Suerth in his activities include those that apply to his people:

> "We train over 3000 people through our learning group to make sure that they can meet our quality standards, and we work closely with our partners to help them be more efficient. Our product and experience is very labor intensive, and it is critical that our partners understand the tangibles and intangibles of the Starbucks product."

Suerth's group shares what they do well with their partners who generally work very hard to absorb that knowledge. Suerth commented:

"Regarding our people and the people we work with within our partners, it's important to draw upon everyone's past experiences from diverse backgrounds and to look at things from your partner's point of view. We constantly challenge ourselves to answer the following questions: How can Starbucks be considered easy to do business with? How can we make our partners more profitable? We always consider the partner and try to understand and anticipate their points of view. We look at our efficiencies from an operations standpoint and see how we can use those to help our partners. Margins can be helped in many ways so my major focus is how I can help my partner to do better in their business in general, and in specific, with us."

Suerth has an interesting approach to competitors:

"I respect the competition. I also respect our customers greatly. We like to learn from everyone. There are markets and channels we have not pursued and are now on my radar screen, so sometimes competition makes you look at new ideas a different way."

The focus of the business alliances group is on metrics which mainly concern alliance implementation. Many alliances are in the startup stage, some are in hockey stick, and a few are in the mature stage. The approach at Starbucks is to apply the same energy, brand quality education, and commitment to all their alliances, regardless of the life-cycle stage, because the company sincerely believes that every single customer experience, whether in a retail store or a nonretail environment, has a cumulative effect on the value and sanctity of their brand.

Starbucks does not like to think of itself as a process-driven company. There are no reams of charts, intricate processes, and levels of paper that need to be plowed through at the company. It's a company that communicates a lot—people to people, more than memo writing. But there is no doubt that the company has definite rules, expectations, boundaries, and mores, all of which have to do with the tenets of the Gandhi philosophy—but especially the one that says there can be no "*Business without Morality.*" When it comes to the metrics of their alliances, measuring morality, integrity, values, cultural fit, and consistency of beliefs are the key metrics that differentiate them both as a company and as a partner from the world around them.

In Chapter Twelve, I will show you an 'out-of-the-box' perspective of the world that has to do with multiplayer gaming principles before I summarize what we have covered in our alliance metrics journey together and give you an action steps template to apply to your company and experiences.

Computer Games and Alliance Metrics: The Un-Metrics

B ecause this chapter is about the 'un-metrics' and this book is about metrics, it will be a short chapter! There are a couple of thoughts about computer gaming that have interesting relevance to alliances and may not be generally known.

Computer games have defined an entire generation of young people along with thousands of mature adults who *play to win in a world within their control.* Begun on-line originally as a side activity by students using the Internet as a communication and gaming tool, computer games have developed into a multibillion dollar ($7 billion) industry. In 2001, the development time of a computer game was approximately 18 months from the design specification to the release.[1] This phenomenon is changing the way vast numbers of people interact with each other—virtually, globally, and fundamentally. As J. C. Herz, an expert in the multiplayer game industry says:

> "If the gamer doesn't understand something, there is a continuously updated, distributed knowledge base maintained by a sprawling community of players from whom he can learn. Newbies are schooled by more skilled and experienced players. Far from being every man for himself, multiplayer online games actively foster the formation of teams, clans, guilds, and other self-organizing groups. The constructive capabilities built into games allow players to stretch the experi-

---

[1] *Gaming the System: What Higher Education Can Learn from Multiplayer Online Worlds* by J. C. Herz (@joysticknation.com). Unpublished paper.

ence in new and unexpected directions to extend the play value of the game, and, in so doing, garner status—customer maps, levels of characters, and game modifications are all forms of social currency that accrue to the creators of customer content as they are shared among players . . . games fully leverage technology to facilitate edge activities—the interaction that happens through and around games as players critique, rebuild, and add onto them, teaching each other in the process. Players learn through active engagement not only with software but with each other."

What is the relevance of this multiplayer game theory in a book on alliance metrics? In multiplayer games, the players contribute their intelligence to the artificial intelligence that is engineered into the system. The system's architecture is so designed that it encourages players to innovate. Not every player will contribute and innovate. But if only a small percentage of them do, for example, 1 percent of the players who are playing a specific computer game called Quake, which has 1 million players at any given time on-line and playing the game, constitutes 10,000 people who are innovating or in research and development. The group dynamic that has been created around Quake was not the result of any game company telling the players to do it. As Herz continues:

"These group dynamics are best represented by the large network of self-organized combat clans that vie for dominance on the Internet. They just emerged in the beta test for Quake and have persisted for years. There are thousands of them. The smallest have five members and the largest have hundreds and have developed their own politics, hierarchies, and system of governance. They are essentially tribal groups and each has a name, its own history, and signs of identification. They even cluster into transnational organizations adopting a share moniker (way to be recognized) across national boundaries and a loose federalist structure . . . it is a highly cooperative system (even though clans are competitive) . . . that runs far more efficiently than any 'official' organization . . . because clans have a set of shared goals. They are mutually dependent on the shared spaces where gaming occurs whether those spaces are maintained by gamers for gamers or owned and operated by game publishers like Sony, Electronic Arts, etc."

Sound like business environments? The game and the gaming process develop relationships between players, between groups of players with individuals, and also with groups. The system itself evaluates and measures those who participate in it. What this means for alliances is that if given the opportunity, people will create and innovate, contribute, and gain energy from each other if the environment is right and supportive of this activity. Certainly computer gaming on-line is a voluntary activity; it's fun, absorbing, interactive, and can be done any time of the day or night. Can alliance work be reconstituted in this way so as to create the same energy? One might think that metrics would put a cold compress onto alliance activity, along with the freedom to exchange information in a networked environment because there are competitive issues and contractual constraints in place. But the gaming environment teaches us that it's possible to create an environment where the culture can grow independently and encourage participation and innovation.

You cannot measure everything in an alliance. Some things require self-generation, an ecology of connections that generates excitement and innovation, the desire to contribute, and the excitement that goes with the newness, the creativity, the outcomes, and the people involved.

NASA's space program has created that kind of dedication and dependency among those who participate. The tragedy of the Challenger and Columbia shuttles and the losses of their teams were what received huge publicity and accolades. Yet, no less were the losses suffered by the thousands of those who worked on every aspect of the shuttles from design to maintenance as well as training, evaluation, and more. The ecology of that community was fractured and damaged with great pain at the loss of lives, but the commitment, belief systems, dedication, and faith of those many who were affected enabled the system and delicate internal alliances that had formed to re-grow, re-position, and re-launch the program again so as to achieve the greater vision and goal that is humankind's exploration of space. The game was real.

Alliances must be given that chance. The focus on metrics must take into account the more intangible element of what happens when people interact, grow to respect each other, have fun, and create something new and valuable that contributes to their companies and, in some instances, to society as well (see Starbucks' dedication to the community and environment in Chapter Eleven).

It is important that these concepts be kept in mind in a book on alliance metrics because it is easy to become so structured, so quantitative, and so process-driven that you allow the joy, the fun, and the potential for inter-personal innovation and group dynamic growth that evolves so skillfully in a multiplayer gaming world to slip away.

How does one include this evolving spirit and gaming ecology in an alliance with an external company? It depends on the creation of a teaming approach. I have placed a lot of weight on the development of the team, its selection, the need to have more than one person as a champion because that is too risky in these days of lateral moves, downsizing, and job changes. But the creation of a team is merely the first step. As Jeff Clarke of HP mentioned at the beginning of the integration process, "They were just names." The initiative and project developed its own momentum. As people who were the best in what they did were selected and they themselves selected those they thought were best in their own departments, the momentum took off and the community began to grow.

Developing a community around the alliance is a critical element of enabling the self-powered, innovative environment where energy, fun, excitement, and the psychic rewards can inure to the participants.

This could take the following form:

1. Co-locating the teams in a separate environment, which could also solve the knowledge transfer concern of having potential competitors' employees wandering around your offices or plants. This kind of setup is one that the division of IBM, Lotus, has done on occasion when co-developing software with companies that are actual or potential competitors in other market applications. What will happen is that a different culture will develop between the players in this kind of alliance. If that is acceptable and desirable, the geographical co-location could be an excellent solution for the multiplayer alliance.

2. Co-locating the teams in one of the partner's environments could be beneficial if one of the partners has a culture that is desired to be the dominant culture in the relationship. Namely, if there is great value to both partners in having the one partner learn and adopt for the purpose of the alliance, the other partners culture. A good example here is Starbucks who wants very much for its partners to learn all about its culture, its approach to the customer, its attitude, its knowledge of coffee, and its perspective in the marketplace. It is pleased to have its partner representatives in its teams reside in their offices in Seattle in order to better imbibe and adapt to the Starbucks experience.

3. Marketing symbiosis means putting together a series of logos (monikers and logos become part of the gaming communities as they create clans and tribes to compete with other groupings of clans and tribes). We (The Lared Group) were working with a series of food-service companies who had strong feelings about how the alliance would be presented. Their corporate logos were jointly branded, but the alliance itself had a mini brand that was for their internal use only. The corporate brands were of global significance and the teams of image makers that work in public relations and corporate branding as well as their outside advertising consultants worked long and expensive hours to be sure that the brands were the same size, located in the appropriate space on every document, and so on. But the real brand that had lasting value to the teams that were working on the group activity was that which they created themselves. Those with artistic ability created the logo, and the various departments who had the skills and techniques put the internal mini brand on clothing which the team would wear, as well as other products such as mugs, bags, and so on. This internal activity led the group to feel more like a community. Because the internal branding happened, innovation and information transfer have increased. The metrics that have been applied have been after the fact. In other words, the real happening here was the creation of the logo, then the community that followed. Measuring the output of the teams, and the various metrics of the implementation of the alliance were the benefit. But the real issue is that the measurable results of the alliance may well have been less impressive had the community of the teams not developed.

4. Recognition by the partner companies as a subculture worthy of respect means that the partner companies are willing to allow the development of a subculture. The same way that those in marketing may look upon those in engineering as a subculture, the subculture of blended alliance teams can add great value to both companies and the activities of the alliance, as long as their subculture is not seen as a threat. An example would be The Walt Disney Company (Disney) alliance team that is employed by HP but work on the Disney alliance. They are not employed by Disney but have a deep understanding and appreciation of the Disney culture. Similarly, with those of the AOL Time Warner team who are at HP, their goal is to integrate themselves as well as possible into their alliance partner's culture. In this way, the alliance managers who may do well on a particular alliance should be selected for his or her ability to

subsume themselves into the culture of the partner so well that they can get into their heads, understand their needs, and anticipate areas for present and future collaboration. The more symbiotic the relationship of the managers becomes, the more likely it is that the environment of innovation, learning, and partnering mutual contributions will increase. In this way, value can be created in new alliances by using great care in team member selection with the gaming community insights in mind of the value that can be added when communities are left to grow and bond themselves. This is also a good technique for *re-launching* stagnant alliances. Moving them into different environments, creating different teams, merging the groups into a working environment that encourages the development of a subculture will set up the natural biological organism that approximates those found to be so successful in multiplayer game environments.

The final chapter, Chapter Thirteen, summarizes where we have been and how your alliance metrics journey can benefit from what you have learned in our time together.

Wrapping It All Up: Summary and Action Items

The best approach to alliances is to see them as a continuum of activities, rather than only a huge effort at the front end, with heavy negotiations and diminishing energy over the life of the alliance. The alliance development metrics will assist you to put the emphasis where it should be—not leaving out any area in the process of conceptualization to planning to partner qualifications and evaluation to launch. The companies that are superb in this inception stage are IBM, with their major commitment to process and partner nomination and evaluation, and Hyundai who sees the partner continuum as many years, even several decades and, therefore, worthy of great upfront care, planning, and relationship development.

The alliance life cycle stages are a perspective—a way of looking at your partnerships with metrics that change as the life-cycle stage changes and with a flexibility of approach that will facilitate change, for that will surely happen in every alliance. Remember that the metrics which may be put into the contract are the inception and development metrics because a company cannot contemplate all the relevant metrics that will come up as the alliance grows, matures, and possibly declines sooner or later in its life. This part of the metrics game is best demonstrated by HP as it integrated the Compaq acquisition by looking at the integration as a process, not an event, and its continuation long after the companies became one entity. They have continued to manage according to the integration metrics and have made those expectations part of their operating plans.

The five stakeholders of alliances are managed with excellence by Valley-Crest Companies. As a company, it takes to heart the world of its customers, employees, and its industry. It sees those relationships as integral to its success, as does Starbucks. These are companies that do not consider profitability to be the most critical part of their value. Regardless of the fact that one is public and the other private, the way they consider and treat their employees and customers is the very essence of what they are about. The external public is well served by the environmental awareness of both companies as they derive their very existence from the earth, that is, ValleyCrest from the surrounding landscape and Starbucks with the coffee they sell. They consider their social responsibilities to be more than enabling their employees to earn a living and providing their customers with good products and service. They believe they need to be good citizens of the world, too. Their relationships with all their partners, internal and external, represent best practices worthy of emulation.

Chapter Five, Avnet: The Master Distributor, presented the best in class of those companies who are in the middle of supplier and customer and are always serving two masters. They have grown, thrived, survived, and prevailed in reinventing themselves and their divisions as the technology industry has changed around them from high growth to depression. Their ability to lead, serve, and partner with those who have different interests on each side of the supply continuum while providing service and innovation has become a gold standard for managing alliances with companies who could at one time be a competitor as well as a partner. The best practices they espouse in global partnering, supply chain management, and customer customization are excellent takeaways for you to apply to your own business.

Local, state and federal governments in any culture are not easy partners. They are generally large, demanding, bureaucratic, and inflexible. However, two businesses have taken the assets of these relationships and leveraged them into profitable, meaningful, and mutually beneficial businesses for both the governments which they serve and the entrepreneurs who have built them. Lurita Doan of New Technology Management and Beverly Bailey of Stronghold Engineering have refined partnering with the government into processes that work. Through their constant focus on quality with their own suppliers and partners, they have delivered consistently excellent results in their private and public partnerships and have grown substantial private companies. Their approaches are good role models for those focused on government partnering.

Few compare with the broad scope and reach of the IBM approach to alliances in their ISV and software group. However, what works for them may not work for you in that the program requires full buy-in from all levels of management in the company and resources which may be beyond some companies. Nevertheless, following a process with the IBM level of intensity is a good example of what can be done if the will is there. The metrics implemented across the continuum of the alliance life cycle by IBM are an impressive example of best practices.

I do believe that the HP/Compaq integration reflected upon in Chapter Eight will be seen as the prototype of what should be done to integrate two firms for consolidation reasons. The results that HP has reported in cost savings are an important metric of proof of the merger's success. Keep your eye on HP. Regardless of changing or difficult times in the technology world, the company has staying power, inspirational leadership, and commitment to their core beliefs and values. It is an example of how to blend seemingly incompatible cultures together.

Staples is a company that partners with a defined focus on their ultimate customer—the small business owner. In their partnership with Fleet they have applied the down-to-earth commitment and simply stated value system of being the best option for that customer with one-stop shopping for all customer needs. They have few partnerships, relatively speaking, and devote careful attention to each of them. This approach is important for companies with a clearly defined mission and a focused customer base. Perhaps their best practices fit your company's profile.

Starbucks is comparable to none. They are a phenomenon that created and defined an industry. One of the takeaways from their story is that alliances can, if measured effectively, expand the brand into a level of critical mass that makes it eventually appear omnipresent, more valuable, and explode the core business effectively into worldwide markets. Using the alliance strategy that Starbucks did, where it created partnerships wherever its customers might travel—airports, hotels, international locations, as well as right near customer homes and bookstores—created an industry and a niche where none had lived before. Measuring customer satisfaction and employee commitment as well as social responsibility are key metrics for Starbucks in its alliances that you might want to think about with respect to your own company.

Finally, the concept of computer gaming is intellectually mind stretching for you to consider. What aspect of your alliances could be augmented by the vital nature of the gaming industry? How could utilization of your product, service, and partnerships be enhanced by applying some of the adoption principles that have evolved out of multiplayer games? Pondering these thoughts will hopefully help you to think out of the box, similar to the way the Peninsula Beverly Hills, The Balsams in the northeastern United States and Hoon

Chung, former chairman and CEO of Hyundai, have made their mark in their worlds. Alliances can be an area of great risk and reward, infusing true innovation, market penetration, energy, and new life into any company.

Choosing Metrics

The time has come to put together an action plan for your company using many of the principles we have covered in the past twelve chapters. Here are some suggestions for that template:

Remember the areas of investigation that must be asked of every alliance so you will know which set of metrics are appropriate:

➤ Alliance life cycle—the *activities* in each life cycle, the *culture* of each life cycle, the *managerial personality* most suited to each cycle, and the *priority* of the alliance and how it changes through each cycle as seen in Chapter One.

➤ The five stakeholders—analysis of the steps covered in Chapter Two, that is, the metrics that are relevant to each stakeholder, which means looking at: 1) the alliance from the points of view of the partners; 2) management; 3) other functions within each partner; 4) external analysts and competitors and the market; 5) the alliances group and managers; and 6) answering the questions as to where you are, where do you want to be, and what do you need to do to get there, then developing action steps to implement the answers.

➤ Alliance metrics group—Alliance *development* metrics (Chapter Three) and alliance *implementation* metrics (Chapter Four).

Alliance Development Metrics

An analysis of the steps covered in Chapter Three, that is, conceptualization, strategic alignment, development, strategic fit, planning, selection, structuring, negotiation, and team selection should answer the questions of: where are you? Where do you want to be? What do you need to do to get there? Out of this analysis will come your list of action steps.

Alliance Implementation Metrics

An analysis of the steps covered in Chapter Four, that is, operationalization, implementation launch, remediation, restructuring, re-evaluation, re-negotiation, re-launch, and termination should answer the questions of: Where are you? Where do you want to be? What do you need to do to get there? Then, you can develop action steps to implement these answers.

The lessons learned from Chapters Five through Twelve apply to all the alliances in your company and your schedule of action steps, that is, timing, resources, and results contemplated, as well as the metrics of your action steps, that is, what, when, how much, why, where, milestones, priorities, resources, buy-in, alignment, termination, and competitive factors.

If you complete this template of both analysis and action, you will be well along the road to adapting your alliance management to take into account the myriad of metrics that are relevant to its every aspect. You are now the implementer of best practices for your company and I congratulate you!

Postscript

Since this book was originally published in 2005, I have sold my shares in Vantage Partners LLC, and although I remain as Partner Emerita, my partners are the ones who continue to grow the firm and consult in the arena of Strategic Alliances.

I now have a portfolio career as a Board member of public and private companies, as well as serving on the Board of The National Association of Corporate Directors for Southern California, The Board of Trustees of Southwestern Law School, the Entrepreneurs Board of UCLA Anderson School of Business and as Chair of the Foundation and Vice Chair of the Governing Board of a global Women's CEO's Group, The Committee of 200.

Alliances continue to be an integral part of every position I hold, including offering Strategic Advisory services to a number of Entrepreneurial companies. They apply also in the private/public sector partnerships that are part of the philanthropic world in which I now play a role. I have created two endowment funds for up-and-coming young women in business and in law, and continue to observe how important structure and process is for 'paying it forward' to future generations in the alliance world. I can be contacted through my email lsegil@lsegil.com or my website www.lsegil.com.

Index

A

Account manager, channel
   partnerships, 31
Adopt and go theme, Hewlett
   Packard/Compaq merger, 164–165
Adventurer manager, 21–22
Aerospace market, Avnet Electronics
   Marketing (EM), 93–94
Agilent, 164
Alliances
   alliance metrics stages. *See*
      Development stage;
      Implementation stage
   development stage, 39–62
   environments for participants, 258
   implementation stage, 63–84
   life cycle, 7–24
   stakeholders, 29–38
   subcultures in, 259–260
Alliances, case examples
   Avnet, 87–115
   BALSAMS, 228–231
   Hewlett Packard/Compaq merger,
      159–192
   Hyundai, 216–221
   IBM, 135–157
   New Technology Management, Inc.
      (NTMI), 124–133
   Peninsula Beverly Hills, 232–236
   Staples, 194–205
   Starbucks, 237–253
   Stronghold Engineering Inc., 117–124
   ValleyCrest Company, 193, 205–214
American Express Company, and
   Staples, 199
Analysts, as stakeholders, 36–38
AOL Time Warner, subculture of
   alliance, 259–260

Asia *See* China; Japan; Korea
Australia, Starbucks in, 247
Automatic Data Process (ADP),
   Staples, 197
Automobile industry, Hyundai, 216–228
Avnet, 87–115
   as hockey-stick stage alliance, 12
   and Intel Corporation, 90, 92, 98
   investor relations, 113–115
   number of alliances, 87
   shared services, 111–113
   supply chain solutions, 89
   See also Avnet Applied Computing;
      Avnet Computer Marketing; Avnet
      Electronics Marketing (EM)
Avnet Applied Computing, 96–103
   alliances, types of, 97–98
   basic operation of, 97
   customer alliances, 98
   daily discipline model, 102
   process builder tool, 99–102
Avnet Computer Marketing, 103–106
   and Cisco Systems, 103
   customer information management
      system, 106
   customer relations, approach to,
      104–105
   and Digital Equipment, 103
   global strategy, 104
   and Hewlett Packard, 103, 107–109
   and IBM, 103, 109–111
   strategic areas of metrics, 105–106
Avnet Electronics Marketing (EM),
   88–96
   aerospace market, 93–94
   connection with supplier products,
      91–93
   evolution of, 90–91

Avnet Electronics Marketing
  (*continued*)
  future market focus, 94
  global strategy, 90, 94, 96
  Internet alliances, 90
  products/services continuum, 95–96
  professionalism, concept of, 95
  success, measure of, 88–90, 94
  value propositions, 91, 95
Avnet Enterprise Solutions, 104
Avnet Fast Build, 97–98
Avnet Hall-Mark, 109, 111
Avnet Manufacturing Spec, 98
Avnet Partner Solutions, 104
Azzi, Michael, 148, 155

B

Bailey, Beverly, 117, 119–120
BALSAMS, 228–231
  customer recognition program,
    229–231
Banking, global alliances, 227
Barba, Steve, 229
Bark, David, 111–112
Barnes and Noble, and Starbucks, 252
Behar, Howard, 238–239, 241–243,
  245–247, 250
Best value approach, government
  contracts, 121
Bet-the-farm stage, 24–25
Blackmore, Peter, 177–178, 189
Bouchard, Gilles, 163
Bowick, Sue, 164
Branding, IBM, 145
Braun, Barbara, 172, 174
Bryant, Andy, 88, 90, 92, 94, 95
Business development plan, 42

C

Camp David accords, 59
Capellas, Michael, 14, 160, 164, 167,
  176, 189
Carlyle Group, and KorAm Bank, 227
Chaebol (Korean consortium), 216–225
  corporate structure, 216–217
  executive roles, 216

  Hyundai, 216–221
  inbreeding type, 221
Challenger shuttle disaster, 257
Chambers, John, 135
Change, change management skills, 9
Channel partnerships, 29–31
  account manager, 31
  challenges to, 30–31
  executive, 31
  marketing manager, 31
  operations manager, 31
China
  investment areas in, 223
  U.S. alliances, 90
China ECNet, Avnet alliance, 90
Chung, Hoon, 216–228
Church, Steve, 91
Cisco Systems
  acquisitions, approach to, 173
  and Avnet Computer Marketing, 103
  portfolio management, 35
Clarke, Jeff, 160, 164, 168, 173–174,
  190–191
Clone and go theme, Hewlett
  Packard/Compaq merger, 164
Coffee master, Starbucks, 250
Columbia shuttle disaster, 257
Communication
  Hewlett Packard/Compaq merger,
    166–169
  in hockey stick phase, 10
  IBM method, 145–148
  protocol for alliance, 68
  at relaunch stage, 81
  Staples method, 196
Communities
  of Chaebol (Korean consortium),
    216–225
  one IBM team, 142–145
  of Starbucks, 244–247
Compaq Computer Corporation
  Digital Equipment acquisition, 160,
    167, 191
  executive sponsorship, 14
  See also Hewlett Packard/Compaq
    merger

Competition
  competitors as stakeholders, 37–38
  Starbucks approach, 253
Computer games
  and human interactions, 255–257
  Starbucks, 250
Conceptualization, 40–43
  high level screens, 42–43
  vision for alliance, 41–42
Conflict, in mature stage, 15
Conflict resolution
  implementation stage, 76–77
  issue escalation ladder, 124
  termination stage, 82
Conservation International, Starbucks,
  245–247
Core competency test, 47–48
Costco Wholesale Corporation, and
  Starbucks, 239–240
Creighton, Scott, 30
Crudup, Robert, 212
Cuen, Fred, 111
Culture/ethnicity
  and partner selection, 52
  See also Global strategy
Culture of organization
  communicating to organization,
    66–67
  cultural integration, Hewlett
    Packard/Compaq merger, 167–170
  and location of team environment,
    258
  and Mindshift approach, 6
Currency factor, 74–75
Customer relations
  Avnet, 98, 104–105
  BALSAMS, 229–231
  Peninsula Beverly Hills, 232–236
  ValleyCrest Company, 210–211

D
Daewoo, and General Motors Company
  (GMC), 220–221
DaimlerChrysler, pyramid analysis,
  55–57
Decline stage, 17–18

issues to consider, 18
  and re-launch, 17–18
Department, as stakeholders, 35–36
Development stage
  analyst functions in, 37
  conceptualization, 40–43
  department functions in, 36
  management functions in, 33
  managerial personality, 21–22
  metrics, summary of, 83
  negotiation process, 57–59
  partner functions in, 34
  partner selection, 50–53
  planning, 49–50
  pre-launch development, 44–45
  strategic fit, 45–49
  strategy alignment, 43–44
  structure of alliance, 53–57
  team selection, 59–62
Development team, selection of, 60
Digital Equipment
  and Avnet Computer Marketing, 103
  Compaq acquisition of, 160, 167, 191
Dispute resolution. See Conflict
  resolution
Distribution agreement
  defined, 68
  and implementation, 68
Distribution arrangements, termination
  stage, 82
Distribution business, Avnet, 87–115
Doan, Laura, 124–132
Documentation, of relaunch, 80
Documentation team, selection of, 61
Donnelly, Tom, 213

E
Eisner, Michael, 14
Employee relations
  New Technology Management, Inc.
    (NTMI), 129–130
  ValleyCrest Company, 206–210
Engineering company, Stronghold
  Engineering Inc., 117–124
Engineering Construction Company,
  216

Erdman, Cynthia, 143, 149, 151, 154
Ethics, and partner selection, 52–53
European Agency for the Evaluation
  of Medicinal Products (EMEA),
  104
Evaluation. *See* Reevaluation
Executive level
  of Chaebol (Korean consortium),
    216
  channel partnerships, 31
  in IBM team, 142–143
Executive sponsor
  IBM, 144, 149, 152
  selection criteria, 61–62
  Staples, 195
Experimental stage, 26–27

F
Farmer manager, 21–22
Fingerman, David, 201–202
Fiorina, Carly, 159–160, 164, 167, 170,
    176, 188–191
Fisher, George, 34
Fisher, Roger, 58
Fleet Bank, and Staples, 201–204
Fogg, Jennifer, 120, 123
Fontana, Emilio, 45–46, 65
Ford Motors Company, and Hyundai,
    218–219
Friberg, Fane, 103

G
Gallagher, Phil, 95
Gandhi, Mahatma, 237, 253
General Motors Company (GMC)
  auto financing by, 222–223
  and Daewoo, 220–221
Gerstner, Lou, 135
Gifford, Chad, 204
Global strategy
  Avnet Computer Marketing, 104
  Avnet Electronics Marketing (EM),
    90, 94, 96
  Hyundai, 218–227
  Staples, 200
  Starbucks, 240–253

Global strategy. *See also* individual
    countries
Go-to-market team, Hewlett
    Packard/Compaq merger, 175–178
Goals, restructuring, 16–17
Government contracts
  best value approach, 121
  New Technology Management, Inc.
    (NTMI), 125–130
  Stronghold Engineering Inc., 118–121
Greece, Starbucks in, 249–250

H
Hall-Mark Electronics, 104
Hamada, Rick, 103–105, 109–111
Harvard Project on Negotiation, 45, 57
Heal, Mike, 175, 177
Herz, J.C., 255–256
Hewlett Packard, and Avnet Computer
    Marketing, 103, 107–109
Hewlett Packard/Compaq merger,
    159–192
  adopt and go metric, 164–165
  clone and go metric, 164
  communications program, 166–169
  compensation metric, 173
  cost savings from merger, 166, 170,
    171, 190
  critical players in, 160–161
  cultural integration, 167–170
  employee characteristics, 168–169
  go-to-market project, 175–178
  integration plan of record (IPOR),
    170–172
  integration steering committee, 164
  integration team selection, 161,
    163–164
  integration team structure, 165–166
  launch day, 188–190
  as merger of consolidation, 165–166,
    190
  sensitive data, handling of, 163–164
  success of alliance, factors in,
    190–192
  timeline of merger, 162
High level screens, 42–43

Hockey stick phase, 9–12
  characteristics of, 9–11
  managerial personality, 21–22
Homeland Security, and New
    Technology Management, Inc.
    (NTMI), 127, 129
Hotels
  BALSAMS, 228–231
  Peninsula Beverly Hills, 232–236
Hovis, John, 113–114
Hunter manager, 21–22
Hyundai, 216–221
  and Ford Motors Company, 218–219
  and Mitsubishi Motors Corporation,
    219–220
  pyramid analysis, 218–220
  size of, 216
  types of alliances of, 221

I
IBM
  alliance process, summary chart, 156
  and Avnet Computer Marketing, 103,
    109–111
  communication metrics, 145–148
  communities in team, 142–143
  examples of, 12
  executive sponsor, 144, 149, 152
  as hockey-stick stage alliance, 12
  implementation of alliance, 153–157
  leadership reviews, 151–152
  matrix structure of, 139, 140
  measurement metrics, 139–142
  one IBM team, example of, 142–145
  partner selection process, 143–144
  recent strategic moves, 135–136
  roles and responsibilities matrix,
    148–153
  solution maps, 141–142
  and Staples, 200
  strategic fit, importance of, 140–141
  strategy development, 153
  weekly reviews, 151
IBM software group
  announcement of alliances, 137–138
  communication in, 146

independent software vendor (ISV)
    partnerships, 136–140, 157
  Partnerworld program, 136
  and Siebel Corporation, 136–137, 151
Implementation launch, 68–73
  change in mutuality metric, 69–70
  and distribution agreement, 68
  Hewlett Packard/Compaq merger,
    191–192
  and joint venture, 68
  portfolio management, 70–73
Implementation stage, 63–84
  analyst functions in, 37
  conflict resolution, 76–77
  department functions in, 36
  IBM example, 153–157
  launch, 68–73
  management functions in, 33
  metrics, summary of, 83
  operationalization stage, 63–68
  partner functions in, 34
  re-evalution, 78–81
  remediation, 73–77
  restructuring, 77–78
  termination, 81–84
Implementation team
  Hewlett Packard/Compaq merger,
    161–166
  selection of, 61, 64
Inbreeding Chaebol, 221
Independent software vendor (ISV)
    partnerships, IBM software group,
    136–140, 157
Information technology provider
  IBM, 135–157
  New Technology Management, Inc.
    (NTMI), 124–133
Integration of alliance
  importance of, 10–11
  process of, 11
Integration plan of record (IPOR),
    Hewlett Packard/Compaq merger,
    170–172
Intel Corporation, 90, 92, 98
Intellectual property, return on
  investment (ROIPI), 78

Intelligent Business Alliances (Segil),
    3, 53, 120
Interbrand Consultancy, 244
International expansion. *See* Global
    strategy; individual countries
Investor relations, Avnet, 113–115
Iran hostage crisis, 59

J
Japan
    collective mentality, 226
    companies compared to Korean, 226
    Mitsubishi Motors Corporation,
        219–220
    Starbucks in, 241–242
Joint venture
    defined, 68
    and implementation, 68
Jurcy, Jan, 114

K
Kamins, Ed, 96–98, 101–103
Kasikci, Ali, 232–235
Kent Datacomm, 103
Knowledge, as metric, 221–222
Knowledge capture initiative,
    Starbucks, 248–249
Knowledgebase.net, 71
KorAm Bank, and Carlyle Group, 227
Korea
    banking alliances, 227
    Chaebol, 216–225
    companies compared to Japanese,
        226
    Daewoo, 220–221
    Hyundai, 216–228
    Starbucks in, 245
    women as leaders, 225
Korea Telecom Corporation, and
    Parsons Corporation, 226
Kraft, and Starbucks, 252

L
Labor hours worked, return on, 78
Landscape company, ValleyCrest
    Company, 193, 205–214

Lared Group, 45–46
    operationalization, 63–65
    strategic alliance plan, 46
Launch
    implementation stage. *See*
        Implementation launch
    pre-launch development, 44–45
    reevaluation stage relaunch, 80–81
Legal counsel
    as documentation team, 61
    and restructuring, 77
    in sustaining phase, 20
    and termination, 81–82
Life cycle
    decline stage, 17–18
    hockey stick phase, 9–12
    mature stage, 14–17
    professional stage, 12–14
    startup stage, 7–9
    sustaining phase, 18–24
Life-cycle stages
    and managerial personalities, 20–21
    Mindshift approach utility, 5, 26–27
Location factors, environments for
    participants, 258
Logos, for alliance, 258

M
McKinney, Harry W., 160–161, 163–164,
    168, 173–174, 190–191
Management
    and alliance implementation, 33
    and development stage, 33
    managerial personalities, 21–22
    as stakeholder, 32–34
Market opportunity cost, return on
    (ROMOC), 78
Marketing
    logos and alliances, 258
    marketing development, 11
Marketing manager, channel
    partnerships, 31
Maslen, Peter, 240, 242–245, 247–251
Mature stage, 14–17
    characteristics of, 15–17
Mediation, in mature stage, 17

Metrics stages. *See* Development stage;
   Implementation stage
Mexico, Starbucks Conservation
   International in, 246–247
Microsoft Corporation, and Staples,
   197–198
Middle-of-the-road stage, 25–26
Milton, Jim, 175–177, 189
Mindshift approach, 3
   alliance culture, 6
   basic premise, 5
   managerial personalities, 22
   project priorities, 23–27
   relationship development, 4
   usefulness and lifecycle stage, 5,
      26–27
Minority workforce, ValleyCrest
   Company, 209
Mitsubishi Motors Corporation, and
   Hyundai, 219–220
Morrison, Leigh, 14, 174–177, 188–190
Mutuality
   analysis of change in, 69–70
   as metric, 69
Mutuality advocate, Starbucks, 252

N
Napier, Bob, 164
National Aeronautics and Space
   Administration (NASA), human
   dependencies of, 257
Negotiating team
   IBM, 143
   relationship manager, 60–61
   selection of, 60–61
Negotiation, 57–59
   negotiation metrics, 58
   negotiation training topics, 58–59
   re-evaluation stage, 79–80
New Technology Management, Inc.
   (NTMI), 124–133
   alliance metrics of, 131–132
   annual high-visibility project, 131
   CEO, background of, 125
   emerging test-bed (R & D), 129–130
   employee relations, 129–130

evolution of, 125–126
government contracts, 125–130
subcontractors, 127–128
New Zealand, Starbucks in, 245
North America Enterprise Systems,
   Country Managers Playbook,
   178–188
North American Coffee Partnership,
   252

O
Office supplies, Staples, 194–205
Operating unit plan, 42–43
Operationalization, 63–68
   Hewlett Packard/Compaq merger,
      190–191
   Lared Group example, 63–65
   steps in, 64–68
Operations manager, channel
   partnerships, 31
Organizational culture. *See* Culture of
   organization
Outsourcing
   as alliance, 219
   subcontractors, 127–128

P
Palmisano, Sam, 135, 150
Parsons Corporation, and Korea
   Telecom Corporation, 226
Partnering workshop, agenda items,
   123–124
Partners
   adding partner, 25–26
   change in mutuality, 69–70
   channel partnerships, 29–31
   culture/ethnicity factors, 52
   ethical factors, 52–53
   partner selection metrics, 50–53
   stakeholder characteristics for, 29
   as stakeholders, 34–35, 38
Partnerworld program, IBM, 136
Peninsula Beverly Hills, 232–236
   alliance development stage, 235–236
   alliance implementation stage, 236

Peninsula Beverly Hills (*continued*)
    twenty-four hour check-in service,
        232–236
Penzel, Ed, 163
PepsiCo, and Starbucks, 252
Personality traits, managers, 21–22
Philippines, Starbucks in, 245
Philosophical goals
    philosophy before structure concept,
        53–55
    pyramid analysis tool, 53–54, 218–220
    and structure of alliance, 53–55
Planning, 49–50
    discussion topics for, 50
    metrics, use of, 49–50
Politician manager, 21–22
Portfolio management, 70–73
    for senior management reviews,
        71–72
    software tools, 71
    tasks in, 35
    utility of, 70–71
Pre-launch development, 44–45
Presidential Award, New Technology
        Management, Inc. (NTMI), 127,
        131
Process builder tool, Avnet Applied
        Computing, 99–102
Process transfer, 11
Professional stage, 12–14
    characteristics of, 13–14
    managerial personality, 21–22
Project priorities, 23–27
    bet-the-farm stage, 24–25
    experimental stage, 26–27
    importance of, 23–24
    middle-of-the-road stage, 25–26
Project stakeholders, Stronghold
        Engineering Inc., 122
Pyramid of alliances
    DaimlerChrysler, 55–57
    Hyundai, 218–220
    philosophy before structure concept,
        53–55, 220
    and structure of alliance, 54

Q
Quality standards, and partner
        selection, 52–53

R
Rapier, David, 99
Re-evalution, 78–81
    issues in, 79
    re-launch, 80–81
    re-negotiation, 79–80
    validity test, 78–79
Relationship manager, role of, 60–61
Relationships
    and alliance building, 224
    and computer games, 255–257
Re-launch
    characteristics of, 8–9
    and decline stage, 17–18
    innovative methods for, 260
Remediation process, 73–77
    conflict resolution, 76–77
    internal currency factor, 74–75
    situation analysis for, 73–74
Remote technologies, New Technology
        Management, Inc. (NTMI), 124–133
Research and development, New
        Technology Management, Inc.
        (NTMI), 129–130
Resource allocation
    in hockey-stick stage, 12
    in professional stage, 13
Restructuring, 77–78
    metrics for, 77–78
Return on intellectual property
        invested (ROIPI), meaning of, 78
Return on market opportunity cost
        (ROMOC), meaning of, 78
Risk management, and restructuring,
        77–78
Ritz-Carlton Hotel, 230

S
Sadowski,, 113–114
Sargent, Ronald, 193, 196, 200
Scheman, Jeff, 194, 195–196, 199, 201

Schultz, Howard, 129, 238–239
Screens, high level
    business development plan, 42
    corporate values, 43
    operating unit plan, 42–43
    strategic plan, 42
Shared services, Avnet, 111–113
Siebel Corporation
    and channel partners, 30–31
    and IBM software group, 136–137,
        151
Smith, Orin, 237, 243–247
Socialization, into culture of
    organization, 66–67
Software tools, portfolio management,
    71
Solution maps, IBM, 141–142
Sperber, Burton, 205–207, 209–213
Sperber, Richard, 205, 213
Sperber, Stuart, 205, 212
Stakeholders, 29–38
    analysts as, 36–38
    of channel partnerships, 29–31
    competitors as, 37–38
    department as, 35–36
    management as, 32–34
    and partner selection, 51
    partners as, 34–35, 38
Staples, 194–205
    alliance development metrics, 199
    alliance evaluation metrics, 194–196
    Automatic Data Process (ADP), 197
    communication process, 196
    evolution of, 193, 196–197, 200
    and Fleet Bank, 201–204
    global strategy, 200
    as hockey-stick stage alliance, 200
    and IBM, 200
    and Microsoft Corporation, 197–198
    and Starbucks, 198
    and Taylor Printing, 197
    and United Parcel Service (UPS), 198
    and Upromise, 198
    value-sharing arrangements, 198
    virtual alliances, 197–198

Starbucks, 237–253
    coffee master, 250
    coffee of origin country activities,
        245–247
    communities of, 244–247
    competition, approach to, 253
    Conservation International, 245–247
    and Costco Wholesale Corporation,
        239–240
    domestic alliances, 251–252
    evolution of, 238–240
    global strategy, 240–244
    international market implementation
        metrics, 247–253
    knowledge capture initiative,
        248–249
    mutuality advocate, 252
    partner selection process, 249
    partnering philosophy, 237–238, 251
    partnership failure, reasons for, 251
    quality standards, 53
    and Staples, 198
    Star team, 250
    training, 252
Stark, Pamela, 208
Startup stage, 7–9
    characteristics of, 7
    re-launch, 8–9
Stemberg, Thomas G., 193, 196, 204
Strategic fit, 45–49
    IBM example, 140–142
    meaning of, 45
    versus moving target, 48–49
    and Staples, 195
    SWOT analysis, 47–48
Strategic plan, 42
    importance of, 48
Strategy alignment, 43–44
    check at implementation stage,
        67–68
    as interactive process, 44
    and vision for alliance, 42
Stronghold Engineering Inc., 117–124
    evolution of, 117–118
    government contracts, 118–121

Stronghold Engineering Inc.
  (*continued*)
  partnering workshop agenda,
    123–124
  project evaluation criteria, 121–122
  project stakeholders, 122
  scope of projects, 118–119
Structure of alliance, 53–57
  and philosophical goals, 53–55
  pyramid of relationships, 54
Subcontractors, New Technology
    Management, Inc. (NTMI), 127–128
Subcultures, recognition by partner,
    259–260
Suerth, Hank, 243, 251–253
Sustaining phase, 18–24
  characteristics of, 19–20
  managerial personality, 21–22
Swiss-Austrian Business Group, and
    Starbucks, 251
SWOT (strength, weakness,
    opportunity, and threat) analysis
  facilitation of, 47
  Starbucks, 248
  testing outcome, 47–48
  utility of, 35

T
Taylor Printing, and Staples, 197
Tazo Tea, 251
Teams
  development team selection, 60
  documentation team selection, 61
  enhancement of, 12
  executive sponsor, 61–62
  in hockey-stick phase, 10
  IBM communities in team, 142–143
  implementation team selection, 61
  in mature stage, 15
  member selection criteria, 8, 59–62
  negotiating team selection, 60–61
  in professional stage, 13
  in sustaining stage, 19
  training and education, 10
  transition team, 63–64
Termination of alliance, 81–84

  legal metrics in, 81–82
  in mature stage, 17
Thailand, Starbucks in, 247
Timson, Bob, 137–138
Transition team, 63–64
Trust issues, in professional stage, 13

U
United Airlines, and Starbucks, 252
United Kingdom, Starbucks in, 247
United Parcel Service (UPS), and
    Staples, 198
Upfront Income Verification of Public
    Housing, 127
Upromise, and Staples, 198
USAA, 224

V
Validity test, 78–79
Vallee, Roy, 87, 94
ValleyCrest Company, 193, 205–214
  alliance development metrics, 214
  alliance implementation metrics,
    214
  clients of, 205, 211
  customer relations, 210–211
  employee satisfaction, 206–210
  employee training, 213
  ethics statement of, 206
  evolution of, 205, 210
  as family venture, 210, 212–213
  maintenance division metrics,
    208–209
  minority workforce, 209
  preconstruction department, 213
ValleyCrest Golf Course Maintenance,
    212–213
ValleyCrest Tree Company, 212
ValleyCrest University, 213
Value-sharing arrangements, Staples,
    198
Values, corporate, and alliance
    development, 43
Vance, Cyrus, 59
Vantage Partners, 45, 57
  contact information, 267

Virtual alliances, Staples, 197–198
Vision for alliance, 41–42
    screens, high level, 42–43
    unifying among stakeholders, 41–42
Visionary manager, 21–22

W
Walt Disney Company, subculture of
    alliance, 259–260
Warrior manager, 21–22
Wayman, Bob, 164
Wipro, 78
Wolfensohn, James, 228
Women leaders
    and Asian companies, 225
    Fiorina and Hewlett-Packard,
        159–160, 164, 167, 170, 176, 188–191

New Technology Management, Inc.
    (NTMI), 124–133
Stronghold Engineering Inc., 117–124
World Bank Group
    banking functions of, 228
    governance of, 228
    knowledge as metric, 221–222
Worst case scenarios, use in planning,
    124

Y
Yong, Chung Ju, 216

Z
Zeitler, Bill, 111
Zetsche, Dieter, 56
Zino, Roger, 207–208